CONTEMPORARY EVANGELICALISM
and the RESTORATION OF THE PROTOTYPAL CHURCH

CONTEMPORARY EVANGELICALISM
and the RESTORATION OF THE PROTOTYPAL CHURCH

Alan J. Delotavo, Ph.D.

FreshIdeasBooks
Enlightens, Inspires, Revolutionizes

Contemporary Evangelicalism
and the Restoration of the Prototypal Church

Copyright©2012 by Alan J. Delotavo. All rights reserved. No part of this book may be used or reproduced in any manner whatsoever without written permission from the publisher except in the case of brief quotations embodied in critical articles and reviews. Published by FreshIdeasBooks. The photo of an old man sitting in an empty church by © Emmacharle is acquired as royalty free from Dreamstime.com, ID: 10089431. Cover design by FreshIdeasBooks © 2012.

ISBN: 978-0-9866306-7-5

For other books by Alan J. Delotavo, please visit his website at www.delotavo.com

CONTENTS

Introduction of the Study	9
Chapter	
Part I: Analysis of the Phenomenon of Contemporary Evangelicalism	
1. Overview	16
2. The Prototypal Ecclesial Life Framework	20

    A. The Life-Oriented Ecclesiological Framework
    B. The Prototypal Ecclesial Life Structures
    C. The Projected Significance
3. The Deformation and Re-Formation of the Prototypal
   Ecclesial Life Framework   55
    A. The State of the Pre-Reformation Church
    B. The Emergence of the Reformation Movement
    C. The Emergence of Puritanism and Pietism
4. The Emergence of Contemporary Evangelicalism   73
    A. The Frontier Precursors
    B. The Immediate Precursor
    C. The Emergence of Contemporary Evangelicalism

Part II: Analysis of the Theological Framework of Contemporary Evangelicalism

5. The Theological Framework of Contemporary Evangelicalism   84
    A. The Formative Stage
    B. Survey of Characterizations
    C. Synthesis
6. The Core of Contemporary Evangelicalism   100
    A. The Layers
    B. The Core
    C. The Message
7. The Evangelical Agenda   111
    A. The Nature and Purpose of Contemporary Evangelicalism
    B. The Challenge!

Part III: Contemporary Evangelical Ecclesiology as the Paradigm of Prototypal Ecclesial Regeneration

8. Contemporary Evangelical Ecclesiological Codes   123

    A. Transdenominational Nature

    B. Missional Cause

    C. Empowerment of the Holy Spirit

    D. Christological Essence

    E. The Projected End Result

9. Characteristics of Contemporary Evangelicalism as the Paradigm for Ecclesial Regeneration   147

    A. Contemporary Evangelical ecclesiology is a full-grown paradigm

    B. Contemporary Evangelical ecclesiology is a synthesizing paradigm

    C. Contemporary Evangelicalism is an ecclesially-friendly and non-threatening paradigm

    D. The Call!

10. Why the Need for Global Ecclesial Regeneration?   159

    A. The regeneration of the church is a historical process that is finally climaxing

    B. The ecclesial reaction to Reformation movement was separatist rather than integrative

    C. Christianity is still very denominational rather than transdenominational

    D. Ecclesiology is still fragmentary rather than unifying

    E. The church is now more eschatological than ever

    F. The Vision!

Part IV: Peoplehood of God as the Essence of Prototypal Church

11. The Calling of the People of God Preceding the Christian Church   180

    A. The Calling of God's People Preceding Israel

    B. The Calling of Israel as the People of God

    C. The Condition of the Call

12. The Christian Church as the New People of God   205

      A. The Emergence and Identity of the Christian Church
      B. The Development of Christian Church.
      C. The Church as One People of Christ
      D. Characteristics of a More Truly Christian Church
      E. The Reason for Transcending Denominational-Self
      G. The Warning Call

Summary and Conclusion   239
Bibliography   241

In memory of:
    My Dad and Mom, LEOPOLDO and GENOVEVA,
    who, despite poverty, supported my expensive theological education
    hoping that someday I will have a much better life than them.

Dedicated to:

Prof. Conrad J. Wethmar, of the University of Pretoria, who sparked my interest in evangelicalism and the church.

And to the churches of Christianity, that they may transcend their sectarian and racial bigotries and be more truly the people of God.

Acknowledgement

The memories of people I am grateful with still linger in my mind. I am thankful to Prof. Conrad Wethmar, former head of the Department of Dogmatics and Christian Ethics of the University of Pretoria, who has long since retired, for guiding me in my research on evangelical movement. I still remember the wonderful fellowship we had in the ministerial association way back in 2001-2006 in the land of the tarsands. We were like one family despite the segregated churches we led (Catholic, Pentecostals, Protestants, and Independent Native). About twelve years ago the British Society for the Study of Theology awakened my interest in theology. And about seven years ago, the American Academy of Religion annual conference kindled my interest for world religions. And to all the churches (Protestants, Pentecostals, Catholic, evangelicals, liberals, ethnic, etc.) and Christian institutions (church, parachurch, colleges, seminaries, universities, etc) I sought refuge amid my long years of struggles in life—for making realize that recognition of equal human value, love and compassion are still subservient to bigotries entrenched in religious institutions.

Introduction of the Study

What really is Contemporary Evangelicalism? It is seemingly an enigmatic phenomenon. While it is missionally and globally prolific and pervasive yet its theological and ecclesiological identities are not yet clearly understood. On the one hand, J. I. Packer is sure that "evangelicalism is an identifiable form of Protestant

Christianity" and even sees it as "the true mainstream Christianity."[1] On the other hand, John Stott speaks of the problem of "uncertain evangelical identity."[2] While Carl F. Henry discusses the evangelical's search for identity.[3] And Donald Bloesch sees that:

> The need for evangelicalism to rediscover its identity and to present a united witness to the church and the world is particularly acute this time when a new modernism threatens to engulf mainline Christianity.[4]

But with its missional prolificacy and pervasiveness, there must also be something theologically and ecclesiologically very significant that is yet to be discovered.

Mark Noll and his colleagues observe that it is easier to recognize evangelicalism than to define it because:

> What we have . . . is a lot of fancy evangelical hybrids: radical evangelicals, liberal evangelicals, liberals who are evangelical, charismatic evangelicals, Catholic evangelicals, evangelicals who are Catholic, evangelical liberationists, evangelical ecumenicalists, ecumenicalists who are evangelical, evangelical feminists, young evangelicals, and orthodox evangelicals.[5]

This entangling diversity is further compounded by the evangelical academic atmosphere they criticize as un-conducive to scholarly growth. They noted that the energy of a small number of evangelical scholars is diffused by a po-

---

[1] J.I. Packer, "Maintaining Evangelical Theology," in *Evangelical Futures: A Conversation on Theological Method*, ed. John G. Stackhouse, Jr. (Grand Rapids: Baker Books, 2000), 183, 186.
[2] John Stott, *Evangelical Truth: A Plea for Unity, Integrity & Faithfulness* (Downers Grove, IL: InterVarsity, 1999), 12.
[3] See Carl F. Henry, *Evangelicals in Search of Identity* (Waco, TX: Word Books, 1976).
[4] Donald G. Bloesch, *Essentials of Evangelical Theology* (Peabody, MA: Prince, 2001), I:1.
[5] Mark Noll, Cornelius Platinga, Jr., and David Wells, "Evangelical Theology Today," *Theology Today* 51 (January 1995): 495.

larity of academic commitments and congregational engagements resulting in a "contemporary malaise in evangelical theology."[6]

This malaise, unless overcome by a well-focused and wholehearted scholarly endeavor, could hinder the formulation of a definitive evangelical theological framework. The absence of a distinct conceptual framework amid academic malaise and ecclesial confusion could spontaneously threaten the evangelical identity. This poses a theological risk to what is generally considered as an integrative missional movement that has globally proliferated. Without a definitive theological framework, mission is not only ironical, but also kerygmatically, ecclesiologically, and societally risky. For the theological structures are both the definition and the content of mission. However, evangelical theology too, could not merely be constructed out of an ivory tower but needs to be relevant to the everyday life of individual believers and corporately of congregations.

Theology shapes both the content and function of the church's proclamation and societal ministry. Further, it shapes not only the ecclesial mission but also the nature of ecclesial life. A theological problem would have a corresponding ecclesiological problem, and vice versa. Thus Richard Beaton identifies the evangelical problem as ecclesiologically rooted, that is, rooted in theologically defining what the church really is from an evangelical point of view. He sees that "evangelicalism is in the throes of identity crisis, and at the heart of the crisis is a lack of clarity concerning the nature and function of the church."[7] Richard Mouw also sees evangelicalism as operating in a weak ecclesiology.[8] And John Stackhouse, Jr. warns:

---

[6] Ibid., 501. Thus Williams talks of the renewal of evangelicalism in relation to the retrieval of evangelical tradition. See D.H. Williams, *Retrieving the Tradition and Renewing Evangelicalism: A Primer for Suspicious Protestants* (Grand Rapids: Eerdmans, 1999).

[7] Richard Beaton, "Reimaging the Church: Evangelical Ecclesiology," in *Evangelical Ecclesiology: Reality or Illusion?*, ed. John Stackhouse, Jr. (Grand Rapids: Baker Academic, 2003), 217.

[8] Richard J. Mouw, "Evangelicals in Search of Maturity," *Theology Today* 35 (April 1978): 32. Mouw identifies this ecclesiological weakness as caused by evangelicalism "not being an organized movement but a *de facto* coalition." Ibid., 35. Grenz adds, "Evangelicalism's

When the church is confused about who it is and whose it is, it can become just another institution, just another collective, just another voluntary society. So we need ecclesiology—the doctrine of the church —to clarify our minds, motivate our hearts, and direct our hands. We need ecclesiology so that we can be who and whose we are.[9]

Bruce Hindmarsh further observes a complication in evangelicalism in his characterization of the evangelical movement as "always a restless 'movement,' iconoclastic of all forms of order, often guilty of schism, and in danger of turning the proclamation of the eternal gospel into matters of popular suasion and the politics of public personalities."[10] This restlessness could be rooted in a lack of explicit theological and ecclesiological framework that could provide distinct identity and direction to evangelical ecclesial life and ministry.

Evangelicalism could not just remain surfing over a crowd of distinct ecclesial identities;[11] for oftentimes, these entities are exclusivist, divisive, and fragmentary—and these characteristics contradict the unifying nature of evangelicalism. Further, not only is there a necessity for academic endeavors, but also evangelical theological-ecclesiological construction should also be life-oriented, that is, focused on life-concerns as opposed to mere theoretical concerns. As Alister McGrath challenges, "Perhaps the greatest challenge to evangelicalism in the next generation is to develop an increasing intellectual com-

---

parachurch ethos work against the ability of the movement to develop a deeply rooted ecclesiological base from which to understand its own identity and upon which to ground its mission, whether it sees that mission as being as, to, or on behalf of the body of Christ." Stanley J. Grenz, *Renewing the Center: Evangelical Theology in a Post-Theological Era* (Grand Rapids: Baker Academics, 2000), 290.

[9] John G. Stackhouse, Jr., "Preface," in *Evangelical Ecclesiology*, ed. Stackhouse, 9.

[10] Bruce Hindmarsh, "Is Evangelical Ecclesiology an Oxymoron?: A Historical Perspective," in *Evangelical Ecclesiology*, ed. Stackhouse, 36. Thus the compilation of essays edited by Wells and Woodbridge talk about evangelical identity and its evolution; refer to David F. Wells and John Woodbridge, eds., *The Evangelicals: What They Believe, Who They Are, Where They are Changing* (Nashville, TN: Abingdon, 1975).

[11] The work edited by Stackhouse (ref. *Evangelical Ecclesiology*), resulting from the 2002 Theological Conference in Regent College, still indicates lack of definite evangelical ecclesiology. Evangelical ecclesiology is portrayed as surfing over varied established ecclesiological traditions.

mitment without losing its roots in the life and faith of ordinary Christian believer."[12]

Moreover, the denominationally transcending nature of evangelicalism implies theological and ecclesiological formulations that are also denominationally transcending yet unifying. Bloesch recognizes the "need for a catholic evangelicalism that will maintain continuity not only with the heritage of the Reformation but also with the whole catholic heritage."[13]

Howard Snyder sounds this call:

> Today evangelical ecclesiology is (as usual!) in a major transition. Precisely for that reason, it faces a large opportunity. What better time to elaborate an ecclesiology that is soundly biblical and evangelical, prophetic and movemental, theologically coherent and sociologically aware, and functional for effective witness to the kingdom of God in an age of rapid globalization.[14]

Statement of the Problem. Thus this work attempts to address the following problems in Contemporary Evangelicalism:

1. The ambiguity of its identity and theological framework.
2. The need to identify its ecclesiological structures.
3. The confusion of its ecclesiological identity.

The Theses. In spite of the aforementioned problems, it is, however, perceived that:

1. The phenomenon of Contemporary Evangelicalism can be definitively characterized and its theological structures can also be clearly identified.
2. That there is an apparent ecclesiological framework profoundly em-

---

[12] Alister McGrath, *A Passion for Truth: The Intellectual Coherence of Evangelicalism* (Downers Grove, IL: InterVarsity, 1996), 243.
[13] Donald G. Bloesch, *God, Authority, and Salvation*, 21.
[14] Howard A. Snyder, "The Marks of Evangelical Ecclesiology," in *Evangelical Ecclesiology*, ed. Stackhouse, 103.

bedded in Contemporary Evangelicalism.

3. And Contemporary Evangelicalism has its own distinct ecclesial identity that is even ecclesiologically paradigmatic for the whole Christian church.

The Importance of the Study. Therefore, this work is very important because it will attempt to address the aforementioned problems and prove the aforementioned theses about Contemporary Evangelicalism. This will attempt to present:

1. The definitive framework and identity of Contemporary Evangelical theology.
2. The distinct framework of Contemporary Evangelical ecclesiology.
3. The very identity of Contemporary Evangelical ecclesiology that is paradigmatic of the identity of the whole Christian church.

Methodology. A literary study will be conducted on literatures related to Contemporary Evangelical theology and ecclesiology. This work will analyze and expound the theological and ecclesiological framework of evangelicalism and the phenomenon of the movement with the intention of constructing fresh yet holistic, synthesizing, and integrative theological and ecclesiological perspectives on Contemporary Evangelicalism.

Delimitation and Conclusion. This work is not intended to expound the details of the plethora of ecclesiologies that are regarded as sources of the evangelical ecclesiological heritage. Rather, this work focuses on an attempt to characterize the phenomenon and theological-ecclesiological structures of Contemporary Evangelicalism, and point out its core intent for the whole Christian church.

McGrath predicts that the "debate over evangelical identity is likely to remain a subject of debate and discussion,"[15] and this work will attempt to clarify the identity of Contemporary Evangelicalism. Further, in doing this research I

---

[15] McGrath, *A Passion for Truth*, 22.

bear in mind the challenge of Darrell Bock, a past president of the Evangelical Theological Society. He writes, "To evangelicals, especially those who are beginning their work, I say let your research pursuits keep the lost in mind."[16]

I foresee that this work will present a new understanding of Contemporary Evangelicalism and what the church really is. And perhaps offer fresh meanings and significance of Christian Faith to the "lost".

---

[16] Darell L. Bock, *Purpose-Directed Theology: Getting Our Priorities Right in Evangelical Controversies* (Downers Grove, IL: InterVarsity, 2002), 110. He adds: "My invitation to my generation and those that came before us is to encourage the next generation to work on projects that may also reach the church at large... Give them room and permission to address the culture they are familiar with in ways that may be different from how we do it... If they package things   differently, assess it on substance, not on style or because it is different. Try not to confuse content and form. Such difference may be matters of generational culture or personal taste....do not forget that no period has a monopoly on truth or method. History shows this." Ibid., 112.

Part I
Analysis of the Phenomenon of Contemporary Evangelicalism

1
Overview

Contemporary Evangelicalism is usually understood as a missional movement resorting to interdenominational evangelistic crusades and parachurch organizations. As neo-evangelicalism, it is considered as a reaction movement against Fundamentalism, resulting in another denominational movement within the Christian church. But there is something beyond these common views on Contemporary Evangelicalism that evangelicals in particular, and the church in general, have missed. Something that if it has not been missed, could have ushered a second wave of Reformation grander than the first. It could have sparked a global conflagration that could have consumed the common fragmentary ecclesiological preconceptions or misconceptions, to pave the way for a new ecclesiological synthesis that is holistic, unifying, and purposeful. Why? Because Contemporary Evangelicalism offers the much needed ecclesial life framework for the church to be truly the prototypal church.

To understand the deeper significance of Contemporary Evangelicalism, there is a need to know the characteristics of the original church in contrast with the historical ecclesiological framework. Knowing the characteristics of the church as it moves along history is very essential because it presents the context for understanding the deeper intent of Contemporary Evangelicalism and preceding ecclesial movements.

Recovering what the Bible meant before formulating what the Bible means is essential in every evangelical theological endeavor. For what it means, without the control of what it meant, oftentimes result in diverse eccentric views. And ironically, at times, these views regarded as theologically peculiar, are not only considered by their respective proponents as truths in contrast to beliefs of other denominations—they are also esteemed as the absolute whole truth. Thus Christian theology is loaded with all sorts of contradictions, from Roman Catholicism to Protestantism, conservatism to liberalism, deism to theism, fundamentalism to evangelicalism, activism to monasticism, etc. Christian theology in general and Christian ecclesiology in particular is fragmented and divisive.

There is a need to recover a synthesizing theological model for the Christian church. Gordon Lewis and Bruce Demarest see a similar need for an integrative theological method.[17] What I am proposing, however, is not just an integrative theological method, but an integrative and holistic approach to historical ecclesiological revelations. However, I also recognize that the process of recovering an ecclesiological synthesis is very challenging because of the risk of confronting mindsets. But a skeptical disposition is not also an option, for this will undermine the value and efficacy of the Bible as the divinely-ordained revelatory medium. Neither is a status quo stance productive—for the church expecting the soon Parousia of Christ—needs clear and fuller understanding of the purpose of its existence. The church needs to be purpose-driven. And the purpose should be original rather than an artificial reconstruction. The church as the body of Christ, not as mere association of divergent bodies of Christ, needs an ecclesiological framework that could engender natural, yet deep ecclesial unity and holistic ecclesial life.

Contemporary Evangelicalism offers an astounding blueprint that could answer the needs of the church in the present time—more than the Reformation answered the needs of the past. This seems a surprising assertion but it is not. When the phenomenon of Contemporary Evangelicalism is analyzed in a holistic sense with due recognition of the operation of the Holy Spirit in the history of the church—we could see it as the most significant and meaningful ecclesiology

---

[17] See Gordon R. Lewis and Bruce A. Demarest, *Integrative Theology* (Grand Rapids: Zondervan, 1996).

ever, since the Reformation. In fact, we could see it as the climax of all ecclesiological revelations!

However, Contemporary Evangelicalism has also detoured from its original intention. Its embodiment in the form of parachurch organizations and insular categorization within the ecclesial archipelago are alternate routes. Why? It is because these are not the deepest intentions of Contemporary Evangelicalism. And the most profound intention of Contemporary Evangelicalism including the preceding movements will be unfolded in this work. Paradoxically though, in spite of its being an alternate route—Contemporary Evangelical parachurch ecclesiology still end up presenting ecclesiological frameworks that are paradigmatic and prototypal.

In coherence with evangelicalism's Bible-centeredness; it is proper to consider the biblical framework as the foundation of every evangelical theological endeavor. Thus this work will start by plainly considering the New Testament ecclesial life framework. I identify the plain biblical approach because Contemporary Evangelicalism is not preoccupied with highly technical exegetical approach developed or influenced by the Liberal movement. Evangelicals content themselves using word studies, historical background, and plain contextual consideration of the message of a text. This defines their Bible-centered epistemology. As Richard Mouw, the President of Fuller Theological Seminary which is the leading evangelical seminary, points out:

> Evangelicals have long worried about ecclesiological perspectives that are so highly detailed and all-consuming that they crowd out other important theological concerns. So we respond by emphasizing some things, such as the need for personal relationship with Jesus Christ and for evangelizing the lost, that are often neglected by people who take delight in detailed ecclesiologies.[18]

---

[18] Richard Mouw, "Evangelical Ethics," in *Where Shall My Wond'ring Soul Begin?: The Landscape of Evangelical Piety and Thought*, eds. Mark A. Noll and Ronald F. Thiemann (Grand Rapids, MI: Eerdmans, 2000), 75.

The significance of considering the original biblical characteristics of the church will be seen in the context of subsequent ecclesiological phenomena. Further, because of the historical progression of evangelicalism, it is also proper to note the characteristics of ecclesial movements preceding its emergence. To understand the deepest intent of evangelicalism, we also need to discern the profound implications of varied ecclesial phenomena in different times—from the New Testament church, to Reformation, Pietism and Puritanism, the Awakening movements, then, eventually to Contemporary Evangelicalism.

2
The Prototypal Ecclesial Life Framework

A. The Life-Oriented Ecclesiological Framework

We usually see the New Testament church from different points of view, namely, from its nature, to the systematization of its beliefs, to its being an institution, to its rituals, to its socio-political role, etc. There is nothing wrong in expounding the different aspects of the church. What is problematic though is when a theological exposition on an aspect of church life is regarded as absolute and as the whole of what the church is. This results in fragmentary ecclesiological formulations. And indeed, in the history of Christianity after the New Testament period—we see the propagation and proliferation of restrictive ecclesiologies. An aspect of the nature of ecclesial life is usually over-focused, overshadowing the whole picture of church life. Further, there is also a need for the laity to see the practical significance of scholarly ecclesiological formulations to their everyday Christian life. A narrow ecclesiological focus could result in, not only varied but also, conflicting ecclesiologies—that could polarize the one body of Christ and threaten the integrity of its internal and external spiritual unity and witness.

An option that tends towards synthesis and holism is a life-oriented rather than philosophical ecclesiological approach, that is, seeing the church from the overall perspective of ecclesial life. Life here means the natural life of the actual church as the result of believers' act of congregating. Not a mystical life attributed to a transcendental church or an institutional life attributed to a religious institution that is independent from the congregating believers. The church was not a product of a theoretical formulation, but a spontaneous consequence of believers' act of congregating because of common life experiences. The preoccupations of the early Christians were things practical not things mystical or philosophical. They were concerned about the reality of human life in the context of the Messiah that has come.

Even when confronting Roman, Greek, or other crossbred's philosophies; their message was always life-oriented rather than theoretical. Their preoccupation was the proclamation of the gospel so that people could repent, accept Jesus as their personal Savior, and live a new life. Faith for them was not speculative or merely a subject to be discussed—but life-oriented—something that concerns everyday real life.

Thus even when John uses the "Word" (*logos*), he did not intend to expound a speculative philosophy but to proclaim a practical life-oriented message. As Kittel points out:

> It might seem to be speculative . . . . Yet it is not speculative for the Evangelist (as distinct from many of his expositors), since his emphasis is on the fact that the statement does not derive from reflection or from a mythical theological idea of pre-existence but from the θεασθαι of the historical figure of Jesus (1:14, cf. 1:51; 2:11, etc).[19]

He further adds, ". . . this apparently speculative statement arises out of, and gains its only light from, the historical process of seeing and hearing Jesus in faith."[20] D. H. Johnson also sees a practical evangelistic concern in John's use of *logos*:

> The meaning of *logos* in the Johannine prologue is clear. The Word is the person of the Godhead through whom the world was created, who took on human nature in history and who is the source of life and light for humanity . . . . John uses *logos* because it is the natural word expressing the meaning of the Hebrew word *dabar* when that word was used in the context of God's revelation. Beginning with its first sentences the Gospel asserts that Jesus is God's final Revelator (cf.

---

[19] *TDNT*, s.v. "λογος," by Kittel.
[20] Ibid.

Heb 1:1-2). This assertion corresponds to the evangelistic purpose of the Gospel (Carson) and fits well with the recent hypotheses that the original historical context of the Fourth Gospel was a debate with first-century Judaism over the locus of revelation.[21]

John, like other Gospel evangelists, was a contextual evangelist. He proclaimed the gospel of Christ using words understandable to his audience; then redirected them to Christ. And in the process of redirecting them from a non-Christian object to Christ—he also transformed the word he used into new Christ-centered meaning.[22] J. N. Sanders agrees that John's use of *logos* was an attempt "to put into language intelligible and acceptable to his contemporaries, pagan as well as Jewish Christians, the basic Christian conviction" about Jesus "as a new revelation from God."[23] Thus John concluded:

> So the Word became human and lived here on earth among us. He was full of unfailing love and faithfulness. And we have seen his glory, the glory of the only Son of the Father. John pointed him out to the people. He shouted to the crowds, "This is the one I was talking about when I said, 'Someone is coming who is far greater that I am . . . .' " We have all benefited from the rich blessings he brought to us—one gracious blessing after another.[24]

The phrasal-vocabularies "became human," "lived here on earth among us," "John pointed him out to the people," are not expressions of something esoteric and hypothetical but something John experienced as actual and real that

---

[21] *Dictionary of Jesus and the Gospels* (1992), s.v. "*Logos*," by D.H. Johnson.
[22] Thus Johnson emphasizes, ". . . verbal similarities do not necessarily imply conceptual similarities. The use of similar words in seemingly similar ways can deceive us into thinking that two authors are discussing the same concept. Only when one document is understood in its own right can it be understood in its own right." Ibid. He further adds, ". . . one must seek to understand words and concepts first and foremost within the immediate literary context in which they occur. Therefore, it seems preferable to search for the meaning of *logos* in the Fourth Gospel itself before looking at religious or literary backgrounds outside the Gospel . . . . " Ibid. See also his survey of various views on John's use of *logos*.
[23] *The Interpreter's Dictionary of the Bible* (1962), s.v. "Word, the," by J. N. Sanders.
[24] John 1:14-16. *Holy Bible*, New Living Translation (Wheaton, IL: Tyndale, 1996). Subsequent biblical quotations are taken from this version.

affect the life of humanity. What we see in John's Gospel prologue is a realistic life-oriented theological outlook rather than a speculative one. The phrases "full of unfailing love and faithfulness," and "we have all benefited from the rich blessings he brought to us" signify practical life-concern.

So is Paul's message of the indwelling of the Holy Spirit in believers in 1 Corinthians 3:16, a life-oriented message. As P.T. O'Brien notes, "By means of the temple imagery he makes plain, first, that the congregation at Corinth is the temple of God because his Spirit dwells among God's assembled people."[25] And the context is a practical-relational concern over jealousy and quarrel—"You are jealous of one another and quarrel with each other," v. 3. These unholy attitudes for Paul indicate that their character is still "controlled by sinful desires," v. 2. And this is a symptom of distorted relationship with Jesus—"acting like people who don't belong to the Lord," v. 3. Thus Paul warned them of divine judgment—"God will bring ruin upon anyone who ruins this temple," v. 17, as a consequence of their church-fragmenting squabble inconsistent with the holiness of God. Thus Paul confronted them, "Don't you realize that all of you together are the temple of God, and that the Spirit of God lives in you?" v. 16. The context here is not a speculative mystical embodiment of God in human nature—but real congregational problems that threatens the holiness of the church.

So is Paul's use of the "body of Christ" metaphor. 1Corinthians 12 gives a clear picture of its metaphoric yet practical use for relational issues confronting the church. As Paul Minear points out, the "body of Christ" image is a "phrase which connotes the many-faceted relations between Jesus Christ and those who belong to him . . . ."[26] There are three points that we need to note here:

First, Paul's metaphoric use of the "body" (*soma*) in relation to the church is not an exposition of a sort of Hellenistic concept of a transcendental

---

[25] *Dictionary of Paul and His Letters* (1993), s.v. "Church," by P.T. O'Brien.
[26] *The Interpreter's Dictionary of the Bible* (1962), s.v., "Christ, Body of," by P.S. Minear.

mystical church. Gerald Hawthorne and Ralph Martin bring out a very important point that could shed light to those engrossed in mystical ecclesiology.

> That Christ, the head of the body, is the exalted heavenly Lord is beyond doubt (Eph 1:20-21), but to argue that in Colossians and Ephesians "the 'body' image is used to denote a *heavenly entity*," since his body the church is also where he is, in heaven . . . is to forget the nature of the body of Christ as metaphor. When believers are said to be raised and seated in the heavenlies with Christ (Col 3:1; Eph 2:6), this is not done in conjunction with the body image.[27]

There is no Pauline or other New Testament indications of the existence of a transcendental entity, tagged church independent from the believers' act of congregating into which believers mystically come into and lodge. Why? This leads to the next point.

Second, the "body" is simply an ecclesiological metaphor of the ministerial relationship that exists in the church. Mitchell Reddish sees a ministerial emphasis of the phrase "body of Christ":

> . . . the phrase "body of Christ" can also be used to emphasize the diversity that exists among believers. A variety of gifts of the Spirit are in evidence within the fellowship. No one is to think too highly of his or her own gift (Rom 12:3-8), nor to disparage the gifts of others (1 Cor 12:4-31). Rather, all gifts are to be used for the mutual benefit of the body of Christ (Eph 4:11-16).[28]

Let us take a look at the immediate context of Paul's use of the body metaphor. Paul points out:

> The human body has many parts, but the many parts make up only one body. So it is with the body of Christ.[29]

---

[27] *Dictionary of Paul and His Letters* (1993), s.v. "Body of Christ," by Gerald F. Hawthorne and Ralph P. Martin.
[28] *Mercer Dictionary of the Bible* (1990), s.v. "Body of Christ," by Mitchell G. Reddish.
[29] 1 Corinthians 12:12.

In the preceding verse he emphasizes:

> There are different kinds of service in the church, but it is the same Lord we are serving .... A spiritual gift is given to each of us as a means of helping the entire church.[30]

Then he continues to explain the different gifts and point out its common purpose for the ministry of the church. Then he compared the church to a human body with different parts and roles yet belonging together to one body, that is, the body of Christ.[31] In succeeding verses he points out:

> Now all of you together are Christ's body, and each one of you is a separate necessary part of it. Here is a list of some members that God has placed in the body of Christ:
>
> > first are apostles,
> >
> > second are prophets,
> >
> > third are teachers,
> >
> > then those who do miracles,
> >
> > those who have the gift of healing,
> >
> > those who can help others,
> >
> > those who can get others to work together,
> >
> > those who speak in unknown languages...[32]

Herein we clearly see the ministerial context of the use of the body of Christ metaphor. The concern here is the interdependent ministerial relationship in the life of the church rather than an exposition of a sort of mystical body. In fact the body of Christ is not only an image of a non-mystical church but also of a non-institutional church. As S. Wibbing points out, "In order to preserve it [church] from false teaching and schisms, it is presented not with an institutional form, but with the reflection that the head and the body are mutually related

---

[30] 1 Corinthians 12:5-7.
[31] As Minear puts it, "Within the one body, the gifts of the Spirit are apportioned in such interdependence that each gift nourishes and is nourished by the whole, love being the "bond of perfection" (Rom. 12:4-8; 1 Cor 12-14; Eph. 4:10-12...)." Minear, "Christ, Body of."
[32] 1 Corinthians 12:27-28.

in love and truth."³³ This may seem a demeaning of the "body of Christ" for theologians and denominations who are preoccupied with a mystical view of the body of Christ. But recognizing the "body" as just one of the many metaphors of church life—places this and the rest of the metaphors in their proper use—practical illustrations for the betterment of ecclesial life. As Kevin Giles emphasizes:

> The understanding of the church as the body of Christ, we may agree, is one of the most profound insights of St Paul, but it would seem to be but one metaphors among several he uses—with each one having its own distinctive contribution to the overall picture, and none on its own providing a comprehensive definition of the church. ³⁴

Third, the body image is used to illustrate the spiritual and vocational unity that should exist amidst diversities in the church. Reddish interprets the phrase body of Christ:

> The phrase "body of Christ: describes the new community of believers created through Christ. The various parts of the body are united in Christ....³⁵

And Bruce Fisk emphasizes that Paul uses the "body of Christ" image in 1 Corinthians "to demonstrate dramatically both diversity within unity (12: 12a, 14-19) and unity out of diversity (12:12b, 20-27)."³⁶ These diversities could be charismatic (that is, in terms of spiritual gifts), or ethnic (that is, Jewish or Gentiles), or social (that is, slaves of free) but all are one (1 Cor. 12: 8-11, 28, 13, 27). This oneness is not a quality inherent in an independent self-existing entity where believers just come into, but the consequence of the believers' Spirit-filled inter-

---

³³ *The New International Dictionary of New Testament Theology* (2003), s.v. "συμα (soma) body," by S. Wibbing."
³⁴ Kevin Giles, *What on Earth Is the Church: An Exploration in New Testament Theology* (Downers Grove, IL: InterVarsity, 1995), 11.
³⁵ Reddish, "Body of Christ."
³⁶ *Evangelical Dictionary of Biblical Theology* (1996), s.v. "Body of Christ," by Bruce N. Fisk.

relationship ensuing out of Spirit-empowered life centered in Christ. Thus the church, in the metaphor of the body of Christ, is both one in Christ and one in Sprit. Minear points out:

> Oneness in him is inseparable from the work of the one Spirit which implies power, hope, peace, and love throughout the whole body (Rom. 8:9-11; 1 Cor. 6:17; 12:1-13; Eph. 2:14; 4:3-4; Col. 3:19).[37]

Further, the believers' coming "into" the body at baptism describes the believers' act of congregating together for "all of . . . [them] together are Christ's body." (1 Cor. 12:13, 27). The church is not seen as independent from the believers' congregation.

Thus, the "body" metaphor of the church is used by Paul—to illustrate in practical sense the importance of smooth interpersonal relationship that should exist in the church. And what is the purpose? The purpose was to illustrate the unity and smooth interpersonal relationship that the church needs in fulfilling the "different kinds of service in the church" (1 Cor. 12:5).

This practical life-oriented perspective is not a rare idea in the New Testament, but an overall perspective of the New Testament ecclesiology. It is, of course, obvious from Pauline to other letters, and even in Revelation with its usually assumed mysterious backdrop. The letters to the Seven Churches of Asia in Revelation clearly emphasize transformation of ecclesial life. The message to the church in Ephesus in 2:4 was the restoration of love to God and fellow believers:

> You don't love me and each other as you did at first! Turn back to me again and work as you did at first.

For the church in Smyrna, "Remain faithful while facing death . . ." (Rev. 2:10). For the church in Pergamum, it was the message of repentance from spiritual apostasy (Rev. 2:14-16). For the church in Thyatira the message was to remain faithful amidst evils and apostasy, "I will ask nothing more of you except that

---

[37] Minear, "Christ, Body of."

you hold tightly to what you have until I come" (Rev. 2:24-25). For the church in Sardis the message was to go back to the kind of life it originally had (Rev. 3:1-3). For the church in Philadelphia the message was to remain faithful and victorious (Rev. 3:11). And the message to the Laodicean church was to get over with its being lukewarm and live a Spirit-led life of faith and righteousness (Rev. 3:15-18).

In this context, the conclusion that we could draw here is that, the New Testament ecclesiology is practical and life-oriented. The concern is on the life of the church. In this chapter, we shall see that the prototypal ecclesiology was focused on the life of congregating believers in terms of their life of faith in and witness for Jesus, and the empowerment of this life by the Holy Spirit. In this regard, may I propose a trinitarian ecclesial life perspective composed of the life of faith, the life a witness, and the life empowered by the Holy Spirit? These structures form the framework of what the church is truly meant to be.

B. The Prototypal Ecclesial Life Structures
a. The Life of Faith

May I propose seeing the life of faith of the New Testament church as composed by a triad of binary constituents, namely, belief and identity, spirituality and fellowship, and commemoration and worship? These binary triads are foundational constituents, because the whole life of faith would collapse with the absence, discordance, non-functionality, or dissection of one from the rest of the constituents. Why? Because this tells us something about the nature of church life, which common ecclesiology have either overlooked or subconsciously ignored—the church is not a fragment, nor could be profoundly meaningful when seen merely from its fragment.

i. Belief and Identity

Paul, in Acts 20:21, succinctly emphasizes the foundational belief of the church, "I have had one message for the Jews and Gentiles—the necessity of turning from sin and turning to God, and of faith in our Lord Jesus." Christ-centered regenerative faith is the only way to salvation. Further, we also need to note that the anticipated redemptive eschatological state of the saved is not a phantom life. It is a real life reminiscent of the primal state the Creator ideally designed for humanity. It is a life of perfect divine-human communion. It is a life where humans are essentially and actually reunited with God and do not turn to sin. In the context of the Fall, the anticipation of that life would mean that humans are turning from sins and turning to God. Thus the objective of faith is hardly mystical but life-oriented. In the church we see the proleptic reconciliation of humanity to God and of humanity to one another. Thus Craig Van Gelder, although taking the concept of ecclesial sociality further, thinks that, "The church is a social community, a community made up of people who are reconciled with God and one another."[38]

Faith here comes with conviction and enlightenment that the original condition of human life designed by the Creator-God is the best suited for humanity. Regeneration is the process of restoring that primal life. And that it could be restored through no other means except faith in Jesus Christ. Further, the Pauline pronouncement, emphatic as it is, is neither expressive of a mere theoretical or creedal affirmation—but of deep-seated faith focused on regenerative life with Jesus. In this sense Wolfhart Pannenberg, Avery Dulles, and Karl Braaten could call the church "a community of faith and not of doctrine."[39]

Paul's faith pronouncement reflects Christ's pronouncement of the necessity of regeneration, and regeneration as beyond human capability. Christ declared:

> I assure you, unless you are born again, you can never see the Kingdom of God . . . . The truth is, no one can enter the Kingdom of God without

---

[38] Craig Van Gelder, *The Essence of the Church: A Community Created by the Spirit* (Grand Rapids: Baker Books, 2000), 108.
[39] Wolfhart Pannenberg, Avery Dulles, and Carl Braaten, *Spirit, Faith, and Church* (Philadelphia: Westminster, 1970), 25-26.

being born of the Spirit. Humans can reproduce only human life, but the Holy Spirit gives new life from heaven.[40]

Here we find the Christological and Pneumatological foundations of the belief framework of the New Testament believers. Without Christ there is no salvation. Without the Holy Spirit there is no conversion. The role of God the Father, of course, is not ignored for biblical faith is always Trinitarian. However, with due recognition of the Trinitarian faith; the incarnate God, Jesus Christ, is the overarching center of Christian faith.

When a trembling human fearful of his life asked, "Sirs, what must I do to be saved?" Paul and Silas replied, "Believe on the Lord Jesus and you will be saved . . . ." (Acts 16:30-31). The first phase of that "saved" condition is the regenerative life that believers now experienced. The final phase would be completed and perfected in the Parousia. The final phase without the first, and vice versa will not complete the soteriological process. However, at the outset, the soteriological process could not begin without the Christological port. Christ is the only means to salvation.

The apparent primacy of this Christ-centered soteriological faith-declaration, at times in the history of Christian church, has been blurred by ecclesial institutionalism or dogmatism. Hans Conzelmann describes the concise and apparent faith structure of the early believers:

> Their faith is summarized in short, easily remembered clauses. Two types of these emerge. In the first type, the faith is formulated personally, as an expression about the nature of Jesus: 'Jesus is the Messiah'. . . In the second type, the formulation is substantive in character, an expression about the work of salvation: 'God has raised Jesus from dead'. . . . [41]

---

[40] John 3:3-6.
[41] Hans Conzelmann, *History of Primitive Christianity*, trans. John E. Steeley (Nashville, TN: Abingdon), 45.

The church created by the Holy Spirit is supposed to be Christ-centered. Its life is supposed to reflect the primacy of Christ. As Helmut Thielicke emphasizes, "All the NT statements about the essence of the church rest on this kind of reference, i.e., to the identity of Jesus and Christ." [42] The ecclesial systematization of beliefs is supposed to be soteriologically Christ-centered—propagating faith in Jesus that result in regenerative life empowered by the Holy Spirit.

Thus the church does not exist for itself, neither its identity inherent in itself. Its existence and identity are derived—derived from Christ. It exists for Christ, and is identified as Christ's. Christ's headship of the church is not just in the sense of dominion but also, at the outset, in the sense of origination. It originates in Christ and is headed by Christ for the primary purpose of proclaiming the soteriological faith in Christ.

The first mass declaration of the core belief of the New Testament church was clearly preached by Peter—the crucified and risen Jesus is "both Lord and Messiah." And when the deeply convicted people asked, "Brothers what should we do?" Then Peter, in Acts 2:36-38, replied:

> Each of you must turn from your sins and turn to God, and be baptized in the name of Jesus Christ for the forgiveness of your sins. Then you will receive the gift of the Holy Spirit.

Shown in this kerygma are the three prototypal structures of the New Testament ecclesial belief framework:

1. The necessity of regenerative life, that is, the necessity of being "born again."
2. The necessity of being baptized in Jesus' name. Or as in Pauline pronouncement, "faith in the Lord Jesus," that is, "acceptance of Jesus as personal Savior"—publicly declared through the rite of baptism.

---

[42] Helmut Thielicke, *The Evangelical Faith*, ed. & trans. Geoffrey W. Bromiley (Edinburgh: T & T Clark, 1982): 209.

3. The consequence, as corollary to the acceptance of Jesus as personal Savior and experience of regenerative life, is the "receiving of the gifts of the Holy Spirit," that is, the empowerment of the Holy Spirit in the lives of believers.

This belief framework is situated in the general picture of the historical divine call. God has been calling humans, as fallen creatures having radically distorted something original and necessary in their life, to come "out of darkness into his wonderful light" (1 Pet. 2:9) and personally avail of his soteriological offer. Eventually, those who respond to the gospel call would congregate into a "called out" people—the church. The soteriological need is answered by their response of faith—the personal willful response to experience new birth, to accept Jesus as the Savior, and be empowered in life by the Holy Spirit.[43] But then, the response has also a socio-spiritual consequence—the congregation of believers.

Thus, the proper characterization of the prototypal belief framework is—gospel-faith.[44] The gospel-faith is focused on a universal life-oriented concern, that is, the redemptive need of humanity. The faith proclamation was calculated to cause personal response to the gospel. It was intended for people to personally experience regenerative life, personal faith in Jesus, and be personally empowered by the Holy Spirit. People who responded to the gospel call consequently congregate as one body of believers—the church. Thus the church is the product of gospel response. The prototype church was truly gospel-oriented—gospel-oriented in its faith and in its constituents.

---

[43] Conzelmann has this to say about the common life of early believers, "The common life was formed out of self-awareness of the believers, they look backward to the resurrection of Christ and the founding of their beliefs, the forward look to his early 'return' in judgment, and the experiencing of the Spirit." Conzelmann, *History of Primitve Christianity*, 48. Conzelmann here notes the early Christians' early expectation of the Parousia, which a number of biblical theologians see as a common eschatological expectation of the early church.

[44] David Neff of *Christianity Today* talks of evangelical faith as gospel-faith, "As *evangel*-icals, we begin this enterprise with the gospel itself." David Neff, "Inside *CT*," *Christianity Today* 43 (January 14, 1999): 5.

The gospel-oriented nature of the life of the early church was not institutionally self-centered nor societally isolationist but kerygmatic and active. Believers congregated for three reasons:

1. Because they have common faith.
2. Because they need to nurture and encourage one another.
3. So that they could be equipped to witness both in their exemplary lives and proclamation.

God called them "out of darkness into his wonderful light" so that they "can show others the goodness of God" (1 Pet. 2:9). Thus the early believers were both evangelical believers and evangelical missionaries. Since Antioch they were identified as Christians (Acts 11:26), and their Christianity was truly gospel-oriented characterized by—Christ-centered faith, Holy Spirit-empowered life, and kerygmatic calling. Their belief and identity was Christ-centered. Their faith was not merely theoretical but life-regenerating. And they were not spiritually passive but missionally active.

ii. Spirituality and Fellowship

The nature of the New Testament ecclesial spirituality never harmonized with the mysticism of its surrounding culture. Mysticism was preoccupied with transcendental form of spirituality. Mysticism was not concerned with everyday transformational lifestyle, practical nurturing, missional proclamation, spiritual-moral modeling amidst a secular society, and more so of humanitarian service. Thus for James, in 1:26-27:

> If you claim to be religious but don't control your tongue, you are just fooling yourself, and your religion is worthless. Pure and lasting religion in the sight of God our Father means that we must care for orphans and widows in their troubles, and refuse to let the world corrupt us.

The practical and pragmatic nature of ecclesial spirituality is further indicated here—"controlling the tongue," so that it would not destroy other's reputation and threaten the smooth interpersonal relationship in the church. I say practical and pragmatic because of the concerns on practical matters of life, and the validity of their faith was tested by the resultant everyday life practices. Their everyday life of faith tested their religiosity. And humanitarian service too, that reflect Christ's ministry of compassion, is regarded as test and practical application of faith; thus "pure and lasting religion" means "care for orphans and widows." The practical notion of ecclesial spirituality is herein pointed out.

Although the ultimate objective of Christ's incarnate ministry was his redemptive death confirmed by his resurrection, yet his teachings and exemplification of regenerative life and acts of love are also emphasized in the Gospels. An everyday life lived based on Christ-centered teachings of love is the essence of Christian spirituality. This is the message of the Sermon on the Mount (Matt. 5-7). The religion of Jesus is a practical religion. It was never intended as mere esoteric enlightenment or an illusory mystical devotion. The Sermon on the Mount and the rest of Jesus' teachings were essentially about practical life-concerns—regenerative lifestyle in contrast to the prevalent distorted culture. Thus the Sermon on the Mount is loaded with the phrase "You have heard . . . But I say . . ."

We may conjecture that James' faith perspective is isolated and not expressive of the overall New Testament perspective. However, this conjecture is tantamount to disregarding the internal coherence of biblical teachings. But, of course, the coherence of James' practical and life-oriented spirituality perspective is readily noticeable in Pauline and other letters, in addition to the abundance of Christological Gospel discourses. Paul reminded the believers in Ephesians 4:17-24:

> Live no longer as the ungodly . . . . They don't care anymore about right and wrong, and they have given themselves over to immoral ways. Their lives are filled with all kinds of impurity and greed. But that isn't what you were taught when you learned about Christ. Since you have

heard all about him and have learned the truth that is in Jesus, throw off your evil nature and your former way of life, which is rotten through and through, full of lust and deception. Instead there must be a spiritual renewal of your thoughts and attitudes. You must display a new nature because you are new person, created in God's likeness—righteous, holy, and true.

Let us note these points:

1. The teachings and learning's about Christ were hardly hypothetical discourses but teachings and learning's (that is, truths) about re-generative way of life. It was life-oriented rather than philosophical. Thus throwing off the "former way of life," v. 22, and living a new righteous life, v. 24.

2. Righteousness, holiness (orthopraxis), and truthfulness (ortho-doxy) were hardly transcendental and theoretical, respectively. They were recognized as real exhibits of life, that is, exhibits of living a regenerated life.[45] Their faith on Christ-centered orthodoxy was validated by their Christ-centered orthopraxis. This is not quite an ascetical or monastic spirituality but a practical and life-oriented spirituality. Their spirituality was characterized by an active life of faith and witness. Thus they "must display a new nature" or live a new God-like life—"righteous, holy, and true," v. 24.

These subsequent phrases in Ephesians 4 and 5 emphasize this practical spirituality:

-"put away all falsehood and 'tell your neighbor the truth' because we belong to each other," 4: 25.

-"Don't sin by letting anger control over you," 4:26.

---

[45] Lewis Mudge sees the calling of the church in a similar way, when he wrote, "the Church of Jesus Christ is called to be a community of faith-full moral discourse and practice." Lewis S. Mudge, *Rethinking the Beloved Community* (Geneva: WCC, 2001), 191. Although his view is more politically colored, yet it reminds the church of its missional life-concerns.

-"stop stealing," 4:28.

-"Begin using your hands for honest work, and then give generously to others in need," 4:28. This is a very practical work-related spirituality with humanitarian implication.

-"Don't use foul or abusive language," 4:29.

-"be kind to each other," 4:32.

-"Follow God's example in everything you do," 5:1.

-"Live a life filled with love for others following the examples of Christ," 5:2. These reflect the everyday life spirituality of the prototypal church.

Devotion to Christ was not regarded as a mystical self-centered devotion,[46] but an everyday regenerative life—like the everyday life Jesus lived on earth. Thus Paul correlated an immoral way of life to the bringing of "sorrow to God's Holy Spirit" who guarantees salvation on the day of redemption (Eph. 4:30). This indicates that redemptive faith and spirituality are not constituted by mere theoretical assents, but by an assimilation of a whole new way of life[47]—regenerative life in Christ empowered by the Holy Spirit.

Such Christ-centered Sprit-empowered life has both individual and interpersonal consequence congregationally shaping the life of the church.[48] Giles also sees that, "Luke [in Acts] intimately connects conversion and communal

---

[46] Thus Green has this to say about the early Christian piety, "For the Christian's [early Christian's] separateness from non-Christian society must not be overstressed. They did not live in a ghetto, and though regarded with suspicion by some, they had friends and relatives among their pagan neighbors." Vivian Green, *A New History of Christianity* (New York: Continuum, 1996), 12.

[47] Mudge comments, "In the end we are talking about an entire theonomous pattern of life—the whole fabric of justified, reconciled human existence—which the gospel calls into being in the world." Mudge, *Rethinking the Beloved Community*, 192.

[48] As Ralph Martin points out, "The 'shared life' depends primarily on God who by his Spirit joins the separate believers together." Ralph P. Martin, *The Family and the Fellow ship: New Testament Images of the Church* (Grand Rapids: Eerdmans, 1979), 45. John Hitchen agrees, "The church is made into a koinonia or living fellowship through the Holy Spirit." John M. Hitchen, "What It Means to be an Evangelical Today—An Antipodean Perspective—Part Two—An Antipodean Perspective," *Evangelical Quarterly* 76 (January 2004):110.

life."⁴⁹ Thus fellowship in this sense is not only casually social, but profoundly spiritual yet realistic and regenerative.

This practical and regenerative spirituality creates a socio-spiritual psyche among believers engendering humanely fulfilling congregational fellowship and societal service. Thus the church has to meet the needs of both its congregation and the world—the church is both a pastoral and missional congregation. Thus, ecclesial spirituality is a real, regenerative, and everyday life lived for one another within the congregation and for the world. Believers are fellowshipping to interpersonally nurture their personal and congregational spiritual and missional lives. As Richard Burridge points out, "Thus the spirituality of the early church also held together the relationship between prayer and practical actions, individual devotion and corporate fellowship, sacramental acts and scriptural study...."⁵⁰

Therefore, ecclesial spirituality is both a practical personal piety and an active kerygmatic piety. Here again could be seen an evangelical paradigm of spirituality and fellowship, that is, spirituality and fellowship intended as a gospel-oriented ecclesial life.

iii. Commemoration and Worship

When Jesus ascended to heaven there was a commemorative-celebrative sentiment and urgent expectation of the *Parousia* among the early believers. This ambiance engulfed the believers as they fellowship in the Lord's Supper. The fellowship of the Lord's Supper was meant to be a reflection of his sacrifices, anticipation of his Second Coming, and a proclamation of redemption.⁵¹

---

⁴⁹ Giles, *What on Earth is the Church*, 77.
⁵⁰ Richard Burridge, "Jesus and the Origin of Christian Spirituality," in *The Story of Christian Spirituality: Two Thousand Years, from East to West*, ed. Gordon Mursell (Minneapolis, MN: Fortress, 2001), 29-30. Burridge also concludes, "Thus the early Christian spirituality was rooted in fellowship—a 'community' or 'sharing together' in the life of God through the Holy Spirit (2Corinthians 13:14)." Ibid., 28.
⁵¹ Martin also sees both baptism and the Lord's Supper as kerygmatic, "Most importantly, both ordinances are the kerygma in action. That is, baptism and the Lord's table bring into focus God's salvation history in a way that could not be said of other 'ordinances,' however valuable they appear to be." Martin, *The Family and the Fellowship*, 79. He further adds that,

Paul writes in 1Corinthians 11:23-28:

For this is what Lord himself said, and I pass it on to you just as I received it. On the night he was betrayed, the Lord Jesus took a loaf of bread, and when he had given thanks he broke it and said, "This is my body, which is given for you, Do this in remembrance of me." In the same way, he took the cup of wine after supper saying, "This cup is the new covenant between God and you, sealed by the shedding of my blood. Do this in remembrance of me as often as you drink it." For eve ry time you eat this bread and drink the cup, you are announcing the Lord's death until he comes again. So if anyone eats this bread or drinks this cup of the Lord unworthily, that person is guilty of sinning against the body and the blood of the Lord. That is why you should examine yourself before eating the bread and drinking the cup.

Further, the celebration of the Lord's Supper has both personal and interpersonal features.[52] And the personal spirit of participants determines the communal spirit of fellowship; thus Paul necessitates personal examination as requisite of communal participation. The integrity of personal spirit is necessitated because the efficacy of the commemorative act is not in itself mechanically inherent in the rite. It is rather dependent on personal spirituality spontaneously engendering congregational spirituality.

Moreover, although the commemorative act of the Lord's Supper is essential in the fellowship of the church; yet it was not designed a means for substituting personal and congregational experience of the process of regeneration by the Holy Spirit. Neither was it designed as a soteriological mechanism; because the process of salvation is only realized through repentance from sins,

---

"contemporizing of his [Christ's] sacrifice and thanksgiving and renewed participation" is "what the communion service is all about." Ibid

[52] McKinion notes of the Lord's Supper described in early documents, "Often small groups would join together in homes to partake of the bread and wine. By sharing communion with one another, believers expressed their common faith and their membership within the Christian community. Only baptized members of the community were allowed to participate in the rite." McKinion, *Life and Practice in Early Church*, 99.

faith in Jesus Christ, and conversion of life by the Holy Spirit. The original ecclesial celebration of the Lord's Supper was not even an intensely solemn rite, but a socio-spiritual event with socio-humanitarian backdrop. As a socio-spiritual act it was celebrated with good social-etiquette. It should not be hurriedly done without sharing food to others who are hungry. It should not disgrace the church and embarrass the poor (1 Cor. 11:21, 22). Thus Paul in 1Corinthians 11:20-22 rebuked the un-regenerated participants in the Lord's Supper:

> It's not the Lord's Supper you are concerned about when you come together. For I am told that some of you hurry to eat your own meal with out sharing with others. As a result, some go hungry while others get drunk . . . do you really want to disgrace the church of God and shame the poor?

The profound significance of commemorating the Lord's Supper does not mechanically reside in the rite itself without regards to the spirit of the celebrants. Thus Bloesch has this to say about church rites, "Its own rites and ceremonies have little value except when they are used by the Spirit to instruct and edify the saints, that is, those who believe in Jesus Christ as Lord and Savior."[53] The New Testament model was not even in the form of an institutionalized rite that we now have. In fact the celebration of the Lord's Supper was rather homely than churchy. Luke accounts, "They worshipped together at the temple each day, met in homes for the Lord's Supper, and shared their meals with joy and generosity—all the while praising God" (Acts 2:42).

This may seem a demeaning of the Lord's Supper, but indeed the performance of its rites was not originally regarded as the means of salvation. The rite could only have redemptive significance if it leads the participants to a deep communion with Christ, engendering true acceptance of Jesus as personal Sav-

---

[53] Donald G. Bloesch, *The Church: Sacraments, Worship, Ministry, Mission* (Downers Grove, IL: InterVarsity, 2002), 24.

ior resulting in regenerative life. This is more like an evangelical rather than ritualistic view of the Lord' Supper.

The called out ones, the church, worshipped at the temple, and celebrated the Lord's Supper in homes. The celebration of the Lord's Supper was then, not more of a ritual than, to use our modern church cliché, a potluck. But it was a potluck with socio-spiritual grounding formed by a spirit of Christ-centered commemoration, celebration, and eschatological expectation. It was a dinner in honor of Jesus Christ. The difference between a secular honorary dinner and the Lord's Supper is that in the Lord's Supper, the physical presence of the honoree was both reminisced and anticipated, although there is a spiritual sense of his presence.

The description of Acts' and 1Corinthians' celebration of the Lord's Supper as socio-humanitarian is indicated by the words like "sharing" and "generosity"—"shared their meals with great joy and generosity," Acts 2:46. The sharing of meals was an intended fellowship means for the haves to share meals with the have-nots in the spirit of Christ's love (1Cor 11:21). Regarding worship and its socio-humanitarian implications, Everett Ferguson remarks, "The gift which Christians offered in their worship were not only the spiritual sacrifices of praise and thanksgiving but also the physical goods necessary to relieve human needs."[54]

Though the Lord's Supper was an essential feature of the believer's ecclesial fellowship, yet it was not a rite overriding the other essentials of Christian beliefs and practices, like emphasis on personal faith in Jesus, regenerative life, gospel proclamation, baptism, and humanitarian concern. I do not imply to demean the significance of the Lord's Supper as well as other rites for they are also important in nurturing the socio-spiritual and communal psyche of a congregation of believers. But I just would like to point out that the original church

---

[54] Everett Ferguson, *Early Christians Speak: Faith and Life in the First Three Centuries*, 3rd ed. (Abilene, TX: ACU, 1999), 207.

life was a balanced and synthesized life. Church life was not just centered on a commemorative act; although such commemoration plays a role in ecclesial life. And church rites were not regarded as means of salvation itself but as avenues for reconnecting believers to Jesus.

Acts 2:42 accounts for a wider perspective of church life, "They [the three thousand baptized] joined with other believers and devoted themselves to the apostles' teachings and fellowship, sharing in the Lord's Supper and in prayer."

We could see a quadrilateral ecclesial life here. A devotion to:
1. Apostolic teachings
2. Congregational fellowshipping
3. Socio-humanitarian sharing of the Lord's Supper
4. Prayer, which is most probably interpersonal

The response of faith, these devotions, and the missional exigency are the causative factors in the phenomenon of the church. Because people responded in faith to the gospel call, they congregated to meet their spiritual needs, enabling them to fulfill the Gospel Commission. Herein we see the gospel-oriented life of the original church. The gospel-orientation of its fellowship also shapes the gospel-orientation of its worship.

Worship was not sacramental or liturgical itself, but kerygmatic, that is, a proclaiming the gospel—thus teaching, fellowshipping, celebrating, and praying as proclaiming the gospel of Christ. Worship proclaims the salvation in Christ and celebrates the new life in Christ. Worship was Christ-centered. Believers congregated to worship Christ for the purpose:

-of nurturing faith in Jesus,

-commemorating the substitutionary death of Jesus,

-celebrating the redemptive victory Jesus did for humanity,

-and praying for the empowerment of the Holy Spirit,

-so that they could live a regenerated life in Jesus and fulfill their missional calling.

Karen Lebacqz sees both the missional and reflective aspects of worship, "The purpose of worship is not only to strengthen us for the tasks ahead, but to remind us of the *meaning* of these tasks." [55]

Faith and spirituality are not inherent endowments of the church services itself. These are the consequences of personal experience with Jesus enriched by Spirit-led interactions with fellow believers while worshipping God. Spiritual life is neither institutionally endowed nor merely individually fulfilled but relationally caused. It is the result of personal relationship with Jesus and interpersonal relationship with fellow believers. And the regenerative individual divine-human relationship also results in a regenerative social interrelationship. The resultant regenerative interrelationship eventually recreates a regenerative congregational reconciliation of the lost human creatures with the Creator-God. Worship in this sense is neither ecclesiocentric, nor lonely, nor mechanical—but Christ-centered, spiritually interpersonal, and spontaneous. We could see a lot of implications here, but suffice it to say, that the institution of church is not, in itself, the entity that births worship. Rather it is the congregation of regenerated believers that by its spontaneous act of congregating gives natural birth to nurturing fellowship and holy worship of God.

b. The Kerygmatic Life

The parting words of the ascending Christ is of utmost importance to the church! And it is appropriately called the Great Gospel Commission. Matthew 28: 18-20 accounts:

> Jesus came and told his disciples, "I have been given complete authority in heaven and on earth. Therefore, go and make disciples of all nations, baptizing them in the name of the Father and the Son and the Holy Spir-

---

[55] Karen Lebacqz, *Word, Worship, World, and Wonder: Reflections on Christian Living* (Nashville, TN: Abingdon, 1997), 68.

it. Teach the new disciples to obey all the commands I have given you. And be sure of this: I am with you always, even to the end of age."

The early believers were called to fulfill the Great Commission—so is the church today. The vocation of the 11-member embryonic church was neither an ascetical preoccupation nor merely pedantic—but evangelistic and life-oriented. Harrison defines the meaning of discipleship, "Though the word *disciple* means 'learner,' its genius does not lie in the intellectual realm but in the area of devotion and sacrifice."[56] The church was called to make disciples of Christ and to teach the disciples to live like Christ. In the paradigm of the Great Commission, the church is not seen not as a static institution waiting for people to come in, but as a dynamic missional congregation of disciples.

The two other Gospel accounts of the Great Commissioning could further explicate the theological framework of the embryonic church.

Mark 16:15-18 states:

> . . . he appeared to the eleven disciples . . . and then he told them, "Go into all the world and preach the Good News to everyone, everywhere. Anyone who believes and is baptized will be saved. But anyone who refuses to believe will be condemned. These signs will accompany those who believe. They will cast out demons in my name and they will speak new language. They will be able to handle snakes with safety, and if they drink anything poisonous, it won't hurt them. They will be able to place their hands on the sick and heal them."

And Luke 24:46-49 says:

> And he said, "Yes it was written long ago that the Messiah must suffer and die and rise again from the dead on the third day. With my authority, take this message of repentance to all nations, beginning in Jerusalem: 'There is forgiveness of sins for all who turn to me.' You are witnesses of all these things. And now I will send the Holy Spirit, just as

---

[56] Everett F. Harrison, *The Apostolic Church* (Grand Rapids: Eerdmans, 1985), 122.

my Father promised. But stay here in the city until the Holy Spirit comes and fills you with power from heaven."

These three accounts are not diverse but complementary accounts defining the kerygmatic life of the church. Let us take a closer look at the original components of the kerygmatic life of the church.

i. Mission and Evangelism

What is the mission of the church? The aforementioned Gospel accounts compatibly complement each other.

Matthew emphasizes discipleship which is a process of realizing the life of faith in people who responded to the redemptive call. But it should be noted that disciple-making was commissioned to those who are already disciples, that is, the eleven disciples. Thus "Jesus...told his disciples," to "go and make disciples," 28:19. This indicates that discipleship is both a life of faith and a life of witness. The disciples are to live in a regenerated life and proclaim the gospel, both in communication and exemplification. Discipleship is not merely intended as a theological education but as a development of life-oriented faith, that is, faith formation meant to change life. Thus the ecclesial mission is not solely theoretical and denominational but life-oriented and eschatological—that is, focused on changing lives in the context of the *Parousia*.

In the framework of the Great Commission, the church is seen not as mere repository of dogma, an information center, or a mystical entity. But as a vocational school where people are taught about the practice of regenerated life, and as a missional agency that evangelizes people. Thus "go and make disciples." The church is a tangible congregation of believers whose mission is to propagate a model of regenerative life amidst a pattern of degenerative life of the world.[57] The ecclesial mission is about making the lost human creatures

---

[57] Thus as the Carmody's say it, "The church is by definition counter-cultural whenever its primary values of faith, hope, and love contradict the operative values of a given culture." Denise L. Carmody and John Carmody, *Bonded in Christ's Love: An Introduction to Ecclesiology* (New York: Paulist, 1986), 7.

believers of the Creator and of his ideals of the recreated life—thus disciples of Jesus.

Mark emphasizes the kerygmatic and charismatic features of the Great Commission—"go and preach" (16:15), "speak new language" (16:17), and heal the sick (17:18). The mission of the church is to proclaim the gospel. And those who respond to the gospel will not only be saved, but will also be vocationally empowered by the Holy Spirit. The proclamation poses either redemptive or judgmental consequence, depending on response of the hearers—thus "Anyone who believes...will be saved . . . anyone who refuses . . . will be condemned" (16:16)." However, salvation or judgment is not the prerogative of the church, but rather a consequence of faith in Christ—as indicated in the phrase anyone "who believes . . ." or "refuses . . .". Acceptance of Christ, not denominational acceptance, is the mission of the church. In fact ecclesiological formation is just a consequence of kerygmatic response. The church itself is not the essence of the gospel, the essence of the gospel is Jesus.

In this sense, baptism is not intended as denominational itself but Christological. Those who were baptized were those who believed on Jesus as their personal Savior; not those who were sort of institutional endorsed or accepted for denominational membership. Although spontaneously those who accept Jesus as their personal Savior became members of the church. As Harrison puts it this way:

> In Acts and in the Epistles baptism is presented as the rite by which those who have put their faith in Christ are inducted to the church. No doubt it was considered to be a fulfillment of the requirement of confessing him before men—not in an exhaustive sense of course, but rather as a first step.[58]

---

[58] Harrison, *The Apostolic Church*, 122.

This practice of baptism is common in evangelical crusades; [59] although, ironically, may not be still so common in so-called evangelical denominations. Furthermore, charismatic gift here is not regarded as a sign or seal of a redemptive confirmation, but as an empowerment of the Holy Spirit for personal regenerative life and public missional life as the result of faith in Christ.

Luke summarizes the missional, kerygmatic, redemptive, and charismatic component of the Great Commission. Luke accounts, "You are witnesses . . . take the message of repentance . . . there is forgiveness . . . I will send the Holy Spirit" (24:47-49). Here the message of repentance and forgiveness of sins (a message prominent in evangelical crusades); and the anticipation of the outpouring of the Holy Spirit (conspicuous in Pentecostalism) are highlighted. The accentuation of "you are witnesses" stresses that the kerygmatic nature of the church, that is, the church's mission, is both to proclaim and exemplify before the world its Christ-centered faith.

But what is the relationship of mission and evangelism? In the paradigm of the Gospel Commission, the mission of the church is characterized as evangelical, that is, gospel-oriented. The church's mission is to preach the necessity of conversion and acceptance of Jesus as personal Savior, and living a new life empowered by the Holy Spirit. Mission is the intention and evangelism is the action. Evangelism is not about a religious institutionalization of a secular world, nor an expansion of a religious institution. It is the proclamation of the redemptive Christological message with the intention of pervasively making disciples of Christ.

Evangelism, in the context of the Great Commission, is not about a quantification of ecclesial institutional growth itself, but a qualification of people for the kingdom of God. As such, evangelism is not denominational. It is not intended for the expansion of a denomination, or merely a denominational effort

---

[59] As in the early church, Coppedge writes, "In the Great Commission, baptism seems to represent the culmination of the whole process of outreach." Allan Coppedge, *The Biblical Principles of Discipleship* (Grand Rapids: Francis Ausbury, 1989), 115.

of professing Christians. It is intended to prepare people for the kingdom of God. And the mission is the mission of both individual believers and the church as a whole and all believers. Thus appropriately, evangelism should be a transdenominational effort rather than denominational, for the evangelistic content and the focus is always the Christ-centered gospel not denominational doctrines. In this sense, evangelism was truly gospel-oriented.

ii. Life and Proclamation

Witnessing for the New Testament believers was holistic. It was both a communication and an exemplification of their life of faith in Jesus. They witness for Christ both in their proclamation and life modeling. As Vivian Green notes:

> It was the life-style of the early Christians which most distinguished them from their pagan contemporaries. Ideally, belief in Jesus Christ had a life-changing dimension.[60]

And McKinion points out:

> Christians attempted to convert their neighbors and others through evangelism, or the personal proclamation of the teachings of Christ. They did this not simply by sharing the message of Jesus but also by living a life that demonstrate their own conversion.[61]

The means of witnessing were both the proclamation of the message and the life of believers; the kerygma and the life of faith were inseparable. Darrell Gruder speaks of the inseparability of the *kerygma* and *martyria*:

> The *kerygma* is the verbalization of the event that has called forth this community.... To separate the *kerygma* from *martyria* of the Christian church is to make the gospel into propositions to be affirmed rather than to understand it as the opportunity to know God in a personal and

---

[60] Green, *A New History of Christianity*, 9.
[61] McKinion, *Life and Practice in the Early Church*, 115.

life-transforming relationship, called faith, and then to serve his purposes. [62]

In this sense, martyrdom is the proclamation and life of faith so rooted that enforcement of sufferings and death could not sway a witness to unfaithfulness or denial of faith.

Witnessing in the sense of martyrdom reveals two essential features of original kerygmatic life of the church, namely, profound commitment to the gospel proclamation and way of life deeply rooted in the gospel proclaimed. In fact, the New Testament Greek etymology of witnessing is barely verbal but a declaration of both the message and the life lived because of the message. *Vine's Concise Dictionary* defines *martus* as "those whose lives and actions testified to the worth and effect of faith." [63] In a contemporary sense, Mudge points out, "Faith and ethics together are a single spiritual reality which cannot be adequately expressed by either of those two terms alone."[64] Further, the kerygmatic model of the New Testament is life-oriented rather than propositional. As Paul emphasized, "For the Kingdom of God is not just fancy talk; it is living God's power."[65] A life of faith is integral in witnessing.

Furthermore, ecclesial witnessing was never passive and static but active and dynamic. The church did not proclaim the gospel just within the confinement of its infrastructure. In fact, the original church was more truly a movement rather than an institution confined within its own infrastructure. Of course, it would be naïve to propose a non-institutional church in the context of the present global society that has evolved into complexities necessitating societal institutions. But the point here is that the church to be truly prototypal should transcend its institutional confinement and be truly gospel-oriented, missional, and trans-denominational. The church went to proclaim the gospel

---

[62] Darrell L. Guder, *Be My Witnesses: The Church's Mission, Message, and Messengers* (Grand Rapids: Eerdmans, 1985), 50.
[63] *Vine's Concise Dictionary of Bible Word* (1999), s. v. "witness."
[64] Mudge, *Rethinking the Beloved Community*, 192.
[65] 1 Corinthians 4:20.

amidst the crowd. It was not a waiting church, it was a going church. As Frost and Hirsch said it:

> The missional church . . . is a sent church. It is a *going* church; a movement of God through its people, sent to bring healing to a broken world.[66]

The original church went where people were and served where people were. And it was not preoccupied with fancy talks, as in speculative dogmatic engagements but with life-concerns—propagating a life of faith amidst a faithless world.

Regarding the church as a way of life, Rodney Clapp writes:

> Church is a way of life lived not with the expectation that Christians, through managerial arts or sudden heroism, make the world right. It is instead a way of life lived in confidence that God has, in the Kingdom of Christ, began to set the world right—and that someday Christ will bring his Kingdom to its fulfillment.[67]

Thus Paul, believing himself as a cosmological specter-believer ("a specter to the entire world—to people and angels alike")[68] testified:

> I discipline my body like an athlete, training it do what it should. Otherwise, I fear that after preaching to others I myself might be disqualified.[69]

A coherent kerygmatic life is requisite of a coherent kerygmatic message.

In the pattern of the Gospel Commission the trustees were already disciples—this points out the primacy of convertive life before missional function. Believers should first experience Christ and live Christ-like life before they could evangelize. Ecclesiologically, this means that the church should first live the

---

[66] Michael Frost and Alan Hirsch, *The Shaping of Things to Come: Innovation and Mission for the 21st-Century Church* (Peabody, MA: Hendrickson, 2003), 18.
[67] Rodney Clapp, *A Peculiar People: The Church as Culture in a Post-Christian Society* (Downers Grove, IL: InterVarsity, 1996), 200.
[68] 1 Corinthians 4:9
[69] Ibid., 4:27.

gospel before it proclaims the gospel. This is paradigmatic of evangelical missional strategy. Thus spiritual renewal is requisite of missional revival. At present, there is a serious need for global ecclesial renewal before there could be a global evangelistic explosion.

c. The Empowerment of the Holy Sprit

The commissioning of the embryonic church was done when Christ ascended to heaven and the ecclesial empowerment was inaugurated when the Holy Spirit descended upon the early believers on that particular Day of Pentecost. That particular Day of Pentecost marked the beginning of a missional era. As Grenz emphasizes, "the coming of the Spirit marked the inauguration of a new era, the age of the mission of the church."[70] It was the evangelistic activation of church,[71] whose life has been spiritually prepared through fellowship, prayer, and oneness in spirit, life and purpose.

Although the Great Commission was entrusted to the eleven disciples, yet at Pentecost, all the called out ones were empowered and were preaching. This implies that the mission of the church does not belong to an elite clique but to all believers. The church at its missional inauguration was not institutionally sacerdotal but missionally evangelical. The life of the church was focused not on priestly ceremonies, but focused on faith and life in Jesus, and the proclamation of the gospel.

In the context of the Old Testament "called out ones," the "ecclesial entity" did not fulfill its mission. It became spiritually ethnocentric, institutionally static, and even soteriologically exclusivist. Their original vocational call was marred and had deteriorated into a religio-ethnic cultism. Because of its missional failure, the Old Testament "called out ones" failed in its calling and could not be regarded as the church. The Pentecostal phenomenon, "predicted

---

[70] Stanley J. Grenz, *Theology for the Community of God* (Grand Rapids: Eerdmans, 1994), 368.
[71] Looking at the Day of Pentecost as the formative time of the church Harrison comments, "It was just impossible, that the church could have been formed before Pentecost as it was impossible that it should not have been formed after that date." *The New Unger's Bible Dictionary*, s.v. "Church," by R.K. Harrison

centuries ago by the prophet Joel" (Acts 2:16), could have been fulfilled to the Old Testament "called out ones." However, its vocational failure and rejection of Jesus consequently resulted in its forfeiture of the empowerment of the Holy Spirit for missional purpose. Eventually a new non-ethnic, spiritual and gospel-oriented entity was called—what is to be more truly called the church.

Further, at Pentecost the church was not seen as a dispenser of spiritual power, but rather as an instrument of the Holy Spirit for the fulfillment of the Gospel Commission. Thus the spiritual power of the church is not inherent in itself, but derived—it is derived from the Holy Spirit. Furthermore, the Pentecostal phenomenon reveals that the Holy Spirit is both the source of life and the one who directs the church. I emphasize the point that the Holy Spirit directs the life of the church because this reminds the church that ecclesial phenomenon within the framework of the gospel, should be regarded as the Spirit's operation rather than just merely a denominational reaction or an accidental event.

When Christ ascended, the eleven disciples did not see the Great Commission as an end in itself but rather an entrusting of faith that needed to be worked out with the provision of appropriate empowerment. Both Luke and Mark clearly emphasize the empowerment of the Holy Spirit. In Matthew the phrase, "I am with you always, even to the end of the age" (Matt 28:20) is reminiscent of Jesus' pre-ascension assurance:

> I am going away . . . . But it is actually best for you that I go away, because if I don't, the Counselor won't come . . . if I do go away, he will come . . . . And when he comes, he will convince the world of its sin, and of God's righteousness, and of the coming judgment . . . he will guide you into all truth.[72]

What happened at the Pentecost was not sacramental itself, although it signified the fulfillment of prophecy. Nor was it ecclesiocentric, although the outpouring was for the congregating believers. It was however missional,

---

[72] John 16:5-13.

kerygmatic, and evangelistic. Missional because it was for the fulfillment of the ecclesial mission; kerygmatic because it was the power behind the proclamation; and evangelistic because through the Holy Spirit people could be deeply convicted of their sins, repented, believed and accepted Jesus as their personal Savior (John 16:5-13). Here we see that Jesus is the object of faith—the Savior; and the Holy Spirit is the power—the Transformer.

Empowered by the outpouring of the Holy Spirit, the believers were enabled to—live their faith in Christ, proclaim their faith in Christ, and witness for Christ. Only through the Holy Spirit could the church fulfill its purpose. Without the Holy Spirit, the church would just become a conglomerate of likeminded people forming a sort of social club, which may have a societal role to play but with no universal redemptive significance.

Suffice it to say that the New Testament, especially the letters of Paul, is replete with discussions on charismatic gifts. However, we should note that the charismatic endowments of the church were not intended for self-centered purpose. It was intended for the empowerment of the life of faith and witness of both individual believers and the church.

Further, a responding believer could not be regenerated through mere pedagogical, sacramental[73] or liturgical means. The washing of sins is only through Jesus, and the bestowal of new life is only through the Holy Spirit (Titus 3:6). Thus living a regenerated life is living a "new life in the Holy Spirit," and the fruits of such regenerated life are the produce of the operation of the Holy Spirit in a believers' life (Gal 5:16, 22).

However, the receipt of spiritual gifts was not seen as a signifying the seal of conversion itself, as if receipt of a vocational spiritual gift indicates the realization of a salvation; although the Holy Spirit spontaneously indwells in a

---

[73] Regarding life as a sacrament, Lebacqz has this to say, "God's grace is not limited to baptism, marriage, Eucharist, death, or ordination, but infuses all of life. All of life, therefore, has the potential to be sacramental. Indeed, all of life should be lived sacramentally—as an outward and visible sign of an inward grace. Lebacqz, *Word, Worship, World and Wonder*, 68.

truly converted believer. The indwelling of the Holy Spirit is a spontaneous consequence of faith in Christ. Receipt of the Holy Spirit for the empowerment of personal regenerative life and receipt of spiritual gifts for missional purpose was not regarded as a sort of seal of redemptive security. For humans, still awaiting the absolute transformation at the Parousia, may still be lead astray from God through persistent and lifelong willful sinful acts. Charismatic gifts are intended, not for personal redemptive verification but, for congregational ministry, that is, "a spiritual gift is given to each of us as a means of helping the entire church" (1 Cor 12:7). Moreover, these gifts are not inherent in the church itself or in individuals composing the church, for only "the Holy Spirit . . . is the source" (1Cor 12:4).

The recognition of the empowerment of the Holy Spirit as both a personal regenerative and a ministerial necessity is central in the life of the church.

C. The Projected Significance

To conclude, the original ecclesial life framework was Christ-centered in content, with life empowered by the Holy Spirit, and mission-oriented. The original church life was a balanced life of faith in and witness for Jesus empowered by the Holy Spirit. Faith was life-oriented and regenerative. Witnessing was truly gospel-oriented. And believers witness for Jesus both in their everyday life modeling and verbal proclamation.

But whatever happened to this original ecclesial life framework, is a history of blunders in, and challenges for, the Christian church. However, it is in this backdrop of ecclesiological blunders and challenges that we could realize the profound intention and significance of Contemporary Evangelicalism and the preceding movements.

3
The Deformation and Re-Formation of the Prototypal Ecclesial Life Framework

A. The State of the Pre-Reformation Church

The original characteristics of the church after the apostolic time disintegrated. The disintegration was caused by a confluence of complex factors. Non-

Christian religious, philosophical, social, cultural, and political influences were accommodated resulting in syncretistic and misdirected preoccupations of the church. Eventually, the original characteristics of the church broke down and were substituted with characteristics that reflected more of a socio-political institution than the New Testament church. Earle Cairns notes "how far the medieval church had departed from the ideal of the New Testament."[74] He further adds, "The Catholic Reformation was in itself an admission that all was not well in the medieval church."[75]

As the church continued to grow institutionally amidst misdirected preoccupations—it continued to transform its nature from a faith-based congregation to something more like a secular institution. On the one hand, its societal milieu like political and economic exploitations, moral disintegration and secularism also became conspicuous in the life of the church. Justo Gonzalez notes:

> But it was not only at the moral level the church seemed to be in need of reformation. Some among the more thoughtful Christians were becoming convinced that the teachings of the church had also gone astray.[76]

On the other hand, an extremist ascetic reaction also became an alternate form of spirituality. F. Donald Logan points out:

> The defining form of Christian spirituality from at least the late eleventh century was the monastic life. Christians wishing to strive for spiritual perfection, would be told to leave the world and enter a religious community.[77]

The balanced faith-based, mission-oriented, and gospel-centered characteristics of church life were deformed. The following are the characteristics of church life of the pre-Reformation church:

---

[74] E. Cairns, *Christianity through the Centuries: A History of the Church*, 3rd rev. ed. (Grand Rapids: Zondervan, 1996), 271.
[75] Ibid.
[76] Justo L. Gonzalez, *The Reformation to the Present Day*, vol. 2, *The Story of Christianity* (San Francisco: HarperSanFrancisco, 1985), 7.
[77] F. Donald Logan, *A History of the Church in the Middle Ages* (London: Routledge, 2002), 341.

a. The Life of Faith

Faith was redefined. Thus the life of the church was also transformed into something that did not more truly reflect the original ecclesial life of faith. The cross had become a mere object of sentiment if not of fetishism. The apparent centrality of the person of Jesus Christ as the only means to salvation was overshadowed, ironically, by religious relics and, more so, of secular preoccupations. The gospel-oriented soteriology was deformed. Pierre Chaunu emphasizes a departure from Christ-centered to church-centered soteriology of the pre-Reformation church, "With the system of Indulgences, everything rested on the Church, to which God had delegated his power."[78] Salvation became a superficial institutional regulation. Redemptive Christ-centeredness was clouded by an institutional church-centeredness. The Bible was either ignored or manipulatively interpreted. Chaunu notes, "The Church had the key to Scripture to which it alone knew and which it scarcely troubled itself about any more."[79] And Owen Chadwick identifies one of the "inner contradictions in Western Christianity" in the 1500's—"the Church held up the Bible as the source of truth. But it taught various doctrines that no one could find in the Bible."[80]

Faith became institutional rather than profoundly Christological, so was the Christian identity. The life of faith was centered on dogmatic institutional assent, rather than— essentially the acceptance of Jesus as the only personal Savior resulting in a regenerative life empowered by the Holy Spirit. The cross even became a symbol of Christendom's territorial conquest.

Spirituality and fellowship, on the one hand, became ritualistic and formal rather than regenerative and spiritually interpersonal. On the other hand, spirituality also became an ascetical monastic preoccupation devoid of interper-

---

[78] Pierre Chaunu, "The pre-Reformation Climate," in *The Reformation*, ed. Pierre Chaunu (New York: St. Martin's, 1986), 56.
[79] Ibid.
[80] Owen Chadwick, *A History of Christianity* (New York: St Martin's, 1995), 196

sonal fellowship for spiritual nurturing and missional support. Thus the balanced life of faith and witness was deformed.

Worship and commemoration of the Lord's Supper became no more than occasional sentimental rites—without engendering an everyday transformational way of life. The Lord's Supper was even turned into a sort of socio-ecclesiastical control distorting the kerygmatic vocation of the church. By this I mean, the rite of the Lord's Supper was regarded as a means of bestowing salvation. Thus the institution of the church was in itself regarded as the source of salvation rather than Christ himself. The life of faith of the pre-Reformation church was stripped of its gospel-orientation.

b. The Life of Witness

Mission and evangelism were synonymous with, at times, inhumane political exploitations. Territorial expansions, coercion to Christianity, exercise of ecclesiastical power with self-claimed redemptive authority, and exclusive terrestrial claim of the extra-terrestrial kingdom of God—clouded the original Gospel Commission of the church. The church was obsessed with materialistic erection of huge and magnificent infrastructures. And these were regarded as sort of centers of the kingdom of God from which people could be called from to come into. Chaunu notes this missional disorientation:

> From the eight century onwards, the idea of mission imperceptibly gave way to a kind of crusade before the event. A colonizing Christianity, a conquest at once cultural, spiritual and at times political and even military, developed in the north to the east. [81]

Although there was indeed sweeping missionary conquest; however, Cairns emphasizes that the conquest "raised the problem of [mass] baptism without a real experience of faith."[82] Green characterizes baptism in the medieval period:

---

[81] Pierre Chaunu, "A long exodus," in *The Reformation*, ed, Chaunu, 33.
[82] Cairns, *Christianity Through the Centuries*, 174.

> For many converts [in medieval Christianity] baptism must therefore have appeared little more than a mechanical or magical act, and their understanding of their new found faith may have been little more than a transposition of what they really believed as pagans now placed within a comparatively crude framework of Christian beliefs.[83]

The focus on converts' "genuine experience of salvation" was overshadowed by the preoccupation on "wholesale acceptance of Christianity"[84] for the expansion of Christendom. In fact, civilizing the world was defined in terms of political Christianization of the world. That is, a religio-political assent to the symbol of the cross, without deeper personal experience with Jesus Christ, for the purpose of territorial subjugation.

Individual life of faith and witness were obscured by ecclesiastical regulations and secular preoccupations. Even the lives and proclamations of missionary groups were defined according to their respective group's focus, rather than the gospel itself.

c. Empowerment of the Holy Spirit

With the disintegration of the original ecclesial life of faith and witness, ecclesial spiritual empowerment was changed to self-claimed institutional power. The need for the empowerment of the Holy Spirit in the life of the church was substituted by the power of politics, money, and ecclesiastical manipulation of societal psyche. The spirit and life of the church became rooted in ecclesiastical institutional authority—losing its rootedness in Christ and the Holy Spirit. The church became secular and indistinguishable from any secular political institution. In fact, there was the medieval synthesis of religio-political power. As Robert Markus notes the, "Church and empire were fused in a single entity; the

---

[83] Green, *A New History of Christianity*, 51
[84] Ibid.

empire was an image of the heavenly kingdom, its boundaries the limits of Christendom...."[85]

Timothy Phillips and Dennis Okholm point out, "During the Middle Ages the church became an integral part of society, indistinguishable from the world."[86] Ferguson agrees on this state of the church even early on the Medieval Age—"By the end of the fourth century the line between the church and the world was becoming blurred."[87] Francis Clark, both of Pontifical Gregorian University and Oxford's Heythrop College, points out the deformation in the late Medieval Age, "The defects attributed to late-medieval Catholicism fall into two categories: in the first are practical abuses and superstitious observances connected with the altar; in the second, errors in doctrine and belief about the nature of the Mass."[88] Thus as Cairns notes, "Protestant historians considered the Middle Ages the valley of shadow in which the pure church of the ancient era of church history was corrupted."[89]

The church drifted into secularism and was losing the integrity of its life of faith and witness—its integrity as the congregation of the called out ones. Thus the original characteristics of the life of the church in the pre-Reformation church were essentially deformed. And there was an urgent need for reformation. Gonzalez asserts, "As the fifteenth century came to a close, it was clear that the church was in need of profound reformation, and that many longed for it."[90] As Berkouwer puts it, "reformation can mean a criticism of a dangerous process of 'deformation'."[91]

---

[85] Robert A. Markus, "From Rome to the Barbarian Kingdoms (330-700)," in *The Oxford Illustrated History of Christianity*, ed. John McManners (Oxford: Oxford University Press, 1990), 70.
[86] Timothy R. Phillips and Dennis L. Okholm, *A Family of Faith: An Introduction to Evangelical Christianity* (Grand Rapids: Baker Academic, 2001), 167.
[87] Fergusson, *Early Christians Speak*, 197.
[88] Francis Clark, *Eucharistic Sacrifice and the Reformation*, 2nd ed. (Oxford: Basil Blackwell, 1967), 56.
[89] Cairns, *Christianity Through the Centuries*, 160.
[90] Gonzalez, *The Reformation to the Present Day*, 6.
[91] G.C. Berkouwer, *The Church* (Grand Rapids: Eerdmans, 1976), 184.

However, in spite of this situation, we could not still characterize the pre-Reformation church as absolutely lost. For after all, it had also spread Christendom. Perhaps, in a sense, its political exploitations contributed to the survival of Christian civilization that could have been wiped out by opposing non-Christian powers. The church struggled to live in a wipe or be wiped out sociopolitical milieu. It did have its failures, particularly on the essentials of Christian Faith. And had it been more faithful to its original design, probably it could have expanded in ways and consequences unexpected in history. The pre-Reformation church could have been intended to gain societal foothold to further fulfill its kerygmatic vocation. However, the church drifted from its kerygmatic calling and was engrossed in politics and materialism. It mistranslated its kerygmatic vocation into something socio-political and materialistic.

However, in spite of its failures, and recognizing the overriding directions of the Holy Spirit in the deeper history of the church, Cairns could still say that, "Development under the divine direction was continuous even in the Middle Ages."[92] Recognizing the deeper divine direction is essential in understanding the phenomenon of succeeding ecclesial movements and, eventually, in understanding the emergence of Contemporary Evangelicalism.

B. The Emergence of the Reformation Movement

At the outset, Protestantism before becoming an ism was intended, not as a separatist denominationalism but—as a movement for reforming the whole church because of its deteriorating nature. As McGrath emphasizes, "As its name suggests, the sixteenth-century movement was concerned with the 'reformation' of the Christian church."[93] Paul Spickard and Kevin Cragg point out:

---

[92] Cairns, *Christianity Through the Centuries*, 160.
[93] Alister McGrath, *Evangelicalism & the Future of Christianity* (Downers Grove, IL: InterVarsity, 1995), 24.

The Reformation was a complex, multifaceted response to the church experience of the fifteenth and sixteenth centuries. Many Christians realized that the Church was simply not serving the spiritual needs of the people. It had become corrupt, and abuses were widespread.[94]

Dixon also affirms such reformation need within the church:

> On the final decades of the fifteenth century the state of the Church had become a matter of great urgency. Moreover, it was clear that the issues would multiply if the Church did not accept the need for reform.[95]

As pointed out in the preceding sub-section, the original characteristics of the church were deformed. The syncretistic new ecclesial culture that the church took on overshadowed, if not in the process of totally obliterating, the Christ-centered and Spirit-empowered life of faith and witness of the church. The church was becoming, not a kerygmatic congregation of called out believers whose life was Christ-centered and Spirit-led—but a center of religio-political power and materialistic exploitation for institutional gains. The gospel was beclouded by religio-political and materialistic institutional preoccupations. The center of ecclesial life was no longer the gospel of Christ but the ecclesiastical mandates. The clerics not Christ became the object of faith. The church not the kingdom became the destiny of believers.

It was in the overall context of the church losing its gospel-orientation that Berkouwer emphasizes that the "Reformers called the church back to the gospel."[96] Gary Dorrien sees that "Luther and Calvin judged that the gospel message of salvation by faith through grace was obscured, if not fatally subvert-

---

[94] Paul R. Spickard and Kevin M. Cragg, *A Global History of Christians: How Everyday Believers Experienced Their World* (Grand Rapids: Baker Academic, 1994), 171.
[95] G. Scott Dixon, *The Reformation in Germany* (Oxford: Blackwell, 2002), 18. Although Dixon does not see the church that time as radically corrupt, yet ironically he still sees the issue of urgency in the state of the church.
[96] Berkouwer, *The Church*, 184.

ed, by the paganizing tendencies of the Catholic church of their time."⁹⁷ Thus Harold Grimm remarks:

> Luther . . . developed a new conception of grace that, he believed, did not operate magically and mechanically through the sacraments . . . God had made this possible by sacrificing Christ on the cross.⁹⁸

The focus of the Reformation movement could be characterized as an evangelical embryo, that is, a back to the gospel-consciousness movement. The gospel that in a situation of a contradictory concept of salvation by works—proclaimed the Christ-centered *sola fide* or *sola gratia* soteriology, *sola scriptura* epistemology, kerygmatic liturgy, and priesthood of all believers. Regarding liturgical reformation Bloesch points out, "In their reaction against the Latin Mass in which preaching played an insignificant role, the Protestant Reformers placed an emphasis upon the proclaimed Word of God." ⁹⁹

These emphases were left out as the church institutionally expanded amidst secular preoccupations. These emphases if heeded and restored back into the whole life of the church—could have resulted in the transformation of the church back into its gospel and missional orientations, rather than perpetuating an ecclesiastically-centered religious-political institution. As Ronald Nash notes, "The Reformation was a needed corrective for what the Reformers saw as errors that had crept into Roman Catholic doctrine and practice."¹⁰⁰ The Reformation was originally intended as a reformation *within* the church, not as an outside movement of oppositionist denominationalism. As McGrath puts it, "Its

---

⁹⁷ Garry Dorrien, *The Remaking of Evangelical Theology* (Louisville, KY: Westminster Knox, 1998), 4.
⁹⁸ Harold J. Grimm, *The Reformation Era: 1500-1650*, 2ⁿᵈ ed. (New York: Macmillan, 1973), 86. Grimm adds about Luther's concept of grace, "Contrition, which he considered the most important part of the sacrament, resulted in forgiveness without indulgence." Ibid., 91.
⁹⁹ Donald G. Bloesch, *The Evangelical Renaissance* (Grand Rapids: Eerdmans, 1973), 67.
¹⁰⁰ Ronald A. Nash, *Evangelicals in America: Who They Are, What They Believe* (Nashville: Abingdon, 1987), 50.

agenda [was] centered on the need to reform an existing church in a settled Christian cultural context."[101]

However, with the very negative reaction of the church on reforming its life—the Reformation movement within the church was not able to reform the one whole church of Christ. Eventually, it resorted to separatist ecclesial formation. Thus a new denomination emerged. And from it—many more competing and separatist movements emerged. There might have been other factors that caused the untoward opposition against Reformation, but probably one of the weighty factors was the Reformation's attempt to restore the priesthood of all believers. This directly impinged on an ecclesiastical institution that promulgated distinct status categorization (with self-imposed religious, political, spiritual, and even redemptive implications) between the laity and clergy. Further, clergy status was reserved to male. As McGrath describes it:

> The Reformation doctrine of the priesthood of all believers thus gives every believer, male and female, both the *right* and *means* to ensure that his or her church and pastors remain faithful to their gospel calling—authorizes the people to exercise them if necessary.[102]

And this could have been taken to mean the laity's subjugation of ecclesiastical power. As Patrick Collinson notes:

> Negatively, the Reformation entailed various versions of anticlericalism, the urge to reduce the role in society of the clergy and to place limits on the space which priests and other religious persons occupied and the privilege and material rewards which they enjoyed, above all their capacity to overrule the laity.[103]

---

[101] McGrath, *Evangelicalism & the Future of Christianity*, 24.
[102] Alister McGrath, "A Better Way: The Priesthood of All Believers," in *Power Religion: The Selling Out of the Evangelical Church?*, ed. Michael Scott Horton (Chicago: Moody Press, 1992), 311.
[103] Patrick Collinson, "The Late Medieval Church and Its Reformation (1400-1600)," in *The Oxford Illustrated History of Christianity*, ed. McManners, 238-239.

Because as Green points out, "Often selected from the ranks of the aristocracy there was always a danger of the bishops adopting the life-style of the key nobles."[104]

The priesthood of all believers and the rest of foundational reformation framework would mean a radical overhaul of the existing ecclesiastical institutional framework that had become the prevalent and pervasive definition of ecclesial life. Such radical revolution, of course, drew radical opposition that was meant to extinguish the Reformation zeal. The church, instead of imbibing Reformation—rejected it! With the rejectionist stance of the church, the Reformation movement resorted to factionalist ecclesiology that further fragmented the already schismatic church. The church was already split into East and West. However, if it did not resort to separatist ecclesial formation amid internal church opposition, probably the movement could have also died out. The church then became not only fragmented, but also loaded with competing contradictory fragments. The one body of Christ was further divided and contradicting itself. Not because the Reformation was a negative factor—but because the church refused to be restored back to its original characteristics due to being engrossed with materialism.

Later, the Reformation movement was also trapped in mundane political matters that also redirected its full attention to the gospel and its proclamation. This may sound unacceptable to some Protestants, but as Spickard and Cragg point out:

> For most Europeans the Reformation led to war. Lutherans fought Catholics in Germany; Calvinists fought Catholics in France, the Netherlands and Scotland; Puritans fought Anglicans in England.[105]

They noted though:

---

[104] Green, *A New History of Christianity*, 51.
[105] Spickard and Cragg, *A Global History of Christianity*, 233.

In each case religion was but one element in the conflict; social, economic, and political factors loomed large. But the differences in faith provided the quickest and easiest means of identifying the combatants.[106]

In its formative stage the Protestant movement was gospel-centered and was open to further revelations of the Bible. Subsequently though, the variety of Protestant denominations that emerged eventually also have their respective dogmatism and anti-Catholic disposition. This disposition is reflected in common Protestant interpretation of the Revelation's anti-Christ as the Roman Catholic Church. Then Protestantism was also confronted by spiritual and moral problems. Dorrien describes the "spiritual coldness and troubling moral implications"[107] of the sixteenth century Protestantism that gave rise to another reaction movements—Puritanism and Pietism.

The Reformation could have ushered the rebirth of one whole gospel-oriented church. But then the Reformation movement was badly regarded and was rerouted. Thus the Reformation movement, which was supposed to reform the church and restore it back to its original characteristics, was also confronted by predicaments. First, it fell short of reforming the church as a whole church and fell into its own separatist denominationalism. The shortcoming may not be so much because of the failure of the core message of the Reformation movement—but because of the failure of the church to be honest and receptive to progressive ecclesial regeneration. Second, the Reformation movement also fell into its own new bred of dogmatism and spiritual coldness, and even into political temptation. Willard Oxtoby points out:

> The Reformation was marked by division and diversity. Protestantism rejected central institutional control, but that rejection was a mixed blessing. Early reformers often advocated their breakaway doctrines

---

[106] Ibid.
[107] Dorrien, *The Remaking of Evangelical Theology*, 5.

with an ideological strindency that matched the authoritarianism of the Church in Rome they had just left.[108]

However, in spite of the negative aspects of the Reformation movement—it opened the new era of hope for the church of Christ! It provided the inertia for succeeding generations of Christians to be open to the progressive restoration of the original characteristics of the church. It opened the gateway for new ecclesial life. And it started the long process of restoring the church back to its original nature.

As Paul Hanson profoundly notes:

> The Reformation was the work of the Spirit. But the unreformed part of the church was not left without the Spirit's aid. On the contrary, just when the reformed part was settling down to what was eventually to become the routine of the eighteenth Century, the Spirit manifested himself through a series of thinkers and saints . . . . It almost seems as if when a national church becomes dangerously tied by the bonds of the state the Holy Spirit raises up saints and witnesses to compensate.[109]

The Holy Spirit continued to work for the restoration of the church back to its original characteristics—then, Puritanism and Pietism that eventually became the frontier precedents of Contemporary Evangelicalism emerged.

C. The Emergence of Puritanism and Pietism

The regenerative history of the Christian church continued from the Reformation onward. And it continued with the progression of thesis and antithesis that resulted in the periodic emergence of ecclesial movements. From the 1500's Reformation to succeeding ecclesial movements—we could perceive

---

[108] Willard G. Oxtoby, "The Christian Tradition," in *World Religions: Western Traditions*, 2nd ed., ed Willard G. Oxtoby (Ontario: Oxford University Press, 2002).
[109] Paul D. Hanson, "The Identity and Purpose of the Church," *Theology Today* 42 (October 1985): 235.

a continuous progressive emergence of strands that would eventually become one synthesized phenomenon intended as the restoration of the church's full gospel-orientation. And right in our present time, we see this astounding culminating phenomenon—this work is presenting!

Nash describes the situation of Protestantism before the rise of succeeding movements:

> Unfortunately, those who followed the Reformers soon fell into their own errors. Protestantism in many places become characterized by a cold, dead orthodoxy sometimes called Protestant scholasticism. This Protestant scholasticism tended to encase the religious convictions of the Reformation only in the hard shell of creeds, assent to which was often made to appear more important than conversion and inward life of the Spirit.[110]

The original life-oriented, in contrast to mere theoretical preoccupation, and gospel-driven life of the church was again at risk. In the same way the societal milieu of the pre-Reformation church reshaped the life of the church, the prevailing philosophy also confronted the life of the Reformation church or churches. As Rolland McCune points out, the eighteenth century Enlightenment "made severe impacts against Christianity."[111] Nash adds it "helped undermine confidence in the Scriptures."[112]

Further compounding the crises of faith in Reformation churches were—on the one hand, the dogmatism and spiritual coldness in Protestantism; and on the other hand, the impact of the Enlightenment that led the once Bible-centered movement to pursue Rationalism at the risk of its Bible-based epistemology. The *sola scriptura* epistemology was beginning to be substituted by rationalistic epistemology that in essence was really individualistic. Reason rather

---

[110] Nash, *Evangelicals in America*, 50.
[111] Rolland D. McCune, "The Formation of the New Evangelicalism (Part One): Historical and Theological Antecedents," *Detroit Baptist Seminary Journal* 3 (Fall 1998): 7.
[112] Nash, *Evangelicals in America*, 50.

than faith was beginning to be widely regarded as the foundation of Christian belief. Faith was beginning to be substituted by reason. The life of faith and witness was being substituted by theoretical preoccupations. And the need for the empowerment of the Holy Spirit in both individual and congregational life was waning.

By then the Reformation movement has already become an ism—Protestantism in particular. And the various forms of Protestant churches were also propagating their respective dogmatism— rather than propagating a gospel-oriented way of life. Ecclesiological concerns were redirected to something merely theoretical rather than life-oriented. And Paul, as aforementioned in the preceding chapter, warned against making Christianity a mere fancy talk rather than a life of faith and witness.

The Protestant churches were now in a crisis of faith. And unless something phenomenal again happened—the Protestant churches could be in danger of spiritual death. Nash dramatically portrays the crisis of faith amidst the cold and dead orthodoxy:

> There was a definite need for religious revivals to call people to decision, commitment, and conversion and that would once again stir up the fires of religious enthusiasm . . . . Western Christianity was in need of a second Reformation . . . not so much of doctrine as one of spiritual life.[113]

Then at opportune time—two related European phenomena, namely, Puritanism and Pietism, with subsequent North American counterparts emerged! In fact, the North American counterparts were called First (1740's) and Second (1790's) Great Awakenings. These Great Awakenings replicated these European post-Reformation movements. And these Awakenings created another formational circumstance from which Contemporary Evangelicalism finally emerged with its full-blown ecclesial paradigm. George Marsden sees the

---

[113] Nash, *Evangelicals in America*, 50-51.

historical link of North American evangelicalism with European Protestant movements. He writes, "Although evangelicalism is largely an Anglo-American phenomenon, its origins give it ties with European Protestantism."[114] Dorrien portrays the situation from which Puritanism and Pietism emerged:

> The spiritual coldness and troubling moral implications of Protestant orthodoxy gave rise to the first glimmerings of a different kind of evangelicalism in seventeenth-century England and Germany. In England, Puritans ... prefigured a movement away from the creedal intellectualism of Reformed orthodoxy, arguing for a more spiritually integrative understanding of Christian faith.... In Germany ... Pietists launched a more explicit and far-reaching protest against the spiritual limitations of Lutheran orthodoxy ... [the] movement subsequently recovered dimensions of the biblical witness pertaining to spiritual regeneration and sanctification that engendered a new kind of evangelicalism.[115]

Further Dorrien specifies that "later, the evangelical followers of John Wesley and George Whitefield lifted up the biblical themes of holiness, good news, and new life in the Spirit."[116] This was an attempt to bring back the gospel-orientation of Protestant churches. Thus when the church in Rome in the fifteenth-century was deteriorating—the Reformation movement emerged to regenerate the life of the church. Then when the Protestant churches in the seventeenth-century were deteriorating—Puritanism and Pietism emerged to regenerate the life of the church.

McGrath sees Puritanism as a "deep concern for spirituality."[117] Mary Fulbrook describes the Puritan's concern, "Underlying all Puritan activities was the concern to achieve an adequate preaching ministry, capable of bringing the

---

[114] George M. Marsden, s.v., "Evangelical and Fundamental Christianity," *The Encyclopedia of Religion*.
[115] Dorrien, *The Remaking of Evangelical Theology*, 5.
[116] Ibid.
[117] McGrath, *Evangelicalism & the Future of Christianity*, 24.

means of salvation, the Word of the Lord, to all who heard."[118] McCune sees Pietism as:

> . . . a protest against Protestant scholasticism, especially German Lutheranism. Pietism emphasized Christian experience, inner feeling, the individual's personal relationship with God, and high religious idealism. It was a strong reaction to rigid, dead orthodoxy.[119]

But basically, Puritan and Pietistic movements were intended to restore the Protestant church back to its gospel-oriented life—but this time the particular focus was on experiential faith. As B.L Shelby emphasizes:

> The Pietists admired Luther and tried to return to his original emphasis on the gospel. They argued, however, that the state church in Germany was of little help in spiritual venture. The state church had preserved Luther's doctrine of justification by faith by freezing it in creedal statements. What men and women needed most was the regenerating life of the Spirit; they needed to experience justification personally."[120]

Thus as Gonzalez remarks, "Pietism was a response to the dogmatism of the theologians and the rationalism of the philosophers, both of which it contrasted with the living faith that is as at the heart of Christianity."[121] Koppel Pinson describes in more detailed way the nature of Pietism:

> . . . emphasis on a more practical Christianity. Learning was not sufficient. Purity of life, saintliness of behavior, active Christianity came to be regarded as the most essential mark of Christian life. It is this which accounts for the stress of Pietists on prayer, for their development of welfare and philanthropic works, and for their great missionary ac-

---

[118] Mary Fulbrook, *Piety and Politics: Religion and the Rise of Absolutism in England, Wurttenburg, and Prussia* (England: Cambridge University Press, 1983), 106.
[119] McCune, "The Formation of New Evangelicalism (Part One):" 5.
[120] *Dictionary of Christianity in America, s.v.* "Evangelicalism," by B.L. Shelby
[121] Gonzalez, *The Reformation to the Present Day*, 203.

tivity throughout the world.[122]

The Puritan and Pietistic movements provided answers to the deteriorating ecclesial life of faith and witness. And although the emphasis was more of spiritual experiential life, but also corollary to the Pietistic and Puritan movements was the revival of the missional zeal of the church. The church was again becoming more gospel-oriented and missional.

However, like the Reformation movement—Puritanism and Pietism also consequently fell into its own pitfall of isms. Richard Lovelace notes: "Puritanism was leaning toward ascetic legalism as it sought to compete with counter-Reformation piety and to create a distinctive spirituality that would rule out cheap grace."[123] The ascetic tendency redirected ecclesial life to something extramundane. The restoration of the practical life-oriented characteristic of the original ecclesial life was again at risk.

Ironically though, while Lovelace characterizes Puritanism as tending toward asceticism, Grimm also notes the secular tendency of Puritanism in England:

> By the middle of seventeenth century, however, state necessity began to supersede every other consideration and practical expediency to replace religion and moral objectives.
>
> In England, where the Parliament had maintained its party with the monarchy, the same tendency toward secularization made its appearance. Puritanism, a dynamic religious force, became identified with parliamentarianism and the interests of the rising merchant class.[124]

Fullbrook points out, "But by the 1630s, Puritanism had become politically salient; and by the early 1640s, it played a key role in the opposition to attempted

---

[122] Koppel S. Pinson, *Pietism as a Factor in the Rise of German Nationalism* (New York: Columbia University Press, 1934), 14.
[123] Richard F. Lovelace, "Evangelical Spirituality: A Church Historian's Perspective," *Journal of Evangelical Theological Society* 31 (March 1988): 30.
[124] Grimm, *The Reformation Era*, 416. 102.

Stuart absolutism."[125] Here we see the risk of a church when it attempts to socio-politically dogmatize its (theological-moral) theoretical formulations. The church's moral responsibility should remain within the boundary of its kerygmatic responsibility. And Pietism too, in its extreme form was absorbed on religious life that "gave very little attention to self-conscious Christian thought."[126] Such negative inclination to the works of the mind also influenced the formation of succeeding anti-intellectual denominations.

Puritanism and Pietism was intended to revive another aspect of the original characteristics of the life of the church. However, again the church misunderstood the deeper objective of the phenomenon of ecclesial movements. Consequently, Puritanism and Pietism fell into "rigid orthodoxy"[127] and a sort of Christian asceticism. And not able to reform the Protestant churches—they also resorted to separatist ecclesial formations. The 1500's Reformation, Puritan, and Pietist movements—were all intended to bring about the re-formation of the original characteristics of the church. But the church as a whole missed integrating the holistic objective of these movements and many other originally gospel-oriented movements in the history of Christian church. However, the operation of the Holy Spirit in the history of the church did not end there. It continued to the rise of the Contemporary Evangelical movement that have made global impact—but still has to synthesize the various strands of evangelical heritage into a framework of holistic ecclesiology for the regeneration of the original nature and function of the church. And this synthesis is what this study is attempting to present!

---

[125] Fulbrook, *Piety and Politics*, 102
[126] Mark A. Noll, *The Scandal of Evangelical Mind* (Grand Rapids: Eedrmans, 1994), 49.
[127] Thus the *Westminster Dictionary of Church History* speaks about "the rigid orthodoxy of...Pietism." S.v. "Evangelicalism."

4
The Emergence of Contemporary Evangelicalism

A. The Frontier Precursors[128]

British Puritanism and German Pietism spread to the frontier America. Puritanism was particularly zealous on creating a Puritan America amidst a rapidly secularizing society. However, it was also in the context of spiritual apathy and antipathy against a Puritan state religion that the frontier spiritual awakenings, or the Great Awakenings[129] as they were called, emerged. Phillips and Okholm describe the emergence of the First Great Awakening of 1735-1750, "It was in this context of stale religion and spiritual apathy in Puritan New England (as well as in the Anglican South) that a revival swept through all of the colonies, striking all classes of people."[130]

The focus of revival had become personal rather than societal itself, that is, the transformation of individuals rather than the transformation of society into Christendom.

As Shelby notes, "The revivalists of the Great Awakening, like the Puritans, preached the necessity of an invisible transformation of the soul, but they no

---

[128] For a discussion on the emergence of North American evangelicalism as a frontier movement; see Mark A. Noll, *The Rise of Evangelicalism: The Age of Edwards, Whitefield and the Wesleys* (Downers Grove, IL: InterVarsity, 2003).
[129] For a historical study on the Great Awakening; see Joseph Tracy, *The Great Awakening: A History of the Revival of Religion in the Time of Edwards and Whitefield* (Edinburgh: The Banner of Truth Trust, 1976). For a collection on the Awakening writings see Alan Heimert and Perry Millers, eds. *The Great Awakening: Documents Illustrating the Crisis and Its Consequence* (Indianapolis, IN: Bobbs-Merrill, 1967).
[130] Phillips & Okholm, *A Family of Faith*, 241.

longer dreamed of establishing a holy commonwealth as the Puritan Fathers did."[131] Stanley Grenz comments on the emergence of frontier evangelical revival:

> ... committed to the primacy of the new birth, early evangelical leaders ... bemoaned the nominalism they found in the established churches of their day. In their estimation such churches were filled with persons baptized by water but bereft of the regenerative work of the Spirit ... [132]

However, in spite of the Awakening movement, by the 1780's religious interest significantly dwindled with an estimate of only 5 to 10 percent of the colonial population attending church.[133] The pervasive spiritual sustainability of the First Great Awakening could have had been threatened by secularizing societal factors. But there were also other significant divisive ecclesial factors that threatened the integrity of the First Awakening in spite of its proliferation among the masses. One of the notable factors was the controversy over emotional preaching and religious experience. This was regarded by other Protestants as offending reason and harming the peace and purity of the church. Others even doubted whether the source of emotional religious experience is God or Satan.[134] Further, the controversy over emotional religious experience resulted in "the elevation of the laity at the expense of the clergy ...."[135]

Another reason as implied in the statements below about the Second Awakening could have been a misdirected notion of the movement's Calvinistic trend. The message of the sovereignty of God in Puritan Calvinism should have been perceived as emphasizing human inability to save itself—recognizing God as the only One who could save. Yet the recognition of God's redemptive sovereignty should also engender willful acceptance of Jesus as personal Savior re-

---

[131] Shelby, "Evangelicalism."
[132] Stanley J. Grenz, *Renewing the Center: Evangelical Theology in a Post-Theological Era* (Grand Rapids: Baker Academic, 2000), 291.
[133] Phillips & Okholm, *A Family of Faith*, 243.
[134] Ibid.
[135] Ibid.

sulting in new life. Eventually the consequence is an active life of faith and witness. This active life could have sustained the First Awakening.

The Second Great Awakening emerged on 1790 to 1820. Its emphasis as Grenz points out:

> ... shifted from the sovereignty of God (the Puritan Calvinist 'waiting on God in Edwards and Whitefield) to the human role in salvation—a democratic, Arminian, active seeking and coming to God. Conversion and holiness came to be seen as matters of individual choice more than divine action.[136]

He further stresses, "The Great Awakening helped to establish a peculiar brand of American Christianity that involved an active seeking of salvation; it was pro-revival, individualistic, and pietistic."[137]

Darrell Bock distinguishes the two Awakenings while pointing out the European heritage and active element of the second American frontier movement:

> While the first Great Awakening was largely Calvinistic, in the Second Awakening evangelism and pragmatics were wed, along with a pietistic Methodism . . . . Revivalists not only preached the gospel but also were moved to social concern (called 'moral reform' then) for the poor, slaves, women and finally temperance.[138]

The Second Awakening propagated an active type of Christian Faith in the American frontier—it was both spiritually and socially active. The two Great Awakenings, as well as succeeding revival movements—when viewed in the perspective of the historical operations of the Holy Spirit—were not in themselves contradictory but complementary. As Michael Horton sees it, "In the first

---

[136] Ibid., 244.
[137] Ibid.
[138] Darrell L. Bock, *Purpose-Directed Theology: Getting Our Priorities Right in Evangelical Controversies* (Downers Grove, IL: InterVarsity, 2002), 44-45. Thus Sweet points out that. "Evangelicalism stands as the most powerful social and religious movement of the nineteenth-century America." *Encyclopedia of American Religious Experience, s.v.* "Nineteenth Century Evangelicalism," by Leonard I. Sweet.

Awakening, the emphasis is on what God has done; in the Second, on what man can and must do."[139] The Awakenings were intended to revive the spiritual life of the laity. However, these spiritual awakenings were consequently regarded as mere emotionalism. Consequently the significance of the Awakening Movements also dwindled. But in spite of its struggles, the Awakenings gave birth to a culture of spiritual revivalism in North America.

Now, let us go to the modern period in North America when another reaction movement emerged. That reaction movement was considered by historians as the direct descendant of Contemporary Evangelicalism. It was closely identified with Contemporary Evangelicalism so that it was even confusedly regarded as evangelicalism.

B. The Immediate Precursor

When the frontier America became modern, along with technological modernization came a worldview that threatened the *sola scriptura* epistemology of Christian Faith. Scientific explanation was becoming the norm of Christian belief instead of the practical and spiritually-oriented reading of the Bible. George Marsden depicts the reactionary and polarizing atmosphere created by the tug-of-war between secularists and conservative Christians. The secularists "cautiously hoped for an age of prosperity and progress built on science and wealth."[140] While the conservative Christians sensed that "the nation seemed to be slipping into a secular dark age, a decline that spokesmen for ecclesiastical liberalism seemed all too eager to bless."[141]

Christians who were enthusiastic for imbibing a secular modern approach to Christian Faith became Liberals. And as such they began losing, not only the spiritual and emotional aspects of ecclesial life—but also the original

---

[139] Michael Scott Horton, *Made in America: The Shaping of Modern American Evangelicals* (Grand Rapids: Baker, 1991), 41-42.
[140] George Marsden, ed., *Evangelicalism and Modern America* (Grand Rapids: Eerdmans, 1984), vii.
[141] Ibid.

active life of faith and witness. And the need for the power of the Holy Spirit was substituted by the need for the power of reason. Ironically compounding the predicament of the church was the emergence of neo-orthodoxy, that though supposedly was an effort to restore theological orthodoxy—still lacks the wholeness of the original ecclesial characteristics, particularly missional zeal and experiential faith.

With the onset of modernism and theoretically-engrossed evangelistically-uninterested neo-orthodoxy—the church was falling into irrelevancy and spiritual death. It was almost falling back into a new form of spiritless state similar to that of the pre-Reformation age. As McCune notes—"Modernism and neoorthodoxy have no true evangelism and consequently their churches and denominations wither into irrelevancy."[142] Nash warns the serious threat of a highly secularized character of Liberalism—"Liberalism was a religion without a personal God, without a divine Savior, without an inspired Bible, and without a transforming conversion."[143]

Then conservative Christians reacted. And Fundamentalism emerged. It was a back to the Bible movement—a retrenchment of the *sola scriptura* epistemology. As Nash points out, Fundamentalism began as a "reaction to the liberalism that threatened the integrity of the historic Christian faith."[144] It was a back-to-the-Bible movement. It was an attempt to lead the church back to its original gospel-centeredness. However, consequently, the movement became prone to its unfortunate excess.[145] It became literalistic and narrow in its biblical epistemological approach. And it also became spiritually, denominationally, and socially judgmental and separatist—rather than spiritually and missionally integrative. Fundamentalism was intended to restore Bible consciousness—to restore the epistemological integrity of Christian Faith. But again the ecclesial

---

[142] Rolland D. McCune, "The Formation of the New Evangelicalism (Part Two): Historical Beginnings," *Detroit Baptist Seminary Journal* 4 (Fall 1999): 133.
[143] Nash, *Evangelicals in America*, 63.
[144] Ibid.
[145] Ibid., 66.

reaction to Fundamentalism was misdirected. In its over-emphasis of plain Bible study, it also fell into the predicaments of questionable approach to Bible-centered epistemology and anti-intellectualism. Further, it also became dogmatically judgmental.

In this situation, the church was again confronted by a disintegrative ecclesial environment—threatened by spirituality breakdown of Liberalism, the missional idleness of Neo-Orthodoxy, and the theological regression of Fundamentalism. Without the intervention of the Holy Spirit, the life of the church in modern times could disintegrate further into spiritual, missional, and theological meaninglessness.

C. The Emergence of Contemporary Evangelicalism

After 1925 Phillips and Okholm note that Fundamentalism lost its respect.[146] And by the "mid-1930s the more moderate fundamentalists began to part company with those who were more militant."[147] But then—those who parted perhaps never realized that the beginning of a climactic ecclesial phenomenon was emerging through them. An astounding ecclesial phenomenon that would impact on the global community, both the church and society, was emerging—Contemporary Evangelicalism was birthed.[148] And it was born in a global center of power, which though different in form but, with similar socio-political-economic-cultural power status with the Roman Empire where Christianity was first born. The situated realities of life, the venue and timing of its emergence, and its movemental nature tell that the phenomenon is of great significance to the contemporary world!

---

[146] Phillips & Okholm, *A Family of Faith*, 253.
[147] Ibid., 257.
[148] For a discussion on evangelical roots see, Kenneth S. Kantzer, ed., *Evangelical Roots: A Tribute to Wilbur Smith* (Nashville, TN: Thomas Nelson, 1970).

At the outset, the beginning of Contemporary Evangelicalism[149] seemed small. It may just be seen as a reaction movement—a movement reacting against the extremes of Fundamentalism that was theologically, ecclesiologically, and missionally stunting. When the moderate fundamentalists parted ways with the militant ones, they organized in 1942 the National Association of Evangelicals. As McCune emphasizes:

> With the formation of the National Association of Evangelicals (NAE) new evangelicalism was conceived if not born. The distinction between 'fundamentalist' and 'evangelical' was beginning to take shape. . . ."[150]

The formation of the National Association of Evangelicals marked the beginning of two things:

1. The identity formation of evangelical denominations. Mark Ellingsen distinguishes Evangelicalism and Fundamentalism, "Despite the organic interpenetration of the Evangelical movement and Fundamentalism, they are not identical."[151] He further emphasizes, ". . . as its title *Evangelical* connotes, it is a movement which intends a more constructive and less separatist stance than the posture connoted by the term Fundamentalist."[152] McGrath also notes that the pioneers of Contemporary Evangelicalism, namely, Billy Graham and

---

[149] For a collection of essays giving an overview of Contemporary Evangelicalism see, Carl R. Trueman, Tony J. Gray, and Craig L. Bloomberg, eds., *Solid Ground: 25 Years of Evangelical Theology* (Leicester, England: Apollos, 2000).
[150] McCune, "The Formation of New Evangelicalism (Part Two):"109. This distinction is also indicated in a compilation of essays edited by Marsden; see George Marsden, ed., *Reforming Fundamentalism: Fuller Seminary and the New Evangelicals* (Grand Rapids: Eerdmans, 1987). For another discussion see, Harriet A. Harris, *Fundamentalism and Evangelicals* (Oxford: Clarendon, 1998).
[151] Mark Ellingsen, *The Evangelical Movement: Growth, Impact, Controversy, Dialog* (Minneapolis: Augsburg, 1989), 97. This distinction is also indicated in a compilation of essays edited by Marsden; see George Marsden, ed., *Reforming Fundamentalism: Fuller Seminary and the New Evangelicals* (Grand Rapids: Eerdmans, 1987). For another discussion see, Harriet A. Harris, *Fundamentalism and Evangelicals* (Oxford: Clarendon, 1998).
[152] Ellingsen, *The Evangelical Movement*, 97.

> Carl Henry both . . . became disillusioned with fundamentalism . . . ."[153]

2. The coming together of denominations that already sensed their being evangelicals and those who have realized the significance of transforming themselves into evangelicals.

Then in the 1950s Billy Graham[154] crusades were beginning to catch a wildfire of national and international attention—it rapidly impacted both America and abroad. Since then, the miraculous operations of the Holy Spirit could be seen and experienced crusades after crusades, with unexpected huge national and international converts. People in mass were accepting Jesus as their personal Savior. Lives were transformed. Churches were joining hands together to fulfill the Great Commission. Denominational barriers were broken on the ground of a common sense of mission. Individuals and congregations were revived. America and the world—were awakened to Christian Faith in a degree, quality and geographical scope never experienced before since the apostolic time!

Mass media and technology were utilized. Evangelism became high-tech. Thus a new dimension of evangelism was born. The world was proliferated by Christ-centered conversion,[155] transformational piety-culture, ecclesial unity, and global missional zeal and breakthroughs. Even places never thought of before from the Communist Russia to China, to secular cities of New York and London, were beyond expectation—receptive to the gospel. The church was becoming more truly gospel-oriented, that is, evangelical. And the world was being evangelized.

---

[153] McGrath, *Evangelicalism and the Future of Christianity*, 38.
[154] Bock emphasizes, "Billy Graham was the acknowledged figurehead of what evangelicalism stood and believed." Bock, *Purpose-Directed Theology*, 47. McGrath remarks that evangelicalism is "especially associated with the figures of Billy Graham (b. 1918) and Carl F. H. Henry (b. 1913). McGrath, *Evangelicalism and the Future of Christianity*, 38.
[155] In contrast to church membership based on mere doctrinal assent or casual church membership.

To further enrich and widen the movement's impact, *Christianity Today* was founded in 1956 by Billy Graham with Carl F. Henry as the editor. In 1947 Fuller Theological Seminary was established to further evangelical theology, followed by other seminaries and colleges popping here and there. Parachurch organizations and independent ministries were organized. The sense of Gospel Commission proliferated. Gospel-consciousness and Christ-centered life were revived nationally and internationally. The church was being redirected to life-centered focus with church life becoming more Christ-centered and kerygmatic empowered by the Holy Spirit. Joel Carpenter concludes, "By the end of the twentieth century . . . the evangelical forms of Christianity had penetrated every Christian tradition and racial ethnic group in North America"[156]. Churches were becoming evangelical.

Contemporary Evangelicalism had its brief low tide too, but then it resurged with an even greater, wider, and richer impact. Jimmy Carter, a publicly professing evangelical won the US presidency—profession of faith is no longer hidden in public political life. And in 1976 *Newsweek* dedicated a cover to evangelicalism and tagged 1976 as the "Year of the Evangelicals". Nash sees the resurgence of Contemporary Evangelicalism as "may be the most remarkable and noteworthy event in the United States in the twentieth century."[157]

Thus Contemporary Evangelicalism emerged from a seemingly diminutive anti-Fundamentalist movement but eventually became a major missional force in contemporary times. Externally, evangelicalism may be seen as a reaction movement consequently resorting to interchurch cooperation and parachurch organizations. But internally, these parachurch organizations are denominationally unifying missional movements. The parachurch ministry is an

---

[156] Joel A. Carpenter, "The Fellowship of Kindred Minds: Evangelical Identity and the Quest for Christian Unity," in *Pilgrims on the Sawdust Trail: Evangelical Ecumenism and the Quest for Christian Identity*, ed. Timothy George (Grand Rapids: Baker Academic, 2004), 32. For the emergence of evangelicalism in other major countries; see George A. Rawlyk and Mark A. Noll, *Amazing Grace: Evangelicalism in Australia, Britain, Canada, and the United States* (Grand Rapids, 1993).

[157] Nash, *Evangelicals in America*, 15.

embodiment of common missional cause that transcends denominations—and that is what the church should be—the embodiment of common missional cause transcending denominations!

Further, beyond its external characteristics there is a deeper thing about Contemporary Evangelicalism—its inner theological dynamics reveals an astounding phenomenon. As Phillips and Okholm adeptly points out, "Contemporary evangelicalism is recognized as an important spiritual, social, and intellectual force."[158] And indeed it is! The following chapters that analyze the theological framework of Contemporary Evangelicalism reveal that indeed it is the most important ecclesial revelation in modern times.

---

[158] Phillips and Okholm, *A Family of Faith*, 259. Johnston, however, poses a challenge of evangelical survival amidst its popularity; see Jon Johnston, *Will Evangelicalism Survive Its Own Popularity?* (Grand Rapids: Zondervan, 1980). A collection of essays edited by Hutchinson and Kalu explores the global cultural issues confronting evangelicalism; see Mark Hutchinson and Ogbu Kalu, eds. *A Global Faith: essays on Evangelicalism and Globalization* (Syndney: Centre for the Study of Australian Christianity, 1998).

Part II
Analysis of the Theological Framework of Contemporary Evangelicalism

5
The Theological Framework of Contemporary Evangelicalism

A. The Formative Stage

At the outset, modern evangelicalism arose both as a rejection of Fundamentalistic theological suppositions and in "reaction to the perceived deficiencies of fundamentalism."[159] From a sociological point of view, Christian Smith categorizes evangelicalism as "the subset of conservative Protestants whose 'neo-evangelical' movement break from fundamentalism during the 1940s and after."[160] However, consequently Contemporary Evangelicalism ends up offering the whole global church a wider and richer theological perspective. We could even see its significance as the paradigm of the original characteristics of church life. And when we perceptibly heed its intent—it could lead to an ecclesial reformation more fulfilling than never before experienced in Christian history!

Phillips and Okholm outline the fundamentalistic views that evangelicalism rejected with the counterpart evangelical provisions for fundamentalist deficiencies:

1. "First, rejecting the defensive separatism of fundamentalists, evangelicals

    attempted to transform culture by involvement in the world."[161]

---

[159] McGrath, *Evangelicalism & the Future of Christianity*, 41.
[160] Christian Smith, *American Evangelicalism: Embattled and Thriving* (Chicago: The University of Chicago Press, 1998), 15.
[161] Phillips and Okholm, *A Family of Faith*, 258.

2. "Second, evangelicals rejected dispensationalism as the only acceptable theological option . . . evangelicals consciously embraced a range of theological positions."[162]
3. "Third, rejecting social passivity, evangelicals have insisted on active Christian involvement in all segments of society."[163]

Thus Contemporary Evangelicalism at its formative stage, by reacting to the deficiencies of Fundamentalism, consequently offered the church the basics of church life that were threatened to extinction. These basics are non-separatist transformational piety-culture, wider and richer yet conservative theological perspective, and social consciousness bringing the relevance of the church in societal life.

Evangelicalism since the Billy Graham crusades has been prominent in leading missional unity. Because of evangelistic unity denominationalism even took on a new meaning from an ism of separationism to the recognition of diverse ecclesial entities as one church united in the common Christ-centered missional cause. Thus the church is regarded as a sort of Christ-centered university—one body with a variety of united sub-bodies. Richard Neuhaus reminds the church, "The quality of our life together is part of the gospel that we proclaim."[164] The rise of evangelicalism gave rise to a viable form of ecumenism—a functional rather than structural unity. It is the unity that is based on common missional cause. The element of separatist and judgmental attitude of fundamentalism waned because of missional preoccupation and unity. And such a unifying evangelical spirit reflects the missional wholeness of the original church.

Evangelicalism is not only non-separatist denominationally but also non-separatist socially. It does not promote ascetism or self-centered mystical

---

[162] Ibid., 259.
[163] Ibid.
[164] Richard John Neuhaus, "Why Evangelicals and Catholics Belong Together," in *Pilgrims on the Sawdust*, ed. George, 105.

preoccupations but rather spirituality with personal, congregational, societal transformational objective. As Barbara Hargrove said, "A sense of self is inadequate if there is in it no sense of public dimension, of some kind of linkage with the larger society."[165]   Evangelicalism always reminds the church "to confront the secular world with a clear declaration of each individual's ultimate accountability to God and thus his immediate need of redemption through the sacrificial ministry of Jesus Christ."[166]   This evangelical missional stance in secular society is neither separatist nor antagonistic but kerygmatic and transformational. Of all the precedent movements, Contemporary Evangelicalism has become more expert in transforming secular lives to Christian faith. McGrath affirms, "evangelicalism possesses the ability to bring individuals to faith from a secular culture."[167]

When the church abandons its kerygmatic relationship with society, consequently the abandonment would result in the "existential meaninglessness" (to use Hargrove's term) of the church. When the church focuses its life only on itself, the whole life of the church disintegrates into a fragment. Contemporary Evangelicalism engenders wholeness in the life of the church because it reflects the gospel-centered missional-orientation of the original church. Its relationship with society is Christ-centered and kerygmatic, rather than institutionally motivated.

B. Survey of Characterizations

In regards to the structure of evangelical theology, Ramm points out:

1. *"In essence evangelical theology is not literalism."*[168]

---

[165] Barbara Hargrove, "Churches as Mediating Structures," *Theology Today* 39 (January 1983): 389.
[166] Hudson T. Armerding, "The Evangelical in the Secular World," *Bibliotheca Sacra* 127 (April 1970): 137.
[167] McGrath, *Evangelicalism & the Future of Christianity*, 122.
[168] Bernard Ramm, *The Evangelical Heritage: A Study in History and Theology* (Grand Rapids: BakerBooks, 2000), 125.

2. *"In essence evangelical theology is not obscurantistic.* Obscurantism is ignoring or neglecting knowledge or denying its claim to truth."[169]
3. *"The essence of evangelical theology does not presume that the final or non-final statement of Christian theology has been achieved."*[170]
4. *"It is not the essence of evangelicalism to believe that revelation is solely propositional or only conveying of information."*[171]
5. *"In essence evangelical theology is not countercultural, world-denying or inherently pessimistic."*[172]

We could see statements 1 to 3 as reactions to fundamentalist theological notions while statement 4 and 5 as reactions to both Fundamentalism and Liberalism.

The open and rich yet Bible-centered nature of Contemporary Evangelical theology is unique compared to its narrow-minded predecessors. Contemporary Evangelical theology integrates the whole basics of Christian faith. In contrast, the preceding movements often have divergent, fragmentary, and contradictory theological foci. From *sola fide* to *sola gratia*, from predestination to free will, *sola scriptura* to reason alone, etc., the preceding movements fell short of integrating the progressive ecclesial revelations. While Contemporary Evangelicalism covers a variety of interconnected aspects of Christian belief and church life. It covers from Christ-centered soteriology to Spirit-led personal transformational piety engendering a life of faith and witness both within the church and in society. To Bible-centered epistemology, conversional everyday life teachings, to personal and interdenominational revival and missional activities, etc. And all these are regarded as interrelated components of what characterize the Contemporary Evangelical Christian life. It is indeed integrative. Its theological perspective is not only holistic but also life-oriented. Contemporary

---

[169] Ibid., 123.
[170] Ibid., 128.
[171] Ibid., 129.
[172] Ibid., 132.

Evangelical theology is not merely about philosophical theories but about directions for living a Christ-centered Spirit-led life. Its theology guides both individual believers and the church towards regenerative life and mission.

Further, rejecting both passivity and extreme social activism, Contemporary Evangelicalism is able to synthesize personal piety and societal concerns. However, its societal mission is defined within the framework of the eschatological kingdom of God as the absolute hope of humanity. Thus it sees the need to proliferate the secular world with the kingdom of God culture. As Bloesch points out, "The church is the worldly agency of the kingdom, the earthen vessel that carries the new wine of creative transformation."[173] Evangelical piety is viewed with both personal and societal significance. As Sanders stresses, "The best disciplined spirituality that evangelicals have to offer the church and society is the affirmation that the gospel of Jesus Christ fully entails both personal and social transformation."[174] Evangelicals see the need for societal involvement within the parameter of its kerygmatic mission. For they recognize that the "gospel is good news for society as well as for individuals."[175]

In evangelicalism we could see a devotion to both personal Christian Faith and social involvement—from proclaiming Christian values amidst moral degeneration to humanitarian service. An example is the 700 Club which presents a synthesis of personal piety, socio-moral concern, and humanitarian service. Of course, the Billy Graham Evangelistic Association is foremost in propagating a Christ-centered transformational culture from crusades, films, TV and radio programs and to humanitarian services, like the Samaritan Purse. Focus on Family is another example as well as other parachurch ministries like Campus Crusade for Christ, Promise Keepers, etc.

---

[173] Bloesch, *The Church*, 76.
[174] Cheryl Sanders, Disciplined Spirituality," in *Where Shall My Wond'ring Soul Begin?: The Landscape of Evangelical Piety and Thought*, eds. Mark A. Noll and Ronald F. Thiemann (Grand Rapids: Eerdmans, 2000), 66.
[175] McGrath, *Evangelicalism & the Future of Christianity*, 165.

Contemporary Evangelicalism consequently became more that just a reaction movement against Fundamentalism. It has synthesized the Christian heritage revived by precedent movements. Although each preceding movement was a fragment; but in Contemporary Evangelicalism the essences of preceding movements become strands that are twined together to revive the original characteristics of Christian beliefs and practices. George sees a confluence in evangelicalism:

> Its [evangelicalism] theology and piety have been enriched by many diverse tributaries, including Puritanism, Pietism, and Pentecostalism, but its sense of identity as a distinctive faith community, what we might call the *evangelical tradition*, has been shaped decisively by the three major episodes: the Protestant Reformation, the evangelical Awakening, and the fundamentalist-modernist controversy.[176]

In the history of Christian church we could see the progressive and regenerative operation of the Holy Spirit.[177] This regenerative process is climaxing in the phenomenon of Contemporary Evangelicalism. However—this profound synthesizing perspective is missed even by evangelicals themselves! As R. Allen Killen aptly puts it:

> The new Evangelicalism also reacts very strongly against fundamentalism. This is sad, because it reveals the fact that they fail to see that there is a cumulative progress in the development of modern apologetics. Each of the movements ... as well as that which follows, is needed since they all contribute irreplaceable parts to an adequate new apologetic. Furthermore, God has used each.[178]

---

[176] Timothy George, "Between the Pope and Billy Graham: Evangelicals and Catholics in Dialogue," in *Pilgrims on the Sawdust Trail*, ed. George, 126.
[177] Barrett affirms, "Revelation in the Judeo-Christian tradition is distinctive in that it not only affects history but also uses history as its principal medium." Charles D. Barrett, *Understanding the Christian Faith* (Englewood Cliffs, NJ: Prentice Hall, 1980), 178.
[178] R. Allen Killen, "The Inadequacy of the New Evangelicalism and the Need for a New and Better Method," *Journal of Evangelical Theological Society* 19 (Spring 1976): 115. What is inadequate however, is not evangelicalism itself, but how the church regards movements like

Before we could be conclusive on the intent of Contemporary Evangelicalism we first need to see the different layers of the theological framework of evangelicalism. The aforementioned characterization of evangelical theology by Ramm may be considered as external. The deeper we go into the layers of its theological framework, the fuller we could appreciate its theological coherence with its core universal ecclesial intent.

A number of evangelical scholars from historians to systematic theologians characterize evangelical theology in a variety of form categorizations. Although varied, yet we could still see the essential coherence. And in a deeper sense, we could even perceive a direction towards its core universal ecclesial intent; although the core intent seems hidden from, if not lying in, the subconsciousness of the evangelical mind.

Ramm said it in a rather technical way:

1. *"The evangelical believes that Christianity is one and not many and is not capable of radical reinterpretation."*[179]

Ramm's recognition of evangelical belief in one essence of Christianity has an important ecclesiological implication for the church amidst seemingly diverse forms. Further the evangelical concept of Christianity as "not capable of continuous radical reinterpretation" is essential in appropriately interpreting the implications of the operations of the Holy Spirit in the history of the church.

2. *"Evangelical theology is Christological and incarnational."*[180]

The Christ-centered incarnational concept of evangelical theology provides an internal control between Bible-centeredness and contextualization, and between kerygmatic and apologetic theological formulations. It is a balance epistemological approach avoiding the extremes of Liberalism and Fundamentalism.

---

evangelicalism. What we need is a holistic perspective of the ecclesiological operations of the Holy Spirit in the history of the Church.
[179] Ramm, *The Evangelical Heritage*, 140.
[180] Ibid., 143.

3. *"The evangelical believes that faith is the fundamental response of the sinner to the gospel and is the foundation of Christian experience."*[181]

This experiential individual and congregational life is an antithesis of intellectualism, creedalism and formalism in Christianity. Not that evangelicalism is anti-intellectualist or anti-theological formulation but for evangelicals faith is an experience with Christ. Faith is regarded as personal encounter and experience with Jesus, rather than mere theoretical engagement. However, the evangelical Christian life model does not imply relative subjectivism without internal control, for evangelical belief is defined within the perspective of a balanced Christ-centered and Bible-based faith with realistic everyday life consequences.

4. *"The evangelical believes that theology will have genuine dignity if it retains an important and nonnegotiable element of the objective in the doctrine of revelation."*[182]

Evangelical theology is always epistemologically defined as Bible-centered in approach, Christ-centered in content, and Spirit-led in process—this is what objectivity means in evangelical theology.

5. *"The evangelical believes that the real touchstone of a theology is its spiritual power not necessarily its intellectual shrewdness or sophistication or learning."*[183]

Thus Contemporary Evangelical theology is more life-oriented than its historical precedents. This life-oriented framework of evangelical theology reflects the framework of the prototypal ecclesial belief. Its theology is directed towards practical piety. Evangelical spirituality is neither ascetical nor monastic, but practical and pragmatic everyday life spirituality.

Expressing in a less technical form, Packer profiles evangelicalism in terms of the following six belief-and-behavior principles:

---

[181] Ibid., 144.
[182] Ibid., 146.
[183] Ibid., 146.

1. Enthroning Holy Scriptures . . . as the supreme authority and decisive guide on all matters of faith and practice;
2. Focusing on . . . Jesus . . . who died as a sacrifice for our sins . . . and will return to judge mankind, perfect the church, and renew the cosmos;
3. Acknowledging the lordship of the Holy Spirit in the entire life of grace, which is the life of salvation expressed in worship, work, and witness;
4. Insisting on the necessity of conversion . . .
5. Prioritizing evangelism . . .
6. Cultivating Christian fellowship . . . [184]

Herein Packer brings out the framework of evangelical faith as composed of the centralities of the authority of the Bible, salvation in Jesus Christ, the role of the Holy Spirit in whole Christian life ("worship, work, and witness"), the necessity of conversion, evangelism and fellowshipping. Packer's portrayal concretely reflects the orientation of the everyday life of evangelicals as the consequence of their Christian beliefs. Evangelicals' everyday life is a life of faith and witness.

However, Packer also criticizes the unhappy improper reactionary antithesis triggered by five proper Christian priorities that stunt evangelical churchliness:[185]

1. "Salvation-centeredness" resulting in human-centered theology.
2. "Word-centeredness" that marginalized sacrament.
3. "Life-centeredness" in small group that is a "seedbed of sectarianism."
4. "Parachurch-centeredness" that draws away from "congregational life."

---

[184] J. I. Packer, "A Stunted Ecclesiology?: The Theory and Practice of Evangelical Churchliness," (Fellowship of St. James, 2002), Cited April 21, 2004. http://www.touchstonemag.com/docs/issues/15.10docs/packer/church.html.
[185] Ibid.

5. "Independent-church syndrome" that leads to decline in "connectional bond with other congregations."

From Reformation to Contemporary Evangelicalism the Spirit-led ecclesial movements were intended for the progressive regeneration of the church back to its original wholeness. However, as usual, when a movement becomes preoccupied with a fragment, its whole church life is overshadowed by that fragment. The consequence is not only misdirection but also fragmentation to the point that a movement becomes entrapped in its own self-making—rather than be concerned with the furtherance of the restoration of church life back into its whole original nature. Contemporary Evangelicalism, with its potentialities richer than before in Christian history needs to be prevented, if not rescued, from this ecclesial entrapment propensity.

Phillips and Okholm list the following "distinctive elements of evangelical Christianity":

1. *"Evangelicals insist that Jesus Christ is the incarnate God and thus the definitive self-revelation of God."*[186]
2. *"Evangelicals affirm the authority of the Bible as the truthful, absolutely reliable, divinely inspired, and uniquely normative guide for Christian belief and practice."*[187]
3. *"Evangelicals believe that our salvation was established only through Jesus Christ's life, atoning death and resurrection, and that Christ's work must be personally appropriated by faith alone."*[188]
4. *"Evangelicals commit themselves to a life of active piety under the lordship of Christ."*[189]
5. *"Evangelicals engage themselves in evangelism, aimed at the conversion of individuals and of the church."*[190]

---

[186] Phillips and Okholm, *A Family of Faith*, 15.
[187] Ibid., 16.
[188] Ibid.
[189] Ibid.

Phillips and Okholm note here the "life of active piety" which characterizes evangelical calling in contrast to ascetic and separatist inclinations of the precedent ecclesial movements. The theology of evangelicalism is placed in its proper Christ-centered redemptive intent.

John Stackhouse, Jr. points out five characteristics of evangelicalism in terms of the following centralities:[191]

1. Salvation in Jesus Christ
2. The Bible
3. Conversion experience
4. Mission
5. Transdenominationalism

Here Stackhouse, Jr. points out an important element in evangelical ecclesiology—transdenominationalism. Although as aforementioned Packer saw the risks of sectarianism with evangelicalism's small group nurturing medium. But the overall model of evangelical ecclesiology is still transdenominationally and missionally unifying. Because of its missionally unifying characteristic, evangelicalism has championed functional interdenominational relationship on common missional cause. Such unifying transdenominational and missional ecclesial model of evangelicalism indeed reflects the unifying missional wholeness of the original church where the church was viewed as one missional body of Christ.

McGrath presents a clear-cut classification of the central themes and concerns of evangelicalism:

1. A focus, both devotional and theological, on the person of Jesus Christ, especially his death on the cross;

---

[190] Ibid
[191] John G. Stackhouse, Jr. "Evangelical Ecclesiology Should be Evangelical," in *Evangelical Futures: A Conversation on Theological Method*, ed. John G. Stackhouse, Jr. (Grand Rapids: BakerBooks, 2000), 40-58.

2. The identification of Scripture as the ultimate authority in matters of spirituality, doctrine, and ethics;
3. An emphasis upon conversion or a "new birth" as life-changing religious experience;
4. A concern for sharing the faith, especially through evangelism.[192]

McGrath's characterization of evangelicalism in terms of Christ-centered focus, Bible-centered identity, conversional emphasis, and evangelistic concern is an explicit portrayal of the basics of evangelicalism. He further adds that these central themes and concerns are "central interacting themes and concerns."[193] This note is important in reminding evangelicals that its essential theological components are interrelated, thus not to be taken alone by itself out of its whole framework. This sorts of remind Contemporary Evangelicals not to fall into the pitfall of its predecessors' fragmentation.

D. W. Bebbington brings out these famous "isms" of British evangelicalism which also resemble the characteristics of the North American evangelicalism:

> These are the four qualities that have been the special marks of Evangelical religion: *conversionism*, the belief that lives need to be changed; *activism*, the expression of the gospel in effect; *biblicism*, a particular regard for the Bible; and what may be called *crucicentrism*, a stress on the sacrifice of Christ on the cross. Together they form a quadrilateral of priorities that is the basis of Evangelicalism.[194]

Although Bebbington defines activism and crucicentrism in evangelical sense, however contemporary North American evangelicals might confuse activism as a Liberation Theology cliché and crucicentrism as expression of Roman Catholic emphasis.

---

[192] McGrath, *A Passion for Truth*, 22.
[193] Ibid.
[194] D. W. Bebbington, *Evangelicalism in Modern Britain: A History from the 1730s to the 1980s* (London: Unwin Hyman, 1989), 3.

The following scholars narrowed their characterization of evangelicalism from Packer's six profiles to Phillips and Okholm's five, to McGrath's and Bebbington's four—to their respective three fundamental characteristics.

Evangelicalism for Richard Quebedeaux could be:

> ... characterized as a school of Christianity which attests to the truth of the three major theological principles: (1) the complete reliability and final authority of Scriptures in matters of faith and practice; (2) the necessity of a *personal* faith in Jesus Christ as Savior from sin and consequent commitment to Him as Lord; and (3) the urgency of seeking actively the conversion of sinners to Christ.[195]

Bible-centeredness, Christ-centered faith, and active evangelism are Quebedeaux's threefold evangelical characteristics. This seems narrow compared to the previous characterizations, but still carries with it the essentials of evangelicalism.

William Wells also presents similar threefold characteristics when he emphasizes:

> When I use the word *evangelical* ... I have three more specific characteristics in mind:
> 1. Evangelicals believe in the unique divine inspiration, entire trustworthiness and authority of the Bible.
> 2. Evangelicals believe and personally appropriate by faith alone God's promise that he will forgive, redeem, justify and accept them into a personal relationship with himself on the basis of the life, death and resurrection of his only Son, Jesus Christ.
> 3. Evangelicals commit themselves to the pursuits of a holy life and to the disciplines seen as necessary for Christian growth, including Bi-

---

[195] Richard Quebedeaux, *The Young Evangelicals: Revolution in Orthodoxy* (New York: Harper & Row, 1974), 3-4.

ble study, prayer, fellowship with other Christians and evangelism.[196]

Stott presents a simple yet adept way of characterizing what evangelicals hold, "We hold the three Rs—revelation, redemption and regeneration; associating revelation with the Father, redemption with the Son and regeneration with the Holy Spirit."[197] Further, he sets the delimitation of evangelical priorities:

> It would therefore . . . be a valuable clarification if we were to limit our evangelical priorities to three, namely the revealing initiative of God the Father, the redeeming work of God the Son and the transforming ministry of God the Holy Spirit. All other evangelical essentials will then find an appropriate place somewhere under the threefold rubric.[198]

Stott presents a threefold content of evangelical theology. However, this delimitation seems focused on a personal spiritual faith, and lacks the direct emphasis on individual and congregational missional focus that characterizes the evangelical movement.

Bloesch however includes this missional focus in his definition of evangelicalism when he said:

> . . . it is appropriate to define *evangelical* more precisely: An evangelical is one who affirms the centrality and cruciality of Christ's work of reconciliation and redemption as declared in the Scriptures; the necessity to appropriate the fruits of this work in one's life and experience; and the urgency to bring the good news of this act of unmerited grace to a lost and dying world.[199]

---

[196] William W. Wells, *Welcome to the Family: An Introduction to Evangelical Christianity* (Downers Grove, IL: Inter-Varsity, 1979), 10-11.
[197] Stott, *Evangelical Truth,* 122.
[198] Ibid., 25.
[199] Donald G. Bloesch, *The Future of Evangelical Christianity: A Call for Unity Amidst Diversity* (Colorado Springs: Helmers & Howard, 1988), 17.

C. Synthesis

We can understand the varied forms of characterizing Contemporary Evangelicalism, although still carrying the same essential characteristics, because evangelicalism is not a creedal religion formally uniformed by a singular text. It is however, a life of faith and witness movement in whose vein flow the life of one gospel of Christ. In all of the above characterizations, there is no more befitting summary of Contemporary Evangelicalism as the *gospel-faith!* Although a brand may not always cohere with its identity-quality but, evangelicalism really characterizes the quality its name carry—*euangelion*—the gospel!

Thus in the context of the overall gospel-centeredness of evangelicalism, may I present, in the next chapter, my own characterization of evangelicalism and discuss its components? However, what would be distinct in my characterization is that it does not merely describe evangelicalism but directs the discussion towards the deeper and core ecclesial intent of Contemporary Evangelicalism. This directional approach that has been overlooked, could lead us to the recovery of the more profound objective of the phenomenon of Contemporary Evangelicalism. There is something very profound and significant in evangelical ecclesiology that has been clouded by superficial theological approach.

Two renowned theologians sensed the bright prospects evangelicalism offers to the present day church. McGrath points out an intriguing and revealing point—"I have become increasingly conscious that evangelicalism holds the key to the future of Western Christianity."[200] And Packer also poses another intriguing and revealing question and affirms—:

> . . . evangelicals as a whole is strong, certainly in North America, seemingly in other places too, and if anything is getting stronger. Could it be that God is grooming evangelicalism for leadership in the new millennium? It appears that way.[201]

---

[200] McGrath, *Evangelicalism & the Future of Christianity*, 12.
[201] J.I. Packer, "Maintaining Evangelical Theology," in *Evangelical Futures*, ed. John Stackhouse, Jr., 186.

McGrath's awareness and Packer's suspicion could be right. It appears that way!

6
The Core of Contemporary Evangelicalism

A. The Layers

Now, let me characterize the theological-ecclesial life framework of evangelicalism by layers, from the external, that is, what could be easily seen; to its inner core, that is, the core-self of evangelicalism.

The *first layer* of evangelical framework is the *centrality of mission* and missional interrelationship. The fulfillment of the Great Gospel Commission is the preoccupation of the Contemporary Evangelical movement. This kerygmatic-redemptive preoccupation is not regarded as denominationally or institutionally exclusive but missionally unifying or denominationally cooperative.[202] Because evangelicalism is a missional movement rather than a denominational or institutional establishment, the fulfillment of the Gospel Commission is regarded as the common Christian cause. Thus it avoids separatist denominationalism and promotes integrative inter-denominationalism. As Nash points out:

> Evangelicalism is not a denomination in the traditional sense. It may be best to think of Evangelicalism as a transdenominational movement in the sense that it transcends traditional denominational boundaries.[203]

Noll emphasizes:

---

[202] As Ward observes, "Within transconfessional evangelicalism the emphasis has moved from doctrine towards strategy and organizational power." Pete Ward, "The Tribes of Evangelicalism," in *The Post-Evangelical Debate*, eds., Graham Cray, et al (London: SPCK, 1997), 27.
[203] Nash, *Evangelicals in America*, 27. He further adds, "No overarching bureaucracy. No single leader, or group of leaders, speaks for all or even a portion of evangelicals. What evangelicals have in common is a set of beliefs and a set of causes that grow out of those beliefs." Ibid., 39.

'Evangelicalism' is not, and never has been, an '-ism' like other Christian isms—for example, Catholicism, Orthodoxy, Presbyterianism, Anglicanism, or even Pentecostalism (where, despite many internal differences, the practice of sign gifts like tongues speaking provides a well-defined boundary).[204]

It even regards denominationalism in the sense of common missional paradigm, so that denominationalism becomes interdenominational missional cooperation,[205] rather than exclusivist denominationalism. Denominations are regarded as avenues that—together as one, could be instrumental in fulfilling the common Gospel Commission. Evangelicals are passionate about the Gospel Commission.

Stackhouse, Jr. emphasizes that "evangelicals cannot be evangelicals without endorsing the importance of evangelism."[206] As in Billy Graham Evangelistic Crusades, denominations are regarded first as missional cooperatives. Then, as nurturing options, that is, options for fellowship venues that are all both missionally and ecclesially interrelated because of their common gospel-orientation. The church then is seen as one essential Christian body in different locations. Evangelicalism, by virtue of its being a common Christian missional movement, transcends denominational barriers. Its being trans-denominational

---

[204] Noll, *The Scandal of Evangelical Mind*, 8.
[205] It is perhaps because of evangelicalism's natural inclination to diverse forms of missional approaches that either led other scholars to see evangelicalism as fragmented or perhaps led traditionally oriented denominations to misunderstand the common cause as inclining towards organic ecumenicity. The quest for efficient missional fulfillment, without denominational obstruction, caused the evangelical movement to resort to parachurch avenues. Thus John Stackhouse, Jr. points out that "contemporary evangelicalism has been fragmented a thousand ways through the proliferation of congregational, denominational, and parachurch options." John G. Stackhouse, Jr., *Evangelical Landscapes: Facing the Critical Issues of the Day* (Grand Rapids: Baker Academic, 2002), 19. And Jolanston thinks that, "The variety and vitality of worldwide evangelicalism defies easy description. It is best understood as an umbrella category which includes under its spread a wide range of otherwise disparate churches, movements, and ministries." *The Oxford Companion to Christian Thought*, s.v. "Evangelicalism," by Robert K. Jolanston.
[206] Stackhouse, Jr., "Evangelical Theology Should Be Evangelical," in *Evangelical Futures*, ed. Stackhouse, Jr., 54.

makes functional and unifying use of denominations. And this restores the missional wholeness of the Christian church.

The *second layer* of evangelical framework is its *centrality of the Bible*. The Bible is regarded as the final standard of evangelical teachings. As McGrath points out, "There is no doubt that evangelicalism is characterized by its emphasis on the authority and sufficiency of Scripture."[207] However, the evangelical use of the Bible is not literalistic or fundamentalistwithout regard to other avenues of God's revelational tools. Evangelicalism propagates a sense of theological openness with its balanced Bible-centered theology that makes appropriate use of science and technology. As Nash states, "Evangelicals are not at war with science, culture, or technology."[208] It makes use of science as in archeology, thus biblical archeology; in psychology, thus Psychology of Religion; cultural studies, thus contextualization; biological science, thus scientific explanation of creation; medicine, thus bioethics; linguistics, thus contemporary language translation of the Bible; etc.

It also makes use of arts and technology, as in the art of writing thus, the proliferation of evangelical books and other forms of literatures. The art and technology of movie making thus, Christian film productions by World Wide Pictures of the Billy Graham Evangelistic Association as well as other Christian productions. Mass media, thus evangelical radio programs and even lately an evangelical newspaper purported as an option to *USA Today*. Evangelicalism makes use of science and technology[209] both in the understanding and communicating the gospel. That is, appropriately using the advancement of know-

---

[207] Alister E. McGrath, "Evangelical Theological Method: The State of the Art," in *Evangelical Futures*, ed. Stackhouse, 28.

[208] Ronald A. Nash, *Evangelical Renewal in the Mainline Churches* (Worchester, IL: Crossway, 1987), 167.

[209] Diehi however warns and proposes control in the use of science and philosophy in interpreting the Bible, "It is important to recognize, however, that our fallible knowledge through science and philosophy can also distort our understanding of Scripture. This is why I stress a Christological progressiveness in general revelation and our knowledge through it." David W. Diehi, "Evangelicalism and General Revelation: An Unfinished Agenda," *Journal of Evangelical Theological Society* 30 (December 1987): 454.

ledge as a tool in understanding what the Bible meant and also as a tool in communicating the gospel—with the intention of faithfully proclaiming what the Bible means in contemporary times. However, its use of advancement of Biblical knowledge is always oriented toward practical applications of Christian faith without being engrossed in highly theoretical formulations. As Douglas Grothius said,

> God's truth is not provincial, parochial or partial; it is universal in scope and application. Yet it allows for unique cultural expression and creative individuality....[210]

Further, although evangelicals are engaged in apologetics, but basically the evangelical use the Bible is hardly speculative but always kerygmatic and life-oriented. John Davis comments, "Evangelical theology can be defined as a systematic reflection on scripture and tradition and the mission of the church in mutual relation, with scripture as norm."[211]

Even its academic pursuits are intended as proclamations of the gospel so that lives could be changed and people could be saved. It does not occupy itself in overly defending or expounding a particular school of thought, as in a particular prophetic perspective, but in proclaiming the gospel. Its concern is the proclamation of the Biblical gospel of salvation so that people would be saved in God's Kingdom. Evangelical Biblical exposition is usually focused on life-oriented concerns, namely, regeneration, salvation, living a new life, Christian lifestyle, love to fellow humans, faithfulness, socio-moral transformation, and related foci—not highly speculative foci.

The life-oriented and kerygmatic evangelical belief naturally results in evangelical ecclesial piety that is a balance of spiritual and missional devotion to

---

[210] Douglas Grothius, *Truth Decay: Defending Christianity Against the Challenges of Postmodern* (Downers Grove, IL: InterVarsity, 2000), 73.
[211] John Jefferson Davis, *The Foundation of Evangelical Theology* (Grand Rapids; Baker Book, 1984), 43.

Christ. It is neither mystical although there is a sense of the personal indwelling of Christ. It is not activistic although there is a sense of social responsibility. It is not institutionally engrossed although there is a ministry organization. It is not ritualistic although there is a heartwarming commemoration of Christ's passions and also importantly, the rite of baptism. It is not factionalist although there is a essential faith-boundary. And it is not charismatically overshadowing although there is recognition of the need for the empowerment of the Holy Spirit.

However, such life-oriented theology does not also negate scholarship, for the evangelical academe does produce noteworthy scholarly works, from Carl F. Henry, to J. I. Packer, to John Stott, to Mark Noll and numerous other scholars. In fact evangelical scholarship takes on a new dimension in academic pursuits because the passion for redemptive truth is made alive with the passion for life-oriented gospel-centered life of faith and witness. Theology becomes a living faith. As Robert Weber states, "The two characteristics—personal faith and a deep commitment to orthodoxy, result in evangelicals being good worshippers."[212] Thus in Contemporary Evangelicalism we find a perspective of faith that is balanced by pursuits of Biblical orthodoxy and concerns for kerygmatic significance.

The *third layer* of the evangelical framework is the *centrality of conversion* through the work of the Holy Spirit. Grenz identifies "convertive piety as the central hallmark of evangelicalism" that "in turn, [has] given shape to evangelical theology."[213] "You must be born again!" is the common evangelical cliché—so common to the point that evangelical Christians are called "born again Christians." They are born again either in the sense of conversion from secularism or atheism to Christ-centered Spirit-led life; or from Christian nominalism to deeper relationship with Jesus. As Weber points out, "The evangelical spirit is the

---

[212] Robert E. Webber, *Evangelicals on the Canterbury Trail: Why Evangelicals Are Attracted to Liturgical Church* (Wilton, CT: Morehouse-Barlow, 1985), 169.
[213] Grenz, *Renewing the Center*, 47.

inward, passionate, and zealous personal commitment to the Christian faith which is born out of deep conviction that faith in Jesus Christ . . . produces life-changing effects in man and his culture."[214] Evangelicalism is indeed a discipleship movement!

Conversion in evangelicalism is intended as a deep spiritual rebirth, that is, the result of regeneration by the Holy Spirit ensuing out of true repentance and acceptance of Jesus as the only personal Savior. Conversion is not considered as a superficial denominational theoretical assent or an ecclesiastical provision. As Richard Mouw says, "all evangelicals strongly emphasize the need for an intensely personal, experiential appropriation of the claims of the gospel."[215]

In fact, the church is regarded as a nurturing venue rather than the kingdom of God itself. The focus of evangelical devotions is not an ecclesial institution but Christ. It is a Christ-centered devotion rather than church-centered. This is not demeaning the church, but rather placing the church in its appropriate framework, that is, missional and nurturing media rather than the object of devotion itself! Evangelicalism avoids the spiritual danger of substituting the kingdom of God with the earthly church.

The church, of course, is still regarded as holy, being the congregation of regenerated Christians. But the holiness of the church is regarded as derived rather than inherent in itself. Inherent holiness only resides in Christ and imparted to the church by the Holy Spirit. Further, Contemporary Evangelical ecclesiology is even more truly universal by virtue of regarding the church as being joined together trans-denominationally by the common bond of Christ-centered Spirit-created regenerative life, devotion, and mission. Evangelical piety is a Christ-centered Spirit-empowered regenerative piety.

---

[214] Robert E. Webber, *Common Roots: A Call to Evangelical Maturity* (Grand Rapids: Zondervan, 1978), 17.
[215] Richard Mouw, "Evangelical Ethics," in *Where Shall My Wond'ring Soul Begin?*, eds. Noll and Thiemann, 72.

B. The Core

The *core* of Evangelical theological and ecclesial framework is obviously the *centrality of Christ Jesus*. Evangelical faith, mission, Bible-centeredness, and regenerative piety are all characteristics of evangelicalism that spontaneously emerged out of the core conviction of faith and devotion to Jesus Christ. Evangelicalism is not a separatist denominational movement but a driving force towards the formation of the core Christ-centered ecclesial identity. Thus there could be Evangelical Baptists, Evangelical Lutherans, Evangelical Pentecostals, Evangelical Anglicans, or Evangelical Catholics, etc., who are all Christ-centered in their teachings and in their ecclesial life. Such Christ-centeredness engenders an everyday life of Christ-centered love-practices. Evangelicals are always inspired to live a life of love and compassion as reflecting the life of Christ. Christ-centered spirituality is not a mystical preoccupation but a realistic everyday life of love.

Evangelicals are clear and emphatic that there is no other means of salvation aside from Christ, no other core theological focus aside from Christ, no other essential identity and core proclamation aside from Christ. Thus evangelicalism is truly the gospel movement.

Grenz comments:

> Most evangelicals would agree that at the heart of their vision of faith is an emphasis on an experience with being encountered savingly in Jesus Christ by the God of the Bible. This encounter is an identity-producing event. Through Christ, God constitutes us individually as believers and corporately as a community of believers.[216]

He further adds, "The encounter with the God of the Bible through Jesus . . . is foundational to Christian identity."[217] "Except one accepts Jesus as personal Savior there could be no salvation and hope"—is the core evangelical message.

---

[216] Grenz, *Renewing the Center*, 202.
[217] Ibid.

Evangelicals are preoccupied with the propagation of the *euagelion*, the gospel. As Noll asserts, "evangelical religion has always been 'gospel' religion."[218] Stott clearly presents the focus in defining evangelical identity:

> In seeking to define what it means to be evangelical, it is inevitable that we begin with the gospel. For both our theology (evangelicalism) and our activity (evangelism) derive their meaning and their importance from the good news (the evangel).[219]

The evangelism of evangelical movement is the proclamation of the evangel of salvation and hope only in Christ Jesus. Its redemptive proclamation is both crucicentric (to use Bebbington's term) and adventistic. That is, it emphasizes the atoning passions of Jesus Christ (confirmed by his resurrection) and the Parousia—as the absolute realization of the ultimate hope of humanity. Regarding evangelical adventistic emphasis, Bloesch affirms that an, "evangelical theologian is noted for its affirmation of the visible coming again of Jesus Christ in power and glory to set-up the kingdom that shall have no end."[220] The centrality of Jesus Christ as the only Savior and hope of humanity spontaneously creates the core evangelical Christological faith. Such Christ-centered faith engenders Christ-centered Spirit-empowered way of life that affects the personal, congregational, and societal life of evangelicals.[221] Such life is regarded as both personal and kerygmatic, that is, a personal life lived and a life lived as witness. Evangelicalism is faith in and witness of Jesus Christ empowered by the Holy Spirit.

C. The Message

To summarize, the evangelical theological-ecclesial characteristics are:

---

[218] Noll, *The Rise of Evangelicalism*, 16.
[219] Stott, *Evangelical Truth*, 25.
[220] Bloesch, *The Evangelical Renaissance*, 5.
[221] As Bloesch emphasizes that "a renewed evangelicalism must not hesitate to apply the Gospel to the whole life, to the political and economic as well as the private, personal spheres." Ibid., 46.

First:	Transdenominational missional ecclesiology
Second:	Balanced Biblical epistemology
Third:	Christ-centered Spirit-empowered regenerative piety
Core:	The centrality of Christ, that is, Christ-centered Sprit-empowered life of faith and witness.

Now what does this characteristics reveal? Let us take a look again at the characteristics of the original framework of ecclesial life:

1. Christ-centered ecclesial belief and identity.
2. Oneness in Christ.
3. Spirit-empowered regenerative life.
4. An integrated life of faith and witness.
5. Missional preoccupation.
6. Church as a venue for nurturing and equipping of believers.
7. Kerygmatic congregational life.
8. Life-oriented theology.

And in all these the core is Christ—faith in Christ, witness for Christ, and the Holy Spirit's empowerment for new life in Christ and for witnessing for Christ! And this is exactly what evangelicalism is all about! Thus the explicit conclusion that we could draw is that—Contemporary Evangelicalism is the paradigm of the original characteristics of ecclesial life. In it we see the climactic operation of the Holy Spirit in restoring the church back to its original characteristics! This is the core intent of the phenomenon of Contemporary Evangelical movement!

In regards to the direction of the Holy Spirit in the history of the church, Packer has this revealing words to say—"The Spirit has been active in the church from the first, doing the work He was sent to do—guiding God's people into an understanding of revealed truth."[222]

---

[222] J.I. Packer, *Fundamentalism and the Word of God: Some Evangelical Principles*, rep. ed. (Grand Rapids: Eerdmans, 1972), 48.

The Holy Spirit has been progressively revealing what the church can be and ought to be. He has been guiding the restoration of the church back to its original nature and function. However, the church has historically misunderstood the phenomenon of ecclesial movements. It regarded these movements as threats to denominational institutional life. The church, instead of regarding these ecclesial movements as building blocks for the eventual restoration of the church back to its original wholeness rejected the cumulative intent of the phenomena of ecclesial movements[223]. Then the ecclesial movements became separatists. And those involved in the movements ended up in their respective predicaments. The proponents of each movement ended up making exclusive claims of their respective fragments—and institutionalizing them into new denominations with fragmented and separatist outlook.

Now in Contemporary Evangelicalism we see right in our very own time—the full-bloom and synthesizing model of the original characteristics of the church. When the framework of Contemporary Evangelicalism is integrated into the life of the whole church—then there could be a grand global ecclesial regeneration! To conclude in R.V. Pierard words:

---

[223] Oxtoby sees a linkage of evangelicalism with Pietism, Puritanism and the Great Awakenings and considers these as movements rather than boundaried denominations. He writes, "Seen in its broadest compass, twentieth-century Protestant evangelicalism is a multifaceted emphasis or movement cutting across the major denominations. It is not a denomination as such, although some denominations are solidly evangelical. It draws on earlier themes, notably the individual's confident assurance of God's grace and acceptance that characterized Reformation Pietism on the European continent and the revivalist movements of England and North America." Oxtoby, "The Christian Tradition," 313. He further defines Pietism, "The name 'Pietism' designates not a boundaried denomination but a movement that rippled through various Protestant denominations." Ibid., 285. And he regards Puritanism as a purification movement, "Puritanism was a movement in English and colonial American Protestant churches, rather than a boundaried denomination in itself....It began as an effort to 'purify' the Church of England of the remnants of Catholic usage in church vestments, furnishings, and ecclesiastical organizations that it retained after the Catholic reign of Queen Mary in 1553-8." Ibid., 282.

> ... evangelicalism is more than orthodox assent to dogma or a reactionary return to past ways. It is the affirmation of the central beliefs of historic Christianity.[224]

Indeed in Contemporary Evangelicalism we see both—the paradigm—and the call—for the regeneration of Christian church back to its prototypal characteristics!

---

[224] *Elwell's Dictionary of Evangelical Theology*, s.v. "Evangelicalism," by R.V. Pierard

7
The Evangelical Agenda

A. The Nature and Purpose of Contemporary Evangelicalism

The 1500's Reformation was intended to lead the church back to its gospel-consciousness—back to the consciousness of the gospel as the core of church life. But the Reformation's gospel-orientation was still embryonic. It was focused on particular *solas: sola fide, sola gratia,* or *sola scriptura*. It was embryonic because it was just the beginning of the long process of restoring the church back to its whole original wholeness.

However, many Protestant denominations that emerged out of the Reformation movement became separatist and dogmatist. The concept of faith and grace were even seen as contradictory. And although the *sola scriptura* epistemological emphasis eventually opened the floodgate of Biblical curiosity and further studies, yet basically the resulting ecclesial preoccupations were theoretical rather than life-oriented and holistic. And years later, with the influence of Rationalism many theological pursuits were even devoid of profound spirituality. Regarding intellectual pursuits devoid of spirituality, William Abraham has this to say to contemporary Christians:

> What I am suggesting is that this concern with the intellectual and with formal theology be thoroughly relativized. It needs to be subordinated to spiritual renewal."[225]

---

[225] William J. Abraham, *The Coming Great Revival: Recovering the Full Evangelical Tradition* (San Francisco: Harper & Row, 1984), 53.

Contemporary Evangelicalism, however, integrates faith and scholarship. Its theological model offers bright promise to the prospect of Christian theological growth. For as Noll said, "Personal faith in Christ is a necessary condition for Christian intellectual life, for only a living thing may develop."[226] Evangelicalism presents a balance of intellectual theological pursuits and experiential spiritual life. It is a balance of mind and spirit—nurturing the soul to avoid regression to either dogmatic formality or uncritical mysticism.

Reformation played its role in restoring gospel-consciousness but it was not yet the whole of evangelicalism, although the Lutheran church in Germany was called evangelical. As Carpenter puts it:

> This new movement [modern evangelicalism] differed greatly from 'the evangelical churches' of Luther's day. The evangelical persuasion now included a lessened emphasis on the creedal sacramental channels of faith, a preference for voluntary religious affiliation and interdenominational cooperation, aggressive evangelization, conversionist views of salvation, earnest and abstemious living, and revivalistic and millennial expectations about God's work in the days to come.[227]

The Reformation movement and subsequent movements carried with them their respected building blocks for further constructive ecclesial restoration. The Holy Spirit is re-building the church back to its prototype—one block at a time!

Contemporary Evangelicalism started as a reaction against fundamentalist theological notion. But afterwards when one talks about evangelicalism, it is associated with things like—Billy Graham Crusades, movements for societal moral recovery, conservative Christian lifestyle, interchurch cooperation, parachurch ministries, life-changing literatures, world-mission, and above all—born again Spirit-led Christians who accepted Jesus as their only personal Savior.

---

[226] Noll, *The Scandal of Evangelical Mind*, 250.
[227] Carpenter, "The Fellowship of Kindred Minds," in *Pilgrims on the Sawdust Trail*, ed. George, 31.

These characterizations of Contemporary Evangelicalism indicate not a mere hypothetical or mystical ecclesial life but of a rich and balanced personal and congregational life of faith and witness.[228]

The church is not regarded as a mystical body into which believers lodge for redemptive security, but as the venue for nurturing and the means for fulfilling the Gospel Commission. This is also true of the evangelical perspective on parachurch ministries. Interdenominational networking is not placed in the context and motivation of a mere organic ecumenicity but of functional gospel-oriented missional cooperation. That is, a cooperation and unity in fulfilling the common Gospel Commission. And the Gospel Commission is fulfilled in both proclamation and compassionate service.

Further, the church is seen as a congregation of believers who live in conservative but not extremist lifestyle. The church is not regarded as the kingdom of God itself but as a venue, by virtue of the believers' act of congregating, for personal and interpersonal nurturing and missional equipping. Thus within the church small group congregation, that is, a congregation within a congregation, is common for the purpose of more intimate and effective interpersonal nurturing and discipleship. Thus, in this sense could McGrath identify that, "The real heartbeat of evangelicalism is in a church Bible study group."[229]

Furthermore, evangelicals are not just people assenting and propagating a particular set of theological propositions, although it has its own distinct theological and ecclesiological characteristics. Evangelicalism is not a mere apologetic movement itself but a kerygmatic one. By kerygmatic, I mean a focus on living a distinct life that proclaims the *kerygma*, and not just a focus on conceptual defense or exposition. It is a balance of faith and experience, a balance

---

[228] Thus as Payne says, "American evangelicalism exists as a theological construct, a historical phenomenon, and a sociological movement." William P. Payne, "The Social Movement Dynamics of Modern American Evangelicalism," *Ashland Theological Journal* 35 (2003): 37.
[229] McGrath, "Trinitarian Theology," in *Where Shall My Wondr'ng Soul Begin?*, eds. Noll and Thiemann, 53.

of theology and way of life. Bloesch asserts, "to be evangelical means to hold a definite doctrine as well as to participate in a special kind of experience."[230] McGrath observes that:

> ... the reason evangelicalism is growing is not because its experts produce theological tomes, but because it proves capable of relating to ordinary people ... offering them a vision that changes their lives and focuses on the very simple Christ-centered piety.[231]

Because of its balanced framework, evangelicalism has phenomenally grown.

Peter Hodgson sees that evangelicalism could indeed provide the most needed religio-moral answer in contemporary times. He sees that, "The resurgence of conservative and evangelical Christianity in recent years (at least in America) is symptomatic both of the magnitude of the experienced threat and of the deep desire to recover stable ethical and religious foundations in a topsy-turvy world."[232] The heart of evangelical worship which is the proclamation of the Word, gives meanings and significance to life amidst this topsy-turvy world.

Moreover, the society is not seen as an institutional domain of Christendom itself but as a mission field. The society is a vocational, rather than political, field. Social concerns voiced out through mass media or even interchurch mass movements, are not intended to make politics ecclesiastical nor make the church political. The objective of evangelical social responsiveness is either moral regeneration or prevention of moral degeneration. Evangelicals see themselves as having inherent responsibility, by virtue of their faith and kerygmatic life, to proclaim the Kingdom values and propagate the Kingdom culture without usurping political power. This seems debatable in the setting of an almost evangelical partisanship in American politics, but the true evangelical spirit always remains within the kerygmatic parameters. That is, within the

---

[230] Donald G. Bloesch, *Essentials of Evangelical Theology* (Peabody, MA: Prince, 2001), I: ix.
[231] McGrath, "Trinitarian Theology," in *Where Shall My Wond'ring Soul Begin?*, eds. Noll and Thiemann, 53.
[232] Peter C. Hodgson, "Ecclesia of Freedom," *Theology Today* 44 (July 1987): 223.

framework of Christ-centered transformational gospel proclamation and avoiding the risk of secular politics.

Puritanism and Pietism did bring further dimension in the gospel-orientation of the church, that is, the concern on spirituality and witness. They brought another life and witness oriented restorative blocks to the church. However, later Puritanism imbibed a legalistic tendency, and Pietism an ascetic inclination. And Puritanism even attempted to establish another earthly kingdom, a Puritan America. The Great Awakenings revived the personal spiritual and missional aspects of ecclesial life. They brought with them spiritually reviving and missionally active characteristics of the church. These are the other restorative building blocks the church deeply needed. However, later the Movements' national influence also waned. Fundamentalism brought back Bible-centered epistemology amidst a secularizing modernism and liberalism. However, later the movement became literalistic, separatist, and denominationally judgmental.

However, not only negatives could be said about the precedents of Contemporary Evangelicalism. Because the ecclesially restorative building blocks of each movement are all parts of the continuing process of regenerating the church back to its whole original nature and function.

When Contemporary Evangelicalism emerged—it presented to the global church a balanced synthesis of historical revelatory features of precedent movements for the eventual restoration of the whole original wholeness of the church. Contemporary Evangelicalism recognizes the Bible as the basis of Christian belief and teachings; yet brought with it a non-literalistic and richer yet conservative theological perspective. In its Bible-centeredness, it is not entrapped in speculative formulations—but rather uses the Bible as source of meanings, guidance, and inspiration for regenerative everyday life. Noll points out that "Christ-centered, biblically normed religious experience" "remained the defining center of the evangelical movement."[233]

The movement is life-oriented. It integrates faith and life. For as David Wells emphasizes, "An evangelical faith that is not passionate about truth and righteousness is a faith which is a lost cause."[234] But though propagating a new regenerative way of life, it avoids legalism, separatism, and being denominationally judgmental. In fact, it is socially and denominationally unifying. It unites churches and other societal organizations for gospel-oriented causes. And it regards spiritual life as both a communication and an exemplification of the Christ-centered gospel. As Packer said it, "the gospel message individualizes, and faith is always an individual personal matter, and in the God-centered relationship of love and service formed within Christian community...."[235]

The denominationally unifying factor of Contemporary Evangelicalism is not merely institutional, but spiritual, experiential, and missional. That is, the spirit of new life, the experience of being born again, and the common witness of experiencing salvation in Jesus—draw believers and churches together. As Dallas Willard points out, "The three substantive elements of evangelical piety are conviction of sin, conversion, and testimony."[236] These elements common among born again Christians of various denominations internally draw all believers as one in Christ.

Contemporary Evangelicalism emphasizes the common fulfillment of the Gospel Commission. Crusades after crusades are intended to make disciples of Jesus, to prepare people for the *Parousia*. Its proclamation is hardly a dogmatic theory but a redemptive and practical life-oriented message. Its evange-

---

[233] Mark A. Noll, "Evangelicalism at Its Best," in *Where Shall My Wond'ring Soul Begin?*, eds. Noll and Thiemann, 4.
[234] David F. Wells, *The Bleeding of the Evangelical Church* (Edinburgh: Banner of Truth, 1995), 9.
[235] Packer, "A Stunted Ecclesiology?."
[236] Dallas Willard, "Christ-centered Piety," in *Where Shall My Wond'ring Soul Begin?*, eds. Noll and Thiemann, 29.

lism is not intended for the expansion of a denominational institution but for the salvation of humanity only through Christ. Its message proclaims a Christ-centered, rather than church-centered, message. Its way of life is also Spirit-centered for it recognizes and proclaims new life in Christ only through the Holy Spirit. The church too is seen, not as a mystical entity but, as a real and living congregation of believers sharing common faith, and nurturing one another for the fulfillment of the Gospel Commission.

Contemporary Evangelical spirituality is Christ-centered and interpersonal, that is, a personal relationship with Jesus engendering deep Christian fellowship. Further, ecclesial rites from the Lord's Supper to baptism are regarded as regenerative-celebrative acts. They are regarded as acts of reconnecting with Jesus, celebrating the salvation he won for humanity, and anticipating his Second Coming. It is celebrating the salvation Jesus realized at the first coming and anticipating the realization of the full restoration of the ideal primal human life at Jesus' Second Coming. Worship in Contemporary Evangelical sense involves teaching, fellowshipping, celebrating, and praying—with the proclamation of the gospel at its center. In fact, the whole church services from Sunday school to Communion Service to prayer and singing to preaching are all regarded as proclamations of the gospel.

Contemporary Evangelicalism indeed more truly reflects the original characteristics of church life. However, there is one component in Contemporary Evangelicalism that is still loose. This component is the charismatic pastoral and evangelistic empowerment of individual believers. Evangelicalism believes on the priesthood of all believers. However, it still needs a balanced emphasis of the spiritual empowerment of all individual believers. Although in Billy Graham crusades, the role of the Holy Spirit is invoked through massive prayer groups, yet personal spiritual gifts still need appropriate recognition. The emphasis on spiritual gifts is conspicuous in the Pentecostal movement. But, at times, Pentecostalism also distinguishes itself from Contemporary Evangelicalism and vice versa. This is ironical because the recognition of the need for the empowerment of the Holy Spirit in the life of the church and individual believers is an indispensable feature of Contemporary Evangelicalism. The appropriate Pentecostal emphasis on individual spiritual gifts for the personal fulfillment of the Gospel Commission is the post script component of Contemporary Evangelicalism.

Noll present an option for synthesizing Pentecostalism and Evangelicalism while expressing his apprehension:

> For all evangelicals it will remain a challenge to maintain classical traditions of trinitarian theological orthodoxy while absorbing the excitements of Pentecostal and charismatic faith. The ideal will be for our traditional evangelicals to be quickened by movements of the Holy Spirit and for devotees of the Spirit to learn balance and gravity from the traditionalists. But the traditional strengths of evangelical theology could be blown away by winds of the Spirit, and new Pentecostal groups might come to imitate the deadening formalism and enervating moralism that have sometimes characterized the older evangelical movements."[237]

The key to the restoration of the original ecclesial life design is a balanced and holistic framework of Pentecostal Evangelicalism. Glenn Davis emphasizes:

> Jesus never meant for us to fulfill his commission without experiencing his power. The outside world will only know that we are Christ's own by the activity of the Spirit in our lives.[238]

McGrath points out that:

> Charismatics and evangelicals belong to the same group. They may

---

[237] Mark A. Noll, "Foreword: American Past and World Present in the Search for Evangelical Identity," in *Pilgrims on the Sawdust Trail*, ed. George, 18.
[238] Glenn E. Davis, "Who Is the Holy for Us Today? The Person and the Work of the Holy Spirit in John 2;:19-23," in *Pilgrims on the Sawdust Trail*, ed. George, 96.

place the stress in different places, but nonetheless a commonality exists between them.[239]

Contemporary Evangelicalism emphasizes the Christ-centered redemptive faith and witness, and the Holy Spirit's role in regeneration. Pentecostalism emphasizes the personal charismatic missional empowerment in fulfilling the Gospel Commission. Both belong to the whole of ecclesial prototypal framework—and as a synthesis, this could be the most powerful and astounding ecclesial revival paradigm ever in the history of the post-apostolic church!

So in all these, what do we have here? Conclusively—the paradigm for the regeneration of the church back to the prototype of active Christ-centered life of faith and witness empowered by the Holy Spirit! This is the objective, the intent—the very purpose of the phenomena of preceding ecclesial movements finally climaxing in Contemporary Evangelicalism!

George proposes, "I suggest a simple and briefer definition: *evangelicalism is a renewal movement within historic Christian orthodoxy.*"[240] Noll affirms that "the rise of evangelicalism was the manifestation of a special outpouring of the Holy Spirit."[241] Contemporary Evangelicalism is the climax of revelatory and regenerative operation of the Holy Spirit intended to restore the life of the church back to its original New Testament design!

To conclude in John Stott's words:

> . . . evangelical faith is not a recent innovation, a new brand of Christianity which we are busy inventing. On the contrary, we dare to claim that evangelical Christianity is original, apostolic, New Testament Christianity.[242]

---

[239] McGrath, "Trinitarian Theology," in *Where Shall My Wond'ring Soul Begin?*, ed. Noll and Thiemann, 54.
[240] George, "Between the Pope and Billy Graham," in *Pilgrims on the Sawdust Trail*, ed. George, 126.
[241] Noll, *The Rise of Evangelicalism*, 139.
[242] Stott, *Evangelical Truth*, 14.

B. The Challenge!

However, Contemporary Evangelicalism could only have its profound regenerative significance in the history of Christian church—when its restorative objective is heeded and its restorative paradigm assimilated into the life of the whole Christian church. It must be received and worked out in the framework of the one whole Christian church. Ironically though, David Walker notes a non-holistic inclination even within evangelicalism itself. He criticizes, "non-holistic ways of understanding become so common place among evangelicals it often happens that holistic formulations are met with suspicion of being departures from evangelical faith."[243]

As Clark Williamson puts it, "Unless God gives it, there is no revelation; unless someone receives it, there is no revelation."[244] James Thwaites reminds:

> Revivals need not end up in the settling ponds and holding patterns the church has historically made for them.... The first are given for the time of planting, and the latter come in the time of harvest."[245]

But why is Contemporary Evangelicalism still beset by ecclesiological identity confusion? Because there is still an ecclesiological misconception; in spite of the fact that Contemporary Evangelical ecclesiology offers the most explicitly prototypal, holistic and synthesizing ecclesiological paradigm. Richard Beaton contends, "evangelicalism is in the throes of identity crisis, and at the heart of the crisis is a lack of clarity concerning the nature and function of the

---

[243] David S. Walker, *Challenging Evangelicalism: Prophetic Witness and Theological Renewal* (Pietermaritzburg, South Africa: Cluster Publications, 1993), 199.
[244] Clark M. Williamson, *The Way of Blessing The Way of Life: A Christian Theology* (St. Loius, MO: Chalace, 1999), 45.
[245] James Thwaites, *The Church Beyond the Congregation* (Cumbria, UK: Paternoster, 1999), 207. Woodbridge and his colleagues regard evangelicalism as an awakening movement, "From Jonathan Edwards to Billy Graham, from itinerant Methodist preachers to television evangelists, the awakening tradition has had a long career." John D. Woodbrige, Mark Noll, and Nathan O. Hateh, *The Gospel in America: Themes in the Story of America's Evangelicals* (Grand Rapids, Zondervan, 1979).

church."[246] Mouw criticizes many of the professed evangelicals as operating "with an extremely weak ecclesiology."[247] Noll and others portray evangelicals as having "a lot of fancy evangelical hybrids."[248]

These claims seem ironical in the context of the prototypal theological and ecclesial-life characteristics of evangelicalism. But, indeed, there is still confusion in Contemporary Evangelical ecclesiology. And this necessitates an ecclesiology that is coherent with the prototypal, holistic, and synthesizing nature of Contemporary Evangelical theological framework. One of the contributing factors to the ambiguity, if not confusion, in evangelical ecclesiology is perhaps what Stackhouse noted as the implied ecclesiology more than the articulated one that evangelicals have.[249] Hunt emphasizes that the, "diligent effort to rethink the biblical foundations of the doctrine of the church remains a top priority on the theological agenda."[250]

Bock has this to say regarding the survival of evangelical theology as well as the whole Christian theology, "At the start of twenty-first century we see that conservative evangelical theology has survived because many were diligent to remain faithful to scripture, committed to Christ and concerned about the world, even as they pursued doctrinal reflection and spiritual integrity."[251]

The succeeding chapters will show that indeed there could be a coherent and distinct Contemporary Evangelical ecclesiology. In fact, it is this distinct ecclesiology that the whole Christian church needs today if Christianity is to survive, grow, and fulfill its purpose in this new millennium!

---

[246] Richard Beaton, "Reimaging the Church: Evangelical Ecclesiology," in *Evangelical Ecclesiology: Reality or Illusion?*, ed. John Stackhouse, Jr. (Grand Rapids: Baker Academic, 2003), 217.
[247] Richard J. Mouw, "Evangelicals in Search of Maturity," *Theology Today* 35 (April 1978): 32.
[248] Mark Noll, Cornelius Platinga, Jr. and David Wells, "Evangelical Theology Today," *Theology Today* 51 (January 1995): 495.
[249] John G. Stackhouse, Jr. "Preface," in *Evangelical Ecclesiology*, ed. Stackhouse, 9.
[250] Boyd Hunt, "New Dimensions in Church," in *New Dimensions in Evangelical Thought: Essays in Honor of Millard J. Erickson*, ed. David S. Dockery (Downers Grove, IL: InterVarsity, 1998), 338.
[251] Bock, *Purpose-Driven Theology*, 50.

Part III
Contemporary Evangelical Ecclesiology as the Paradigm of Prototypal Ecclesial Regeneration

8
Contemporary Evangelical Ecclesiological Codes

There is a distinct Contemporary Evangelical ecclesiology. In fact, its framework reveals ecclesiological codes that are universal and foundational. These codes are the universal foundations of a more truly prototypal church. And these are the codes that could transform a particular denomination and the whole Christian church to the kind of church faithful to the original design. These codes are already implied in the general theological framework of Contemporary Evangelicalism. And these are: transdenominational nature, missional cause, Christological content, and dependence on the empowerment of the Holy Spirit.

A. Transdenominational Nature

Evangelicalism is not a denomination itself but a gospel-oriented and missional movement. Denominational-centered organizations are usually preoccupied with their own institutional growth through the propagation of what they regard as their unique doctrinal proclamation among other claimants of truth. The denominational identity-centered proclamation is exploited as means, supposedly for the salvation of souls but eventually, of institutional expansion; even if evangelism would simply mean proselytism. Proselytism is even regarded as an effort to salvage deceived souls from what are considered as apostate churches, that is, the "other" churches not conforming to its unique truth-claim. Although this denominationally-centered missional propensity is, in contemporary times, common among cultic sects; yet it also characterized the general missional disposition before the proliferation of Contemporary Evangelical movement.

Further, while the World Council of Churches (WCC) has been externally trying to promote ecumenism, Contemporary Evangelicalism has been internally and spiritually drawing churches together to fulfill the common kerygmatic missional cause. The movement has been very successful in leading churches to transcend their respective superficial self and just focus on Christ and his mission. It has proliferated transdenominationalism worldwide. Thus Pierard defines evangelicalism as, "The movement in modern Christianity, transcending denominational and confessional boundaries, that emphasizes conformity to the basic tenets of faith and a missionary outreach of compassion and urgency."[252]

Hindmarsh sees a new ecclesiological paradigm in evangelicalism:

> From the beginning of the movement in the eighteenth century, evangelicalism has been transdenominational, international, and public in a way that is unique in Christian history. This raises new, important questions about how we are to understand the church.[253]

And indeed, Contemporary Evangelicalism presents a new—or rather prototypically renewed—understanding of the church. At the outset, however, evangelicalism's transdenominational operation was regarded as radical, and was even seen as threat to denominational-self. Others, at times, even supposed it as means of apostatizing the true Christian church through what they regarded as syncretistic missional effort of what they tagged as "false" and "true" churches. That ironical denominational prejudice posed polarity in the fulfillment of the common Christian missional cause that evangelicalism was reviving. However, such prejudice with its polarizing consequence waned as they were over-

---

[252] *Evangelical Dictionary of Theology*, s.v. "Evangelicals," by R.V. Pierard.
[253] Hindmarsh, "Is Evangelical an Oxymoron?," in *Evangelical Ecclesiology*, ed. Stackhouse, 18.

whelmed by the missional zeal and evangelistic fruitfulness of evangelicalism. And eventually evangelicalism succeeded in proliferating global transdenominational missional relationship.

But what is the nature of evangelicalism's transdenominationalism? At the outset, it is significant to note the difference between transdenominational nature and interdenominational association. Transdenominational nature presupposes an internal unifying framework beyond superficial denominational-self. While interdenominational association merely suggests an interrelationship intended for a particular purpose while still subconsciously recognizing calculated denominational motives. A transdenominational framework transcendentally drawing churches together for the regeneration of the one whole Christian church—is on a higher plane than an interdenominational association. Contemporary Evangelicalism is not merely an interdenominational association but a regenerative transdenominational ecclesiological framework. However, evangelicalism's transdenominational nature does not merely propose an institutional organizational restructuring of divided churches into one. But rather sees the transcendence of the operation of the Holy Spirit in restoring the church back to its original and denominationally transcendent nature. Eventually, with the restoration of the original characteristics of the church in every denomination—all denominations internally become one whole body of Christ again. This may sound merely idealistic and impractical to those used to rigid denominational setting, but in Contemporary Evangelical movement we are already seeing bright prospects for internal ecclesial regeneration.

Although there are still other deeper factors that contribute to evangelical transdenominational nature, but what we could immediately see is its missional transdenominational operation. The fulfillment of the Gospel Commission draws churches together to co-operate for greater kerygmatic societal impact. Thus Grenz sees that, "At the heart of the institutional expression of evangelicalism was a new model of Christian cooperative engagement, the voluntary society."[254] The primal purpose of its transdenominational missional cooperation is redemptive, that is, the salvation of sinful humanity. And the church is not regarded as an object of devotion, but as the means for fulfilling the mission of Christ. Evangelicals believed that the mission is entrusted to no other corporate entity than the church. And by the church, what they mean is the congregation of all believers. Thus parachurch ministries as ministries of groups of mission-driven believers are indeed ecclesial bodies. For evangelicals, mission transcends denominations.

However, oftentimes a question is raised, "If evangelicalism believes that the mission of Christ is entrusted to no other corporate entity than the church, why the existence of evangelical parachurch ministries?" As just said, parachurch ministries are indeed ecclesial bodies. In fact, parachurch organizations being distinctively ministry organizations are even more operationally efficient and prototypal than bureaucratized churches. As Carpenter puts it, "parachurch agencies have made a hash out of traditional ecclesiology."[255] Stackhouse, Jr. gives the reason why, "In some accounts, they [parachurch ministries] do what the church in its congregational or denominational form is not doing, is not able to do, or is not doing well enough."[256]

Thus the Billy Graham Evangelistic Association, as well as other parachurch ministries, though may not be sociologically categorized as a church—but theologically, spiritually, and missionally—they are. From the coming together of churches for evangelism to the congregating of people at the Cove[257] for spiritual nurturing, equipping, and worship—it is an ecclesial entity.

---

[254] Grenz, *Renewing the Center*, 293.
[255] Carpenter, "The Fellowship of Kindred Minds," in *Pilgrims on the Sawdust Trail*, George, ed., 38. Thus because of evangelicalism's transdenominational orientation resorting to parachurch ministries, others like Escobar thinks parachurch movement as the predominant definition and make-up of American evangelicalism. Samuel Escobar, "The Church: Help of Hindrance to Evangelism?," in *Evangelicalism: Surviving Its Success*, ed. David A. Fraser (Princeton: Princeton University Press, 1987), 68.
[256] Stackhouse, *Evangelical Landscape*, 27.
[257] The Billy Graham retreat center in Ashville, North Carolina, USA.

Such church transcends the traditional sociological or even sociologically colored theological definition of the church.[258] This may seem a stretch of definition of the church for many traditionalists—but theologically and spiritually, pastorally and missionally faithful parachurches reflect more of the original characteristics of the church than bureaucratized churches. I do not imply the promotion of parachurch organizations over against, or at the risk, of established churches. But I would like to point out the unique characteristics of the nature and function of evangelical parachurch ministry—that pose serious challenge to churches that have become less prototypal. These characteristics transcend denominational enclosures enabling them to focus, without denominational obstruction, on Christ and his mission. This framework serves as paradigm for the missional regeneration of dogmatized, institutionalized, and bureaucratized churches.

Contemporary Evangelical ecclesiology is not a bureaucratized ecclesiology but a movement ecclesiology. It is not something institutionally confined but a movement transcending the traditional bounds of denominations. As McGrath points out:

> Evangelicalism rejects the idea that 'the church' can in a way be equated with one ecclesiastical body. The true church is found wherever the gospel is truly preached and truly received.[259]

The gospel is the center of the evangelical movement, not organizational matters itself. Evangelical ecclesiology is more truly gospel-centered than denomination-centered. Although evangelicalism makes use of institutional means in

---

[258] Thus Snyder disagrees calling "support institutions" as church. "But all ecclesiastical institutions—whether seminaries, denominational structures, mission boards, publishing houses or what have you—are not the Church. Rather, they are supportive institutions created to serve the Church in its life and mission. They are bound and can be sociologically understood and evaluated. But they are not themselves the Church." Howard A. Synder, *The Community of the King* (Downers Grove, IL: InterVarsity, 1977), 60. Snyder's definition of the church, however, tends to be more sociologically oriented. Theologically though, a group of believers nurturing one another and called out to fulfill the Gospel Commission—is a church.

[259] McGrath, *Evangelicalism & the Future of Christianity*, 105.

fulfilling its pastoral and missional mission—it is not trapped in institutional denominational preoccupations.

Further, evangelicalism's transdenominational ecclesiology is not oriented towards theoretical dogmatism but towards the regeneration of the original characteristics of the church. It is an ecclesial life-oriented ecclesiology. This gospel-oriented paradigm offers the church that has been historically deadened by superficial dogmatic preoccupations—new and reinvigorating life of faith and mission. The Christian church has been historically trapped in superficial and fragmentary dogmatic presuppositions and preoccupations. And these varied suppositions and preoccupations consequently resulted in denominationalism. Contemporary Evangelicalism, however, presents a framework for redirecting the church toward the original focus of the church—Jesus and his gospel. This framework for redirection internally reintegrates denominations into one body of Christ—that transcends denominational eccentricities—and is united as one in essence.

The confinement of denominations in their respective dogmatic preoccupations could be a symptom of a deeper ecclesial-theological identity struggle. Christians in general is internally struggling on what it means to be more truly the Christian church. There is in Christianity a post-apostolic, historical and diversely theological ecclesial-identity struggle. When this identity struggle is superficially or improperly answered it results in schism and exclusivist denominationalism with diverse truth-claims. Churches attempting to find answers to what has become an enigma have historically resorted to misdirected religio-ideological approaches that resulted in the polarization of Christian beliefs and disintegration of unifying ecclesial framework. I do not mean that theological formulation necessarily lead to religious ideology. But when a theological formulation is regarded, as not only absolute but also, as tool for exclusivism and its theory becomes the center of ecclesial identity and life rather than Jesus and the Gospel Commission—then theology has become a religious ideology. Whenever churches become preoccupied with their respective dogmatic theoretical formulations, then we also see the Christian church becoming a pile of embellished ecclesial fragments.

It is in the situation of a divided Christian church that ecumenism came with its external approach to uniting separate churches. External because the usual approach to ecumenism assumes acceptance of fragmentary ecclesial identities, while trying to pull them together for, at times, a socio-political cause as in World Council of Churches. The superficial identities of Christian churches as Catholic, Protestants, Orthodox, Pentecostals, etc., are just accepted as what they are. Rather than redirecting churches towards the internal and holistic renewal of the original characteristics of the one church of Christ. To use Ezekiel's metaphor (Ezekiel 37:1-14), this is like trying to glue together old lifeless dry bones. What Christianity needs is the internal gospel-reorientation and enlivening by the Holy Spirit of the whole Christian church.

I do not mean that existing churches are dead itself, although others might be spiritually dying amidst a secular world. But that the internally unifying framework among churches is obviously dead. It is deadened by ideological and institutional process due to unresolved deep identity crises. This may sound a very negative evaluation of the state of the Christian church. But the fact that each of the Catholic, Protestant, Orthodox, Pentecostal, and numerous other sub-categories of churches—remain willfully distinct and exclusivist from one another—validate this evaluation! Churches still insist on divergent superficial identities—each regarded as sacred matter—while ironically, recognizing one Christ. And even more ironical—the objectively regarded one Christ is even subjectively reshaped in some contradictory forms.

Since Reformation there was a call for the gospel-reorientation of the church. However, the Reformation was an embryo that still has to mature later in Contemporary Evangelicalism that is still post-scripted by appropriate Pentecostalism—that all belong to the same regenerative ecclesial process. However, it is not as though the post-script is lacking in Contemporary Evangelical framework. For the need for the empowerment of the Holy Spirit in the corporate life of the church is an essential structure of Contemporary Evangelicalism. Steve Rabey and Monte Unger even trace the development of American Evangelicalism from the Azusa Street Pentecostal phenomenon to Billy Graham.[260] What needs to be appropriately emphasized is the personal spiritual gift for the ministry of the church. Pentecostalism should be seen as the awakening of the church's need for the personal empowerment of the Holy Spirit in the life and ministry of the church in relation to Evangelicalism's awakening of the church's need to be more truly gospel-oriented in its life and ministry.

The church needs to "listen to the word of the Lord"—the gospel needs to be the heart, the mind, the soul, and spirit of the church. Restoration in the metaphor of the old dry bones in Ezekiel's vision starts from listening to "the word of the Lord" (Ezekiel 37:4-8). The proclamation of the gospel is the missional identity of the church, and Christ is the center of life of the church and the content of the gospel proclamation, and the Holy Spirit is the power that enables the church to live its Christ-centered identity and fulfill its kerygmatic mission. These essences transcend denominational enclosures.

The Christian church today needs to rethink of its true identity and functions not based on denominational suppositions but based on the original ecclesial characteristics that are being revived since the 1500 Reformation. D. Lyle Dabney poses this ecclesiological challenge in the postmodern context:

> In such a world I suggest, the Church finds itself facing what amounts to a new and different challenge to its own self-understanding; a challenge that will require us to think through ecclesiology again by thinking

---

[260] See Steve Rabey and Monte Unger, *50 Events of the 20th Century that Shaped Evangelicals in America* (Nashville, TN: Broadman & Holman, 2002).

through the most basic categories of Christian theology anew.[261] However, ecclesiological rethinking could only be faithful to Christian theology while being a fresh theological construction when it truly reflects the prototypal ecclesiology; rather than a new ecclesiological construction based on denominational suppositions or a cultural form. A denominational-based ecclesiology is still a denominational ecclesiology. A culture-based ecclesiology simply becomes a cultural ecclesiology. What the world needs in any denominational or cultural form is Christ-centered, Spirit-empowered, and missional ecclesiology. For it is in Christ that the world finds ever fresh meanings in life. It is through the Holy Spirit that the church lives. And it is through mission that Christ is made known to the world.

Millard Erickson saw the need for apparent ecclesiological understanding:

> At the present time [the mid 1980's] the focus of this [twentieth century] literature is not the church itself, but other entities. It is time to reverse this trend, for if we do not have a clear understanding of the nature of the church, we cannot have a clear understanding of its relationship to these other areas [like relationship to society].[262]

In Contemporary Evangelicalism we see the apparent nature of the church as Christ-centered, Spirit-empowered, and kerygmatic. In it we see the paradigm for church wholeness. Churches could not be made whole through mere associational approach but through the entire gospel-reorientation and deep empowerment of the Holy Spirit, and missional preoccupation. These could result in the restoration of ecclesial wholeness amid denominational fragmentation. Thus, in Contemporary Evangelicalism we could see the paradigm that trans-

---

[261] D. Lyle Dabney, "The Church as a Community of (Un)Common Grace: Toward a Postmodern Ecclesiology." The Christian Theological Research Fellowship Papers 4(July 1991), cited March 28, 2004, http://home.apu.edu/sCTRF/papers/1997_papers/dabney.html.
[262] Millard J. Erickson, *Christian Theology* (Grand Rapids: Baker, 1985), 1027.

cends denominational eccentricities. As Abraham notes—"A most significant change [of neo-evangelicals] was the rejection of the separatist ecclesiology."[263]

Further, we could see another synthesis in Contemporary Evangelical transdenominational characteristics. And this is its life-oriented characteristic that synthesizes spirituality and mission, devotion and proclamation. Christian life in evangelical sense is not a passive spirituality. It is an active everyday life of faith. It is a life personally connected to Jesus, while at the same time a life that proclaims the gospel of Jesus. As Paul testified, "I don't want anyone to think more highly of me than what they can actually see in my life and my message" (2Cor 12:6). Faith for evangelicals is not merely a theoretical assent to creed; although it does include the essentials of Christian belief. Faith is defined in terms of life of faith. A life of faith is defined as a personal experience of encountering Jesus, experiencing regenerative life, and witnessing to others the blessings of being saved by Jesus.

Thus evangelical ecclesial life is focused on proclaiming the gospel. Grenz portrays the advent of evangelicalism as "the quest for the truly Reformed church" whose focus is the proclamation of the convertive gospel "whether inside ecclesiastical structures or beyond them."[264] Thus for the church to be truly evangelical, it should live the life of Christ and proclaims the gospel of Christ. As Grenz further describes it, "the truly evangelical church is a community of faith, understood not merely as the people in whose midst the faith is proclaimed, but as a community of people of faith and of faithful people."[265]

Moreover, not only is evangelical life regarded as gospel-centered, but the gospel proclamation is also life-oriented rather than theoretical. It is in-

---

[263] Abraham, *The Coming Great Revival*, 20.
[264] Grenz, *Renewing the Center*, 47.
[265] Ibid., 338. For further discussion on the gospel and evangelicalism, see R.C. Sproul, *Getting the Gospel Right: The Tie that Binds Evangelicals Together* (Grand Rapids, Baker Books, 1999). In regards to Christian life, Westerhoff states, what evangelicals similarly thinks although in a wider framework than cultus, "Daily life provides the context for expressing the truth we have experienced through cultic life." John H. Westerhoof, III, *Living the Faith Community: The Church That Makes a Difference* (San Francisco: Harper & Row 1985), 56.

tended to change lives rather than to convince people of a particular theological view in contrast to other denominational views. So here we have a synthesis of gospel-centered proclamation and gospel-oriented life. With this overarching character of evangelical life—Contemporary Evangelical ecclesiology is not entangled in a denominational web but rather lifts churches to a higher plane of a life of faith and witness. Grenz realizes that:

> By uniting together all who were born again and therefore members of the invisible church, evangelicals seemed to have found a practical solution to the perplexing problem of ecclesiology.[266]

Thus in all these, the transdenominational characteristic of Contemporary Evangelicalism offers a viably meaningful and fulfilling framework for the restoration of the church back to its unifying nature and wholesome function. This may not be tagged an ecumenical proposal, for ecumenism plots an ecclesial direction different from Contemporary Evangelicalism. But this could just be tagged Contemporary Evangelical transdenominational paradigm for ecclesial wholeness.

B. Missional Cause

A number of established churches are losing membership, succumbing to secular threats, and loosing significance in the life of people amidst a secular global society.[267] Many churches are just struggling to survive if not dying. As Barna observes of the state of American church in the 1990's:

> ... the Church in America is losing influence and adherents faster than any other major institutions in the nation. Unless a radical solution for the revival of the Christian Church in the United States is adopted and

---

[266] Grenz, *Renewing the Center*, 300.
[267] For a challenge on living Christian faith amidst a world getting less Christian see, R.R. Reno, *In the Ruins of the Church: Sustaining Faith in an Age of Diminished Christianity* (Grand Rapids: Brazos, 2002).

implemented soon, the spiritual hunger of Americans will either go unmet or be satisfied by other faith groups.[268]

However, the state of the church is not that all grim. For at the time when the world needed the church most amidst the situation of church decline—Contemporary Evangelicalism emerged. It offers a new hope for the spiritual revival of both church and society. And an aspect of this hope hinges on evangelicalism's revival of the missional life of the church!

Mission is a prominent emphasis of evangelicalism.[269] But what is mission in Contemporary Evangelical sense? The mission of the church in evangelical sense is a kerygmatic-redemptive mission, that is, the proclamation of the gospel for the salvation of fallen humanity. As the model of the prototypal ecclesial mission—Contemporary Evangelicals preach the need for regeneration, accepting Jesus as the only personal Savior, living in a new life, then witnessing for Jesus to others. They emphasize that the only hope of humanity, the only redemptive means, is Jesus.

Mission for evangelicals is primarily soteriological not sociological, political or institutional. It regards the church as a venue for nurturing and equipping believers for the fulfillment of the Gospel Commission. The church is regarded as a corporate resource for accomplishing the mission. And the existence and life of the church should cohere with its missional fulfillment. The church does not exist for itself, nor is the soteriological end, but a means for a soteriological end. The intended objective is not the coming of people to an ecclesial institution but the coming of people to Christ.

As Wade Roof, a professed liberal, states it, "The church is not an end in itself, it is an earthen vessel from which sacrifice and service and proclamation

---

[268] George Barna, *The Second Coming of the Church* (Nashville, TN: Word, 1998), 1. This could describe that state of established churches that are losing missional zeal. However, mega-churches that are more Christ-centered and Spirit-filled are also emerging.

[269] For an articulation of an evangelical missional agenda; see Billy Graham Center, *An Evangelical Agenda: 1984 and Beyond* (Pasadena, CA: William Carey Library, 1979).

must constantly be poured out."[270] The coming of people to church is a natural socio-spiritual outcome of experiencing salvation in Christ. Thus the growth of the kingdom of God, not the growth of the church itself, is the goal of evangelical ecclesial mission. And as Thom Rainer puts it, "The call for churches today is for growth that is soteriocentric."[271] The church is primarily a missional, pastoral, and soteriological means—an instrument rather the origin of salvation. The church nurtures and sent out believers for mission, rather than secures and dispenses salvation. The church is a venue for nurturing spiritual life so that when believers proclaim the gospel there lives cohere with their proclamation. As Phillips and Okholm emphasize, "The church is God's family (Matt. 12:48-50) where his children are nurtured and trained to be his disciples."[272]

Evangelicalism provides a non-confusing definition of the mission of the church—to evangelize, that is, to proclaim the gospel of Christ so that people would have the opportunity to accept Jesus as their personal Savior and be saved. The mission of the church is definitely a redemptive kerygmatic mission. Making disciples is nurturing those who accepted Jesus as their personal Savior. It is not a sort of subjugating people or society as what happened in the Middle Age. Because subjugation impinges on the gift of volition the Creator God imparted to humans. However, evangelicalism spiritually-oriented redemptive mission does not also exclude humanitarian and societal concerns[273]—as in al-

---

[270] Wade Clark Roof, "The Church in the Centrifuge," *The Christian Century* (November 8, 1989):1014.
[271] Thom S. Rainer, "New Dimensions in Evangelicalism and Church Growth," in *New Dimensions in Evangelical Thought*, ed. Dockery, 425.
[272] Phillips and Okholm, *A Family of Faith*, 118.
[273] Freston even identifies evangelical involvement in the politics of Third World Countries, see Paul Freston, *Evangelicals and Politics in Asia, Africa and Latin America* (Cambridge: Cambridge University Press, 2001). However, we should note that political involvement in these countries describes more of the involvement of liberal churches than the crusade and humanitarian oriented evangelicals. For a brief discussion on the development and stunting of evangelical social concern, see Gary Scott Smith, "The Man and Religion Forward Movement of 1911-12: New Perspective on Evangelical Social Concern and the Relationship Between Christianity and Progressivism," *Westminster Theological Journal* 49 (Spring 1987): 91-118. Tinker discusses further on present issues confronting evangelicals, see Melvin Tinker, *Evan-*

leviating sufferings and poverty,[274] and the restoration of societal moral integrity. As the means of fulfilling the gospel of Christ, the church should be naturally replete with acts of love and the propagation of Christ-centered values.

Further, evangelical ecclesiology is not philosophically-oriented engrossed on reflection and exposition of the philosophical being of the church. It is a missional and functional ecclesiology—a dynamic rather than static ecclesiological paradigm. Its missional and dynamic ecclesiology that transcends the traditional philosophically-oriented ecclesiology, confuse some theologians on the real nature of Contemporary Evangelical ecclesiology. Other theologians even doubt if there is really such thing as Contemporary Evangelical ecclesiology. Further, because of Contemporary Evangelical missional preoccupations, churches whose missional zeal has been overshadowed by other institutional concerns—regard evangelicalism as a mere missional movement rather than a holistic ecclesial movement.

And indeed Contemporary Evangelicalism is not an institutional or denominational movement itself, although there are attempts to embody its ecclesiological concepts into an ecclesial institution. Although it is usually regarded as preeminently a missional movement; however, its being a missional movement is just an aspect of its wider intended purpose. While being a missional movement, it is also an ecclesiologically restorative movement. Its pastorate transcends denominational enclosures. It is intended to pastorally regenerate the whole Christian church, so that the whole Christian body could fulfill its evangelistic mission. Thus in essence, its mission is both pastoral and evangelistic.

---

gelical Concerns: Rediscovering the Christian Mind on Issues Facing the Church Today (Ross-shire, UK: Christian Focus, 2001).

[274] Gaebelein poses this challenge to evangelicals amidst a materialistic world, "The prevalent confusion of success with material things and the growing sense of entitlement to more and more possessions—and evangelicals are by no means free from it—can get the nerve of compassionate concern for our suffering brothers and sisters for whom Christ died." Frank E. Gaebelein, "Evangelicals and Social Concerns," *Journal of Evangelical Theological Society* 25 (March 1982):22.

Moreover, mission in Contemporary Evangelicalism is regeneratively life-centered. Its missional objective is not just a theoretical affirmation of Christian beliefs, or a theoretical reconstruction of the church—but the transformation of life of both unbelievers, nominal Christians, and the declining churches. Thus evangelicalism is not just preoccupied with evangelism but also with church revival. The transformation of life is seen as the consequence of true and deep encounter with Christ resulting in the acceptance of Jesus as personal Savior, and experiencing a sustainable new life in Christ through the empowerment of the Holy Spirit.

Christianity, in evangelical sense, is not just a matter of belief but also a matter of life. This regenerative life-orientation truly reflects the discipleship mission of the original church—the disciples were commissioned to teach believers how to observe the teachings of Christ, that is—to live like Christ. The essence of discipleship is living Christ's exemplary life on earth.

Furthermore, evangelicalism's missional cause promotes ecclesiological operational wholeness. With the transcendence of Contemporary Evangelicalism over denominational enclosure; its evangelistic mission become apparently Christ-centered, rather than denominationally-centered. As such it draws Christian believers together both individually and congregationally to fulfill their missional calling. It may be intuitive to say that as in Billy Graham crusades, the Holy Spirit is working among believers and churches, convicting them of participatory need and drawing them altogether to fulfill the one common evangelistic mission. But indeed, experientially and pragmatically the called out individual Christians and churches could be seen as exhibiting Spirit-empowered zeal as they come together and unite to play complementary roles in fulfilling the common gospel proclamation. This is seen and experienced in every Billy Graham crusade and other evangelical evangelistic endeavors.

In evangelical evangelistic crusades, we see the deep spiritual and missional revival of churches. Churches are awakened, become zealous, and

Spirit-enlivened. They are internally and naturally drawn and fitted together into one spiritually alive and evangelistically proclaiming body of Christ. This is quite a contrast to other cause-oriented ecumenical approaches that is merely socio-political, or even academic, but superficial. The gospel-oriented missional cause Contemporary Evangelicalism is reviving in Christian church, promotes another aspect of the internal ecclesial wholeness.

C. Empowerment of the Holy Spirit

Contemporary Evangelicalism recognizes the need for the empowerment of the Holy Spirit in a more appropriate sense than extremist charismatic movements. As aforementioned, I regard Pentecostalism as the postscript yet part of Contemporary Evangelicalism. For as Stott points out, "the indwelling presence of the Holy Spirit is the chief distinguishing mark of the people of God today...."[275] Hans Küng, a Catholic theologian, also see the ecclesial universality of charisms, "So charisms are not special marks of distinction belonging to a chosen few...but a distinguishing mark of the whole church, of the fellowship of all believers." [276] Vanhoozer adds, "The church is . . . the people of God filled with the Spirit of God."[277]

However, evangelicals regard spiritual gifts not merely for liturgical self-centered purpose or merely intended for the emotional trance of liturgical participants. Evangelicals believe on the outpouring of the Holy Spirit but are wary of this kind of Pentecostalism. This does not mean that evangelicalism negates healing miracles, prophecy, or the primal role of the Holy Spirit in regeneration—evangelicals do believe on these. However, the evangelical view of the empowerment of the Holy Spirit is practical rather than basically emotional. The empowerment of the Holy Spirit is viewed in a utilitarian perspective, that

---

[275] Stott, *Evangelical Truth*, 93.
[276] Hans Küng, *The Church* (New York: Sheed and Ward, 1967), 187.
[277] Kevin J. Vanhoozer, "The Voice and the Actor: A Dramatic Proposal about the Ministry and Minstrelsy of Theology," in *Evangelical Futures*, ed. Stackhouse, 103.

is, as the indispensable power for accomplishing the church's mission and conversion of people's life.

Bloesch defines charism in an ecclesiologically utilitarian sense:

> A charism ... signifies a special gift or power which enables one to perform a particular service. The charisms were given by the Spirit primarily for the upbuilding of the church.[278]

Miroslav Volf expresses a similar concept of charism:

> Although all of Christian life is lived in the Spirit, it is not charismatic as a whole. Charisma has a narrower meaning in its reference to a particular capacity given by the Spirit of Christ for a particular ministry in church or world.[279]

However, evangelicalism does not also do away with the spiritual experiential encounter with the Holy Spirit amidst liturgy. But such encounter with the Holy Spirit is always Christologically oriented. That is, an experience with the Holy Spirit leading to a deeper and more meaningful relationship with Jesus. Or for non-believers, it is a spiritual encounter resulting in the acceptance of Jesus as personal Savior. This would at times be emotional but not wildly hysterical and chaotic that is devoid of conversional awareness and apparent Christological consciousness.

The empowerment of the Holy Spirit is seen as a missional and conversional empowerment. As in Billy Graham crusades, numerous networks of prayer groups invoke the operation of the Holy Spirit for evangelistic success. The Holy Spirit is regarded as the absolute power behind the fulfillment and success of every evangelistic effort. The indispensable role of the Holy Spirit in evangelical's redemptive kerygmatic mission is regarded in the following senses:

1. In convicting people of their sinfulness and their need of accepting Jesus as the only personal Savior; and

---

[278] Donald G. Bloesch, *The Reform of the Church* (Grand Rapids: Eerdmans, 1970), 109.
[279] Miroslav Volf, *After Our Likeness: The Church as the Image of the Trinity* (Grand Rapids: Eerdmans, 1998), 229.

2. In charismatically empowering the missional human resources, namely, preachers, singers, and other participants in crusades or other evangelistic endeavors.

With the sense of presence of the Holy Spirit, evangelicals feel enthused and alive in their evangelistic endeavors. Without it they feel un-animated. The Holy Spirit is the power behind the evangelization of people with due regard to their volitional options. I point out due regard to volitional option because altar call for conscious decision for Christ is common in evangelical crusades. This is, however, in contrast to just being unconsciously caught up in trance state as in some charismatic crusades. During the crusade, without the Holy Spirit the preacher and his message becomes a "tingling cymbal" so to speak. It is the Holy Spirit that transforms a human proclamation into words of life that opens the redemptive gateway for the hearers. Gustaf Wingren expresses a kerygmatic view of the Pentecostal phenomenon:

> When the Spirit breathes on man, they begin to *speak* and their words go out to the converted. Thus the kerygma can actually be the means of restoring a fragmented and disintegrated humanity.[280]

Evangelicalism regards the outpouring of the Holy Spirit at the day of Pentecost as a missional kerygmatic inauguration. The outpouring was intended to empower the believers to proclaim the Christ-centered redemptive message. The empowerment was not intended as a spiritual exhibit or as affirmation of redemptive realization in individuals mystically caught up amidst a liturgy. When the Holy Spirit was outpoured, believers began preaching the gospel in understandable languages. The Pentecost was a kerygmatic linguistic empowerment of the zealous yet linguistically incapable believers.

Acts portrays the event:

"These people are all from Galilee, and yet we [Jews coming from vari-

---

[280] Gustaf Wingren, *Gospel and Church*, trans. Ross Mackenzie (Edinburgh: Olive and Boyd, 1964), 106.

ous ethnic-linguistic groups] hear them speaking the languages of the lands where we were born! Here we are—Parthians, Medes, Elamites, people from Mesopotamia, Judea, Cappadocia, Pontus, the province of Asia, Phrygia, Pamphylia, Egypt and the areas of Libya, Cyrene, visitors from Rome (both Jews and converts to Judaism), Cretans, and Arabians. And we all hear these people speaking in our languages about the wonderful things God has done!"[281]

The Holy Spirit enabled the believers to speak in known languages they were unable to speak—for the purpose of proclaiming the message of salvation in Christ Jesus. Contemporary Evangelicalism does not confuse the missional gift of tongue with the personal spiritual groaning amidst struggles in life while praying.[282] The former is for public evangelistic purpose, the latter is for personal spiritual purpose. The essence of the Pentecostal event is seen as the empowerment of the believers by the Holy Spirit in the fulfillment of their evangelistic mission.

The "gift of tongues" was seen as an occasional linguistic bestowment contingent on their present need. Evangelicals recognize the waning of such supernatural need with the conversion of multi-ethnic, multi-linguistic believers who are able to preach in their respective languages. Coppedge sees the Pentecost as a unique event of ecclesial birth. He writes, "Unquestionably, the day of Pentecost was a distinct historical event and in the sense that it represents the birth of the New Testament church, its events are indeed unique and not repeatable."[283]

Evangelicals do recognize the gift of healing and other spiritual gifts; however, these gifts are seen in the perspective of mission and discipleship.

---

[281] Acts 2:7-11.
[282] Paul notes, "And the Holy Spirit helps us in our distress. For we don't even know what we should pray. But the Holy Spirit prays for us with groanings that cannot be expressed in words. And the Father who knows all hearts knows what the Spirit is saying, for the Spirit pleads for us believers in harmony with God's own will." Romans 8:26-27.
[283] Coppedge, *The Biblical Principles of Discipleship*, 122.

That is, as spiritual tools in fulfilling the Gospel Commission and in nurturing fellow believers. These gifts are intended for spiritual and kerygmatic purposes rather than mystical. The missional and pastoral empowerment of the Holy Spirit is an essential structure in evangelical ecclesiology.

Furthermore, empowerment of the Holy Spirit in evangelical sense is also meant for life-centered transformation and sanctification. The spiritual operation of the Holy Spirit in individual believers is not seen as occasional but continuous. Some charismatic movements however, are preoccupied with occasional trance state experience. Aside from the bestowal of spiritual gifts, the role of the Holy Spirit in regenerative sanctification of believers is an essential faith structure in evangelical life. As Bloesch emphasizes, "Certainly true spirituality will also emphasize the outpouring of the Holy Spirit, for there can be no Christian life that is not inspired by the Spirit."[284] New life in Christ is actually a new life in Christ empowered by the Holy Spirit. Ecclesiologically, this implies that the regeneration of ecclesial life is not merely institutional, associational, or liturgical[285]—but essentially the operation of the Holy Sprit.

The empowerment of the Holy Spirit is what the church needs for spiritual revival. Without the Spirit-empowered revival, churches would continue to regress towards its deadening propensity! Bloesch challenges, "If we are to have spiritual renewal in our time, the church must be open again to the special gifts and charisms given by the Spirit of God for the purpose of ministry in the world."[286] As paradigmatic in evangelical missional strategy, spiritual revival of the church is necessitated for the fulfillment of the church's redemptive kerygmatic mission.

The *re*-formation of the prototypal characteristics of the church requires spiritual revival empowered by the Holy Sprit. Ferguson points out the essen-

---

[284] Bloesch, *The Future of Evangelical Christianity*, 133.
[285] As in mere organizational restructuring, formation of associations of churches, or liturgical renewal.
[286] Bloesch, *The Reform of the Church*, 114.

tiality of the Holy Spirit in the existence of the church:

> If the church is the body of Christ, the Spirit is the life of the body. Just as the body without the spirit is dead, so without the Holy Spirit there would be no church, no community at all.[287]

The evangelical perspective of the empowerment of the Holy Spirit is intended for the empowerment of individual conversional and missional life. This emphasis on spiritual empowerment is very relevant in the context of institutionalized and bureaucratized churches. These churches, at times, disfranchise the ecclesial empowerment of the Holy Spirit. Ironically however, the misdirected emphasis in other extremist charismatic churches has also disfranchised centralities of Christ and Biblical epistemology. These are, at times, substituted by emotionalism and subjective revelational claims.

McGrath notes the evangelical apprehension on extremist Pentecostalism: "word-centered evangelicals often express a concern that an emphasis on the Holy Spirit might result in Scripture's being bypassed in favor of an immediate personal revelation to an individual."[288] Lovelace however, identifies the charismatic movement as a Puritan carryover, thus an evangelical heritage at that—but ironically lacking epistemological control. He comments:

> The charismatic renewal continues to express the mystical spirituality of the Puritan and Awakening eras, but often without the rational and theological checks against error and credulity maintained by evangelicals.[289]

Here again is an example of a common blunder in the history of Christian church—a fragmentary ecclesial preoccupation based on an aspect of a progressive historical revelation intended for the regeneration of the church back into its balanced and wholesome state. Indeed, since the Reformation on-

---

[287] Everett Ferguson, *The Church of Christ: A Biblical Ecclesiology for Today* (Grand Rapids: Eerdmans, 1996), 107.
[288] McGrath, *Evangelicals & the Future of Christianity*, 70.
[289] Lovelace, "Evangelical Spirituality," 33.

ward—ecclesial movements were fragmentarily regarded. It is in the backdrop of this ironical and fragmenting ecclesial preoccupation—that Contemporary Evangelicalism offers a balanced holistic framework. How? It positions the components of ecclesiological framework in its appropriate place—the operation is transdenominational, the cause is missional, the power is the Holy Spirit, and the content is Christ!

D. Christological Essence

It might be awkward to call Contemporary Evangelical ecclesiology Christological for this seems not to fit existing ecclesiological models, namely, sacramental, mystical, institutional, etc. Christological is usually regarded as describing a theological content and not an ecclesiological model[290]. However, in the context of evangelicalism being a Christ-centered movement—it offers the renewal of the Christological essence of the Christian church.

As in every ecclesiological model, the ecclesial focus becomes the ecclesiological characterization. When a particular ecclesial body focuses on liturgy, it becomes a liturgical church. When a church focuses on spiritual gifts, it becomes a charismatic church. When a church focuses on its institutional elements, it becomes an institutional church. Thus we have different models that are shaped according to their respective focus. Regarding evangelicalism Derek Tidball observes, "The evangelical's primary concern is not with the fixed ecclesiastical structures but with people who are Christians whatever denominational label they wear or structure they inhabit." [291]

Evangelicalism as a missional movement is a kerygmatic church. And being a kerygmatic church it is not only Christ-centered but also a Christological church. The church exists to proclaim Christ and his message of salvation, and

---

[290] However, Kimlyn Bender's recent publication on Karl Barth's Christological ecclesiology does explore a Christological ecclesiological model, refer to Kimlyn J. Bender, *Karl Barth's Christological Ecclesiology* (Hamshire, UK: Ashgate, 2005).
[291] Derek J. Tidball, *Who Are the Evangelicals: Tracing the Roots of the Modern Movement* (London: Marshall Pickering, 1994), 158.

to guide people to Christ both evangelistically and pastorally. It exists in and for Christ. Its existential derivation and kerygmatic content becomes its ecclesiological essence. Being Christological and Christ-centered—the church could transcend its fragmentary and distortive human frailty. The church is lifted up to its true plane of existence and purpose—that is, existence in Christ for the purpose of proclaiming Christ.

In this context Contemporary Evangelicalism offers not only a regenerative missional movement but also a regenerative ecclesiological framework. Evangelical ecclesiological framework presents a model for the restoration of the prototypal Christ-centered and Christological nature of the church—that were historically marred since the pre-Reformation period. Like the marring of the archetypal image of God in human nature at the Fall, the image of Christ in ecclesial nature has also been marred since the ecclesial fall. The ecclesial fall, of course, did not totally obliterate the image of Christ in the church. However, through the process of assimilating essentially degenerating secular cultures—the image of Christ in the church has been clouded and is not really as apparent as the apostolic church. By re-emphasizing Christ as the essence of the church—Contemporary Evangelicalism is guiding churches to where it properly belongs—to Christ—as his one whole body!

E. The Projected End Result

These aforementioned components properly fitted together in the perspective of Spirit-operated ecclesial regeneration form a distinct Contemporary Evangelical ecclesiology. And this distinct ecclesiology offers hope—not only for the survival of prototypal Christianity but also—for the fulfillment of the very reason of the existence of the church. This is the objective of the codes of Contemporary Evangelical ecclesiology. Indeed these evangelical codes re-present the characteristics of the original church.

But what then are the implications of these Contemporary Evangelical ecclesiological codes? Assimilating these codes into the life of the whole Christian church will naturally result in the grand new regeneration of Christianity! But why is Contemporary Evangelical ecclesiological codes very suitable for ecclesial regeneration? The next chapter will explore the factors why . . .

9
Characteristics of Contemporary Evangelicalism as the Paradigm for Ecclesial Regeneration

Contemporary Evangelicalism presents the most wholesome paradigm for the reformation of the church back to what it was more truly meant to be. However, its ecclesiological paradigm is not appropriately regarded because it does not seem to conform to a highly-detailed and technical ecclesiological formulation. In spite of its holistic characteristics it is even tagged underdeveloped. As pointed out earlier in the Overview, Mouw emphasizes:

> Evangelicals have long worried about ecclesiological perspectives that are so highly detailed and all-consuming that they crowd out other important theological concerns. So we respond by emphasizing some things, such as the need for a personal relationship with Jesus Christ and for evangelizing the lost, that are often neglected by people who take delight in detailed ecclesiologies.[292]

And McGrath argues, "Those who accuse evangelicals of having 'immature' or 'underdeveloped' theories of the church might care to ask themselves whether they might not have hopelessly overdeveloped theories."[293] As pointed out in the preceding chapters, evangelical ecclesiological framework presents a

---

[292] Mouw, "Evangelical Ethics," in *Where Shall My Wond'ring Soul Begin?*, eds. Noll and Thiemann, 75.
[293] McGrath, *Evangelicalism & the Future of Christianity*, 82.

model of the church that is Christ-centered, Spirit-empowered, life-oriented, missional, and transdenominational. These characteristics when fully and deeply integrated into the life of churches would result in transcending denominational eccentricities and rapture of regenerated churches into one whole prototypal church of Christ.

This rapture scenario reflects the resurrection, transformation, and ascension of believers into one whole new humanity at the Second Coming. Before the ascension of Christ after resurrection, there was an apostolic embryonic church of a few people who were wondering what to do. Then finally at ascension, the wondering embryonic church was entrusted the Gospel Commission. Before the Holy Spirit descended, there was a growing church who knew what to do, but did not know how to do it. Then finally at the advent of the Holy Spirit at the day of Pentecost, the church was empowered to fulfill the Gospel Commission. At the Parousia, the church, that is, the assembly of all the called out ones—in fact a great multitude—will receive their reward and be ushered into the fully restored universe—where they all as one—then becomes the restored prototypal humanity. Salvation will then be fully realized.

In this perspective, the church to remain true to itself, should remain true to its redemptive eschatological objective—and not be tied up to superficial institutional concerns. The life of the church should always be oriented towards the redemptive eschatological objective. When the church deviates from its redemptive, kerygmatic and eschatological orientation, it will get entangled in secular affairs. Thus for ecclesiology to maintain its integrity, should maintain its redemptive, kerygmatic and eschatological orientation. It is in this context that Contemporary Evangelicalism offers fresh and prototypically renewed ecclesiology because of its redemptive, kerygmatic, and eschatological orientation. Its focus is the proclamation of the gospel of Christ so that people would be saved in the coming kingdom of Christ. Evangelical ecclesiology is a full gospel-oriented ecclesiology.

Although the embryo of the gospel-oriented movement that began at Reformation matures in Contemporary Evangelicalism, yet evangelicalism does not regard itself as the ecclesial objective. But rather as a movement that, first of all, intends to lead people to the kingdom of God, and as corollary, a movement reviving churches. Thus the movement is truly eschatological-oriented rather than denominational-centered. It regards itself as the instrument of the kingdom of God, rather than the kingdom itself. However, because of the evangelical synthesis of the life of faith and witness—church life becomes the foretaste of the regenerated life in the Kingdom.

As Hodgson says, the "Ecclesia is an image . . . and foretaste of the basilea, embodied in a diversity of historical churches."[294] In evangelical ecclesiology, while church life is regarded as prolepsis of the life in the Kingdom, the church is not equated with the Kingdom. It is clearly regarded as a divine-human agency to usher people in the present realm to the eschatological realm. It is a mediatory congregation, a bridge between this world and the kingdom of God separated by a gulf of sin. It is in this unobstructed and apparent emphasis of the relationship of the church to the kingdom of God that, aside from its holistic characteristics, makes evangelical ecclesiology more efficiently paradigmatic.

Aside from the aforementioned ecclesiological characteristics in the preceding chapter, this chapter emphasizes three more reasons why Contemporary Evangelical ecclesiology is the suitable paradigm for ecclesial regeneration.

A. Contemporary Evangelical ecclesiology is a full-grown paradigm.

There are varied views as to when evangelicalism emerged. Some would trace its emergence from Luther whose followers formed the Evangelical Lutheran Church in Germany. Others trace it from the Pietistic and Puritan[295]

---

[294] Hodgson, "Ecclesia of Freedom," 226.
[295] For a collection of essays on the historical development of evangelicalism from Puritan to Postmodern contexts, see D.G. Hart, *Reckoning with the Past: Historical Essays on American*

movements. Still others considered evangelicalism as a North American phenomenon originating from the Awakening Movements.[296] While others define evangelicalism as a contemporary event;[297] and the pioneers of Contemporary Evangelicalism like Harold Okenga,[298] Carl F. Henry, and Billy Graham considered their movement as Neo-Evangelicalism. Neo-evangelicalism was just eventually tagged "evangelicalism."

Seeing the ecclesiology of evangelicalism from the point of view of its historical emergence could be confusing. This is because evangelicalism, in essence, is not a momentary ecclesial movement. Nor is it merely a reaction to a particular theological view like Fundamentalism. Nor is it simply a movement—but a process. It is a progressive process of restoring the unobstructed and full gospel-orientation of the church. Seeing evangelicalism from the viewpoints of its prototypal regenerative framework implies not regarding it as a new separate denomination. But rather regarding it as an overall revelatory movement and process for the restoration of the whole Christian church.

But is there really the need for restoration of the church when churches seem settled in their respective ecclesial comfort zones? Churches seem settled comfortably in their respective denominational convictions and traditions. And churches seem to hold on to their respective particular theological notions from which they build their denominations. Further denominational distinctive characteristics are not only regarded unique but even regarded as the whole of the original church. In essence though, what are distinct in most denominations are actually fragments of the whole progressive ecclesial revelation.

Evangelicalism from the Institute for the Study of American Evangelicalism (Grand Rapids: Baker Books, 1995).
[296] Noll traces the rise of evangelicalism from the eighteenth century Awakenings, see Noll, *The Rise of Evangelicalism*.
[297] For an account of the British root of evangelicalism, see Graham Storey, ed, *The Evangelical and Oxford Movement* (Cambridge: Cambridge University Press, 1983).
[298] Founding President of Fuller Theological Seminary, a leading evangelical seminary in the US.

Thus when an ecclesial movement emerges, it is generally regarded as the emergence of just another denomination distinct from the already established ones. Thus traditionally, Christianity is filled with historical reloading of fragmentary ecclesiological constructions. This resulted in the proliferation of various brands of competing and exclusivist denominations loading Christianity and the world mission field with ecclesial and spiritual confusions. The secular society is also Christianized in denominational, fragmentary, and exclusivist sense. Thus traditionally, we see converts or believers who identify themselves as Catholics, Protestants, Orthodox, Pentecostals, etc.—rather than just Christians itself. Christianity has become a secondary ecclesial identity for those professing to believe in Christ.

However, in evangelical crusades, as in Billy Graham crusade, what we see are people converted to Christ—and identifying themselves as Christians. And believers coming from different denominations become more faithful Christians itself—they become integrated into one faithful spiritual body of Christ. Thus primarily we see that people are coming to Christ rather than to denominations itself. We do not see the promotion of denomination itself or the emergence of a new denomination. What we see is the promotion of the kingdom of God and the emergence of more truly Christ-centered believers spiritually joined together in Christ. And because of its being more truly prototypal it becomes more spiritually prolific.

We could also see this spiritual fruitfulness in mega-churches who are characterized by Christ-centered proclamation, transformational life-oriented ministry, empowerment of the Holy Spirit, and transdenominational outlook. Mega-churches do not emerge as new denominations itself but as new embodiments of the original ecclesial characteristics re-presented by Contemporary Evangelicalism. These embodiments reveal that the more churches become full gospel-oriented, or evangelical at that, the more they become meaningful to the lives of the people. The more they become missionally prolific and pastorally relevant. Contemporary Evangelicalism is not a new denomination, or a new ecclesiological formulation, or a new movement promoting a denominational ecclesiology. But rather it presents the paradigm for the formation or re-formation of the original characteristics of the church.

B. Contemporary Evangelical ecclesiology is a synthesizing paradigm.

What makes Contemporary Evangelical ecclesiology unique is its being a transdenominational paradigmatic movement rather than a separatist denominational formulation. Thus, there is no single ecclesiastical bureaucracy that centralizes all evangelical churches. As Paul Zahl says, "Centralized church structures have never been an easy fit for evangelicals."[299] It is more of a movement than an institution; although it uses institutional means in fulfilling its pastoral and missional objectives. Thus, the movement is not confined to denominational enclosures. It is inclusive rather exclusive. Although there are ecclesial entities like the Evangelical Lutheran Church or Evangelical Free Church evangelicalism is not confined in these entities or even in parachurch organizations. For these churches and parachurches, though may reflect evangelicalism, are not exclusive confinements of evangelicalism. Moreover, to be truly evangelical, ecclesial entities should reflect not just an aspect of evangelical heritage but all prototypal characteristics.

Contemporary Evangelicalism is prominently embodied in parachurch and other support ministries like the Billy Graham Evangelistic Association, 700 Club, Focus on Family, Gaither Concerts, World Vision, evangelical publishers, etc.[300] Although these organizations are not regarded as traditionally organized churches itself—but they are efficient means of accomplishing the Gospel Com-

---

[299] Paul F.M. Zahl, "Up the Creek: Paddling in the Maelstrom of the Mainline," in *Pilgrims on the Sawdust Trail*, ed. George, 180.
[300] From an organizational point of view evangelicalism, as McGrath sees it is "a broad term embracing a complex network of individuals, seminaries, parachurch organizations, and journals, each with a distinctive 'take' on what constitutes the essence of evangelical identity." McGrath, "Evangelical Theological Method," in *Evangelical Futures*, ed. Stackhouse, 26.

mission that many churches fail to do. Or do not do in a primarily Christ-centered sense without being hindered by calculated denominational motives.

Thus what we could see in evangelical endeavors are missional operations that more truly reflect the original missional endeavors—where the focus is just leading people to Christ and touching people's lives with the love of Christ—not calculated denominational or institutional preoccupations. And this is what ecclesial mission should be—Christ-centered rather than denominational-centered. As Clark Pinnock emphasizes, "All religions make absolute claims at some point, and Christians ought to make them in the matter of the finality of Jesus Christ."[301]

As Hanson puts it:

> The church's purpose is not its own. The church is present in the world on behalf of God by whose grace it has been called into existence. Thus, at the heart of the church's act of self-definition is a basic theological question: What is the nature of God's presence in the world? .... Where there is brokenness, loneliness, and sickness, God is present to heal.[302]

Mission is defined by Stott in a Christ-centered sense:

> The Christian church is called to mission, but there can be no mission without a message. So what is our message for the world? It centers on the cross, on the fantastic truth of a God who loves us and who gave himself for us in Christ on the cross.[303]

With such Christ-centered missional orientation, Contemporary Evangelicals have reached out to people in an incarnate sense without clouding the Christological redemptive essence of the evangel. For as Frost and Hirsch cautioned, "incarnational mission will mean that in reaching a people group we will need to identify with them in all ways possible without compromising the truth

---

[301] Clark H. Pinnock, "The Finality of Jesus Christ in a World Religion," in *Christian Faith and Practice in the World: Theology from an Evangelical Point of View*, eds. Mark A. Noll and David F. Wells (Grand Rapids: Eerdmans, 1988), 155.
[302] Hanson, "The Identity and Purpose of the Church," 344.
[303] Stott, *Evangelical Truth*, 82.

of the gospel itself."[304] The Christ-centered kerygma is what makes evangelical mission apparently distinct from the socio-political mission of so-called liberal churches or the institutional preoccupation of bureaucratized churches. In Contemporary Evangelicalism we see the missional model of apostolic church, not a separatist denominational mission.

Further, evangelicalism is not intended as a denomination separate from other churches. Its ecclesiology is not intended as a formulation to compete with existing ecclesiologies. Nor is the movement intended as a new denomination. But rather it provides a model for the *re*-formation of the genuine ecclesiological framework for churches that has assimilated structures foreign to its original nature and purpose. Or for churches that are miniaturized to an ecclesial aspect or theological notion—to grow into the fullness of the original ecclesial nature and function. Contemporary Evangelicalism provides a framework for the maturation of churches into its complete being! And with its being a regeneratively all-embracing structural paradigm—churches could be internally transformed and reconnected as one whole body of Christ—thus an internal transdenominational reformation of the original oneness of the Christian church!

One of the blunders in the history of the church is the rerouting of an aspect of the restorative ecclesial process from its inclusive intent to an exclusive claim. This is due to a preconceived notion of its being a threat to, rather than a prospect for, an existing ecclesial framework. The fragmentary and antagonistic reactions to the process of the restoration of the church has resulted in revelational misconceptions that caused further ecclesial polarization—
amidst the supposedly bright prospects of progressive reformation. The well-being of Christianity could have been different, that is, in more meaningful and fulfilling terms—if Christianity has been receptive to the Spirit-led gospel-reorientation of the church. The full gospel-reorientation of the church as pre-

---

[304] Frost and Hirsch, *The Shaping of the Things to Come*, 37.

sented in Contemporary Evangelicalism, with appropriate charismatic empowerment is the climactic hope of ecclesial reformation before the *eschaton*.

Contemporary Evangelicalism presents a prototypal pastoral and missional framework that present churches need to fully assimilate—because this describes the very purpose of the church. When the church loses its prototypal pastoral and missional functions—it could lose its pastoral and missional election. And like Israel's loss of its missional and pastoral election to the church—the church too might lose its election to probably a transdenominational parachurch entity or whatever. This seems a bold conjecture but the experiences of the dwindling of static churches and the prolific emergence of mega-churches with prototypal integrity validates this notion. There is a need for denominations to undergo the process of "evangelicalization" and mature into prototypal ecclesial nature and function. When the ecclesial regenerative process becomes pervasive, the world would see a new bred of Christianity being born—an even grander and more missionally and pastorally significant Christianity than the past.

C. Contemporary Evangelicalism is an ecclesially friendly and non-threatening paradigm.

Contemporary Evangelicalism does not threaten the existence of a particular denomination. Rather it presents a model from which denominations could see their respective weakness and allow themselves to be regenerated by the Holy Spirit to become what they were all originally meant to be.[305] Contemporary Evangelicalism is not merely a sort of ecumenical movement that operates in an associational or causal level. It is a regenerative framework that is intended to transform the church back to its original characteristics.

---

[305] Fahlbusch remarks, "In view of the ambivalence of the phenomenon [of the church], a relevant ecclesiology must present both the dogmatically normative premise and the empirical reality in a way that allows us to explain the conditions leading to the distinctive phenomena and to make intelligible the legitimacy and reality of the actual forms." *The Encyclopedia of Christianity*, s.v. "Church: Subject, Tasks, and Problems of Ecclesiology," by Erwin Fahlbusch.

Its regenerative nature spontaneously shapes a regenerative mission, that is, the mission focused on regenerating humanity both individually, congregationally, and even socially.[306] In both ecclesiological ontological and functional senses it is regenerative. It regenerates the nature and function of the church. Thus it is a wholesome ecclesiological paradigm. Moreover, Contemporary Evangelical ecclesiology presents a holistic regenerative paradigm, rather than emphasizing a particular revelation fragment. Further it draws churches together to a higher plane of focus in Christ and his mission. Bloesch comments, "A viable doctrine of the church for our time will involve us in a passionate concern for church unity."[307] Contemporary Evangelicalism goes beyond a mere external ecumenical approach; it rather presents an internal framework for the regeneration of ecclesial wholeness.

Contemporary Evangelicalism is prominently known for its evangelistic crusades and parachurch ministries. However, it is not a movement that merely accentuates crusades and "parachurchism." Rather it presents a balance framework of ecclesial nature and function. It promotes a balanced life of faith and witness both individually and congregationally. Its mission is life-oriented. Its proclamation is Christ-centered. Its everyday life is Spirit-led.

Contemporary Evangelicalism is not a fragmentary ecclesial movement because it does not emphasize a particular ecclesiological aspect as an overarching ecclesial foundation—as common in tradition-oriented churches. For example a mystical church is such, because of its overarching emphasis on the ontological mystical aspect of the church. So is a liturgical church because of an overarching emphasis on liturgy. So is a charismatic church because of the overarching emphasis on spiritual gifts. All these result in ecclesiologies which may seem whole—but are actually merely an outgrowth from a fragment. Such an

---

[306] Even in the early stage of evangelicalism it was already very missional. Noll points out, "The dynamism of evangelicalism [eighteenth century] was revealed most clearly in its missional activity." Noll, *The Rise of Evangelicalism*, 256.
[307] Bloesch, *The Future of Evangelical Christianity*, 129.

outgrowth ecclesiology, at times, invokes the notion of being an ecclesial remnant. However, the Biblical concept of remnant ecclesiology is not an ecclesiology born out of a fragment, but rather an ecclesiology that remains in its holistic integrity amidst the context of theological and spiritual disintegrations. Thus a true remnant ecclesiology is not fragmented or propagating fragmentation—but holistically prototypal promoting original ecclesiological holism.

Further, Contemporary Evangelicalism is a non-separatist and non-denominational ecclesiology. Thus Contemporary Evangelical ecclesiological characteristics could be integrated into existing denominations. Thus there could be Evangelical Catholics,[308] Evangelical Protestants, Evangelical Pentecostals, Evangelical Orthodox, and Evangelical Inter/Non-Denominationals.[309] Why? Because it is not intended as another denominational construction amidst numerous existing ecclesiologies—but a synthesizing paradigm for denominations to rediscover their present ecclesial-selves and be regenerated to their most profound and true ecclesial-selves. Consequently churches will be transformed into one whole new family of Christ! This is a very friendly ecclesiological paradigm.

All these characteristics make Contemporary Evangelicalism ecclesiologically the most original, synthesizing, and friendly ecclesiological model.

D. The Call!

To synthesize, Contemporary Evangelicalism presents a prototypal ecclesiological paradigm offering bright prospects for the Christian church. It is not merely a superficial denominational paradigm. In it we could perceive the profound framework for restoring the church back to its original nature! Like

---

[308] For a brief exploration on Evangelical-Catholic dialogue, see J. Augustine DiNoia, "The Church in the Gospel: Catholics and Evangelicals in Conversation," *Pro Ecclesia* 13 (Spring 2004): 58-69. For further study, see Thomas P. Rausch, ed., *Catholics and Evangelicals: Do They share a Common Future?* (Downers Grove: InterVarsity, 2000).
[309] For a discussion on varieties of American evangelicalism, see Donald W. Dayton and Robert K. Johnson, *The Variety of American Evangelicalism* (Downers Grove: Intervarsity, 19991).

humanity that fell due to accommodation of sin—the church too had fallen due to assimilation of things foreign to its essential nature. And like humanity in the process of regeneration in Christ through the Holy Spirit—there could also be the regeneration of the Christian church back to its original nature and function. And very essential in the life of the church today, as it was after apostolic times—is the restoration of its Christ-centered core and life-oriented missional preoccupation through the empowerment of the Holy Spirit. The process of restoring the church back to its original transdenominational full gospel-orientation is the more profound objective of the phenomenon of Contemporary Evangelical movement—that the whole Christian church has yet to fully discover and explore!

There is the need for Christian denominations to undergo the process of full gospel-reorientation. When denominations undergo full gospel-reorientation, there deeper existence does not disintegrate, but rather they will all be internally and profoundly transformed into one wholesome interconnected body of Christ. And such interconnection is not just superficial or organizational but theological and spiritual, truly ecclesiological and missional, Christ-centered and Spirit-led. This then will be the holistic regeneration of the Christian church. This will result in the emergence of a new era of Christianity—a new dimension in Christian life—and a fresh vision and zeal for the fulfillment of the Gospel Commission—and this will be the New Reformation!

But why is there the need for the New Reformation? Because the need is dire and urgent! The succeeding chapter will point out the serious considerations why...

10
Why the Need for Global Ecclesial Regeneration?

Why the need for global ecclesial regeneration? Because the Reformation sparked by Luther was not the culmination of ecclesial reformation—but rather the beginning of a long process that has finally matured in the present time in Contemporary Evangelicalism. However, like its embryonic stage, the maturation of the process of ecclesial restoration has not also been properly regarded. The Christian church in general has missed the holistic intent of the first and could also be missing the last. When this happens, the bright prospects of churches to be internally integral of one whole church of Christ will continue to disintegrate until probably a new form of ecclesial entity would emerge.

In fact, the emergence of evangelical charismatic mega-churches indicates not merely a sociological trend but profoundly—the spiritual, missional and pastoral significance of non-traditional ecclesial entities that are more prototypal than established churches. These mega-churches are not even emphatically denominations itself but profoundly churches that more truly reflect original ecclesial characteristics. Because of their Christ-centered life of faith and witness, life-oriented missional focus, emphasis on the empowerment of the Holy Spirit, and transdenominational outlook they are naturally prolific. These ecclesial entities are not only adapting prototypal characteristics but, at the outset, are born with prototypal embryo that spontaneously matures along the way. Although we could not deny church growth among institutionalized churches in South America, Asia, and Africa they grow because they somehow assimilated gospel-oriented characteristics. They have become more gospel-oriented in missional and pastoral, spiritual and theological senses. There is a dire need for institutionalized churches to be more truly gospel-oriented and missionally active. There is a serious need for the Christian church to be more truly reformed, so that it could be more significant and prolific amidst a secular world struggling for meanings in life.

Now, why is there a need for global ecclesial regeneration? Let me point out five considerations with profound implications for the whole Christian church.

A. The regeneration of the church is a historical process that is finally climaxing.

The 1500's Reformation started by Luther and followed by other reformers, was intended to bring back evangelical consciousness to the psyche of the church. It was intended to reform the deformed concept of salvation and also to restore the centrality of the Bible as the basis of Christian beliefs. But it was not yet a missional movement itself, nor was there a wide emphasis of empowerment of the Holy Spirit in individual and congregational life.

Further, although there was a sense of faith but, faith was not yet extensively life-oriented, conversional, and missional. There was still no emphasis on active individual redemptive and pragmatic conversion. In fact in the early stage, the Reformation was more of a theological movement inside the church, rather than a missional movement. The concern was the reformation of what had been particularly perceived as a deformed theological structure of Christian faith.

We could viably assume that there was no intention of reforming all churches and transdenominationally integrating them into one whole body of

Christ. There was of course a concept on the universal invisible church, but the transdenominational perspective was merely theoretical rather than missional and pastoral. We could also viably assume that the focus of the Reformation was just the Western Church without clearly emphasizing the whole Christian church including the Eastern Church.

In Contemporary Evangelicalism, however, we see a more transdenominational and holistic framework because it is not confined in a particular denomination. The preceding chapters describing the theological and ecclesiological characteristics of Contemporary Evangelicalism show its holistic orientation and paradigmatic nature. And being the movement that promotes the whole characteristics of the original life of the church, we could conclude that indeed Contemporary Evangelicalism is the full-grown climax of the Spirit-led process of restoring the church back to its original nature, purpose, and function. However, being the climax—it also poses to us the risk of losing the significance of the last call for regenerating the church amidst the present fragmentary life of the church—should we fail heeding it! Thus every denomination that believes on the centrality of Christ and the leadings of the Spirit—need to heed the climactic call for global ecclesial regeneration!

And this is a serious ecclesial need requiring openness and wholehearted reception to the restorative operation of the Holy Spirit in the history of the church. As Hodgson emphasizes, "no viable ecclesiology can surrender the conviction that the church is the continuous creative and redemptive work of God, who indwells and empowers it as Holy Spirit."[310] Hendrikus Berkhof also sees the dynamics of church life:

> The fact of being church is thus not something static, it is a prototypal movement, a bridge-event. Therefore as it moves along it is itself con-

---

[310] Hodgson, "Ecclesia of Freedom," 225.

tinually changing.[311]

We should regard ecclesial transformation, however, as progressive and moving towards the full-grown prototypal ecclesial restoration. The Christian church could not continue to exist in fragmentary life—for fragmentary ecclesial life does not only polarize the one body of Christ it also result in missional breakdown and also threaten the spiritual integrity of the church amidst a secular world. There is a serious need for churches to get over with their respective exclusion and be internally drawn together into one whole prototypal church. As Roof cautions:

> . . . adopting narrow, sectarian notions of the church and ourselves would be alien to our theological heritage and our commitment to be a public church. Historically our churches have been "bridging institutions" concerned with bringing all of life into some meaningful whole.[312]

The fact that the contemporary church is now being further fragmented, not only by theological issues—but even by present moral issues—describes the further disintegration of church's holistic and unifying framework. Not only is the church further fragmented, particularly in North America, by separatist denominational beliefs but also by divisive stands on moral issues like gay marriage, abortion, euthanasia, and use of stem cell for medical purpose. To say that the one Christ of Christianity is the basis for diverse conflicting beliefs is both ironical and polarizing. Although we may argue that varied cultural or historical forms situating different churches presuppose ecclesiological diversities. However, if a cultural or historical form becomes the essence of each denomination—then such denomination is substituting its essential original nature with incidental factors. Further, building a church based solely on a particular theological insight and regarding it as the whole of ecclesial revelation is very frag-

---

[311] Hendrikus Berkhof, *Christian Faith: An Introduction to the Study of Faith*, trans. Sherd Woodstra, rev. ed. (Grand Rapids: Eerdmans, 1986), 415. The change, however, should be regarded as a change of form rather than of essence.
[312] Roof, "The Church in Centrifuge," 1012.

mentary. It is because ecclesial revelation is progressive and should be progressively and holistically integrated into the life of the church.

Fragmentary denominational existence puts at risk the testimonial and kerygmatic integrity of the one whole Christian church. Different and conflicting brands of Christianity present ironical testimonies and proclamations amidst a spiritually hungry world that has overwhelmingly grown by billions. This confusing state of the Christian church poses a serious question about the church's fulfillment of the Great Commission. I do not imply that the conversion of the global society is dependent on the regeneration of the church into wholeness. But the wholeness of the church would enable the church to meet more efficiently the serious missional and pastoral challenges posed to the church by the secular and spiritually broken world. As the Confessing Theologians Commission declares:

> In the absence of faithful Christian witness, society establishes false idols . . . consumerism, materialism, individualism, and hedonism rush in to fill the void . . . a renewed church will reform public life.[313]

If denominational churches still believe on the primacy of Christ, the indispensability of the Holy Spirit, missional cause, and its transdenominational nature being the one body of Christ—then it should, by all means—undergo global ecclesial regeneration in the paradigm of the full-grown Contemporary Evangelicalism.

B. The ecclesial reaction to Reformation movement was separatist rather than integrative.

The restorative features of the 1517 Reformation movement and subsequent movements were not holistically integrated in the life of the whole church. The Catholic Church regarded the Reformation movement as opposi-

---

[313] The Confessing Theologians Commission, "Be Stedfast: A Letter to Confessing Christians," in *Pilgrims in the Sawdust Trail*, ed. George, 210.

tionist. Protestant churches too regard Catholics as antagonistic. And many Protestant churches also regard other ecclesial movements, even other fellow Protestants, as competitions. The oppositionist ecclesial disposition resulted in the formation of churches embodying their respective theological affirmation—rather than integrating the progressively revealed prototypal characteristics of the church.

Thus every restorative theological affirmation has its corresponding denominational formation. Instead of the integrating the progressive restoration of the church back to its whole original nature—the result was the proliferation of separatist denominational formations within the supposed to be one whole church. Instead of restoring the church back into wholeness—the church was further polarized and fragmented. The integrative framework of the Reformation movements was disregarded. Thus as Braaten perceives it, "We have live in strange paradoxical situation in which Protestants have been trying to have the gospel and its freedom without the church and its structure and the Catholics have been trying to have a church with a superabundance of structure without the gospel."[314]

The separatist disposition towards reforming the church resulted in an ironical cycle of ecclesial renewal and decline. There could have been a progressive regeneration of the church had the ecclesial disposition towards Reformation been integrative rather than separatist. Each renewal of an aspect of the original church life—should have been regarded as progressive step toward the full reformation of the church. There is that serious need for progressive renewal and integrative reformation of the Christian church. Os Guiness even sees a need for revival and reformation among evangelicals, "Short of revival and reformation . . . are likely to prevent evangelicalism from making a constructive

---

[314] Carl E. Braaten, *Mother Church: Ecclesiology and Ecumenism* (Minneapolis: Fortress, 1998). 17.

and enduring response to the present moment."[315] Tom Nettles compares revival and reformation to love and marriage, "love and marriage go together" thus so "it is with revival and reformation; when individuals pursue one without proper appreciation for and attention to the other, the result can be very ugly."[316]

What I mean here is not that amidst cultural and geographical factors, there should only be one uniform church. But what I mean is that amidst cultural and geographical diversities—the church still remains essentially whole and one—the one whole church of Christ. Thus one in essence, though may be superficially diverse. Prototypal ecclesial restoration does not inhibit mitotic ecclesial growth—but the mitosis is still within the framework of the progressive holistic growth of the church—not the disintegration of the church into conflicting denominational fragments. Why? It is because the growth is intended as the growth of the kingdom of God—not the growth of the institution of the church itself.

If all the beliefs and ecclesial characteristics revived by various movements were progressively synthesized into the whole life of the church—Christianity could have been experiencing astounding regeneration of the one whole Christian church. From Luther's Reformation there was the restoration of faith and the Bible. From Pietism and Puritanism there was the restoration of Spirit-filled life of faith. From the Awakenings there was the restoration of missional zeal. Then finally from Contemporary Evangelicalism we have the restoration of the full-grown framework of Christ-centeredness, empowerment of the Holy Spirit, life-oriented ministry, conversional life, Bible-based faith, and transdenominational unifying movement. With the synthesis of all the essentials, the church could have been more truly like the body of Christ—more truly

---

[315] Os Guiness, "The American Hour: The Evangelical Movement," in *Evangelicalism*, ed. Fraser, 197.
[316] Tom Nettles, "A Better Way: Church Growth through Revival ad Reformation," in *Power Religion*, ed. Horton, 161.

like the one called out to fulfill the Gospel Commission. Not merely a sort of abstract spiritual umbrella loaded with religious institutions fulfilling their respective denominational institutional preoccupations.

G. R. Evans emphasizes:

> If the ecclesiologies of history have all contained truths, if they describe the same Church, they must cohere. The ecumenical task is to discern their coherence.[317]

However, the ecclesial predicament may not be so much in discovering the conceptual coherence of historical revelations as in having openness to transcend hallowed denominational eccentricities. These hallowed eccentricities blur the psyche of denominations in integrating progressively the Spirit-directed process of restoring the church back to its whole original nature. Many denominations regard itself as already finished products of God that need no more restorative process. What the church needs today before it could fulfill its very purpose is honest and wholehearted openness to the historical leadings and restorative operation of the Holy Spirit.

However, this scenario of ecclesial openness has yet to be realized. And in the context of the emergence of Contemporary Evangelicalism, professing evangelicals have resorted to parachurch ministries, and even ecclesial categorization in contrast to Catholicism, other Protestantism, or Pentecostalism. The movement has also been regarded as a belief categorization of Christian conservatism in contrast to Christian liberalism within the Christian church.

Denominations preoccupied with their respective hallowed eccentricities are hesitant—if not bureaucratically constrained—to assimilate the whole and unifying prototypal ecclesial framework. Mudge expresses regrets, "The opportunity sacramentally to signify God's gathering of the people of the earth into a blessed community is severely compromised by the inability of Christian

---

[317] Evans, G.R., *The Church and the Churches* (Cambridge: Cambridge University Press, 1994), 4.

communions to surmount the ecclesiastical barriers that separate them."[318] At the outset, of course, the sense of self-sufficiency in denominational churches hinders the cumulative ecclesial regeneration. Thus Volf reminds that, "no ecclesiology can proceed in self-satisfied isolation."[319]

What we have in Christianity are incidental churches, rather than one archetypal church situated in different cultural or geographical settings. Because of this situation, the history of Christian church is a history of fragmentation and separationism—rather than a progressively restorative synthesis. This ecclesial landscape necessitates ecclesial regeneration that restores the archetypal nature of the whole ecclesial body.

C. Christianity is still very denominational rather than transdenominational.

The Christian church is still trapped in denominational institutionalism—although not as gravely as before. And Michael Riddel poses this warning:

> God will not be contained. The attempt to construct boxes for the divine presence is doomed to tragedy.[320]

At the onset of Contemporary Evangelicalism, denominationalism was still obvious. At the early days of the Billy Graham crusades, some church leaders and denominations were even negative on involving churches, different from them, in common evangelistic cause. But subsequently denominational barriers began dissipating, and presently we could see greater interdenominational relationship. From scholarly societies, to missions, to crusades, to retreats and conferences, to ministerial associations, to councils or associations of churches, to academe we could see greater ecclesial interrelationship. Even

---

[318] Lewis S. Mudge, *The Church as a Moral Community: Ecclesiology and Ethics in Ecumenical Debate* (New York: Continuum), 120. However, Mudge speaks of this unity in the context of "solidarity with the suffering world." Ibid.
[319] Volf, *After Our Likeness*, 19.
[320] Michael Riddel, *Threshold of the Future: Reforming the Church in the post-Christian West* (London: SPCK, 1998), 174. Refer to this book for challenges on the new reformation.

theological conferences are getting more intentionally inter-ecclesial as in the 2005 joint conference of the Society for the Study of Theology (Protestant) and the Irish Theological Association (Catholic).

However, in spite of the pervasiveness of interdenominational relationship, the church is still in quest for deeper transdenominationalism. And the quest results in varied approaches to ecumenism. Stephen Rose in the late 60's, proposed a concept of decentralized church structure where churches form "the cells of the coming ecumenopolis" where ecumenicity is horizontal and ministerially cooperative.[321] Other approaches are causal and associational.

However, an external ecumenical approach could not really disintegrate exclusivist denominational eccentricities. Each denomination naturally clings on to their respective distinctions. Thus, while joint endeavors are getting common, yet preservation of denominational distinctions is still perpetuated. This is so because such distinctions are regarded as unique ecclesiological hallmarks—ironically implying the notion that the hallmarks of Christian churches are both divergent and contrasting. In this context, because of denominational eccentricities, ecumenical approaches are hardly unifying and synthesizing in deeper sense. It is so because the usual approaches to unifying the body of Christ are external rather than internal. It is like trying to unify human society under one government amidst cultural, geographical and political diversities.

Mudge proposes an approach beyond associational ecumenism. He suggests, "The need today could be to reconstruct different visions of church-in-world not as new 'denominations' but as varieties of spiritual-moral practice lifting up different concerns with the communion of one church."[322] This is a bit deeper approach, is culturally-oriented, and assumes diverse spiritual-moral ministries. Thus churches are regarded as complementary to one another. And indeed the church has evolved into a complex societal institution with complex

---

[321] Stephen C. Rose "Shape and Style of the Church Tomorrow," *Theology Today* 25 (April 1968): 77.
[322] Mudge, *The Church as a Moral Community*, 122.

educational, medical, humanitarian, social, and media roles. The church has become more complex in form than the form of the primitive church. However, we should note that these roles are simply corollary to its most essential kerygmatic role—the proclamation of the gospel primarily intended to lead people to accept Jesus as their personal Savior. This may seem naïve to a highly institutionalized church but this is still the original mission of the church. And the forms of spiritual-moral practice should cohere with the church's essential Christ-centered and Spirit-empowered kerygmatic role. And when culture or particular institutional roles become the distinguishing mark of a church—it becomes either merely a cultural or institutional denomination rather than more fully the church of Christ itself.

However, in Contemporary Evangelicalism, we could see an even deeper and holistic approach to transdenominationally unifying the churches of Christ. It presents a model for transforming the very nature of churches into something archetypal—so that by internal transformation—they would all be regenerated into one whole Christian church.

When churches are regenerated into their respective whole archetypal nature, their nature becomes one—thus one ecclesial nature regardless of their varied locations. Churches then are internally and spiritually knitted together as one people of God—not divergent and conflicting peoples of God. This oneness as people of God is proleptic of the oneness of the redeemed people of God in the *Parousia*. The church being proleptic of the eschatological humanity needs to experience and exemplify before the world its unifying life. But the church still has to experience and exemplify its unifying life—thus it needs a deeply unifying and synthesizing ecclesial regeneration.

B. Ecclesiology is still fragmentary rather than unifying.

Although at present, there is a growing awareness that diverse ecclesiologies could simply be based on diverse metaphors of the church and not one metaphor could be regarded as absolute that excludes others—yet generally denominational ecclesiological absolutism still exists. It is ironical because while there is a proliferation of recognizing the viability of other ecclesiologies—each of the denominational ecclesiologies is still prevalently asserted as *the* ecclesiology among other ecclesiologies. Thus we have Catholic ecclesiology, Protestant ecclesiology, Pentecostal ecclesiology, Orthodox ecclesiology, Nondenominational or Interdenominational ecclesiology—who, while now beginning to recognize the probable validity of one another on grounds of being variant ecclesiological models—are still assertive of their respective ecclesiology as paradigmatic of the whole.

There is still the absence of pervasive acceptance of assimilating the whole prototypal ecclesial framework. The prototypal characteristic that is lacking or weak in a particular denomination is often times avoided for fear that integrating or restoring them could threaten denominational identity regarded as unique. It appears that each denomination wants to be unique rather than be generically called just the church of Jesus Christ. Denominationally-centered ecclesiology perpetuates fragmentary ecclesiology. Thus individualized ecclesiology remains pervasive. And usually every new emerging ecclesiology is regarded as just another ecclesiology in contrast to existing established ecclesiologies.

Ironically though, separatist ecclesiologies are justified on the ground of diversity in the body of Christ. But we should note that diversity in the body of Christ is not an ecclesial diversity, but rather a charismatic diversity. That is, diversity of gifts for accomplishing the various roles in the one body of Christ. The roles are varied but the church is one.

Further, even the usual approach to ecumenical movement is still not that really unifying. It is because it merely attempts to organize an umbrella organization to pursue a particular cause. Thus what is being promoted is a narrow causal and occasional relationship rather than deeper regeneration of ecclesial nature—that could naturally result in a well-focused and undivided effort in fulfilling the Gospel Commission. It starts from the proposition that churches are really diverse but could be occasionally one in cause. One may argue that a causal approach to unifying the Christian churches is more realistic than the ontological approach proposed in this paper. But the latter approach places the church in the context of the whole salvation history.

Humanity is originally intended as one people of God. Because of the Fall, humanity has become superficially diversely and culturally separatist. As Davis emphasizes, "We need renewal, reform, and revival because we live in the midst of the fallout of the Fall."[323] Yet, humanity is still of one essence, and in spite of its superficial diversities. And in the Parousia humanity is intended as one restored, reconciled, and completely regenerated one whole people of God. It is in this wider soteriological-eschatological context that ecclesiology should cohere. The church being the pastoral, missional and proleptic people of God—should also be one. The church's identity as the people of God should be regarded and exemplified as primal identity—rather than superficial denominational identities.

Riddel poses an integrative and holistic spiritual framework for Christianity:

> Life is already split and fragmented, and many people feel the lack of a sustaining center to existence. A spirituality adequate to the missiological task will be one which is integrating and holistic. In the development of New Testament Christology, the drama of the Christ-event reaches cosmological proportions (Colossians 1.15-20, Ephesians 1.3-14). In doing so its binds together creation and redemption so that the purpose of God and the meaning of human existence are united. Contemporary Christian spirituality will need to rediscover the empha-

---

[323] Davis, "Who Is the Holy Spirit Today?," in *Pilgrims on the Sawdust Trail*, ed. George, 93.

sis, and move toward bringing together disparate elements of faith and experience.[324]

The nature and purpose of the church of God is one. Divergent ecclesiological natures and purposes are disintegrative of this essential oneness. Thus there could be no two or more different and conflicting churches of Christ but only one. And there are no original denominational purposes for the existence of the church—there is just the Christ-centered Spirit-empowered kerygmatic redemptive purpose for the church. The external associational approach to uniting the body of Christ may just provide a framework for occasional common endeavors while still perpetuating denominational theological-ecclesiological distinctions. However, when churches assimilate the prototypal ecclesial characteristics—then churches will be regenerated into one church of God. When churches within Christianity become more truly Christ-centered, Spirit-empowered, Bible-based, life-oriented, missional, and transdenominational—their internal commonality will naturally result in profound ontological, relational, and functional unity and oneness.

R. Newton Flew perceived a growing conviction in the late 30's for the church to become more prototypal:

> The conviction is growing that the need of Christian people is a fresh vision of the Church of Christ as God meant it to be, His own creation, the instrument of His age-long purpose, the reconciling Body in which all mankind might meet in a worship and service which would extend to the farthest boundaries of human life.[325]

E. The church is now more eschatological than ever.

The destiny of the church is not in itself. When the church is regarded as the eschatological objective of humanity—then it begins to confine its life in

---

[324] Riddel, *Threshold of the Future*, 133.
[325] R. Newton Flew, *Jesus and His Church: A Study of the Idea of the Ecclesia in the New Testament* (London: Epworth, 1960), 12.

self-absorption and forgets the urgent needs of the world outside its confinement. Hanson warns against "thinly veiled program of self-aggrandizement" and challenges the church to lay "aside all triumphalism and placing not its own needs but the needs of the world at the forefront."[326] Max Stackhouse and colleagues pose the urgent needs of the world confronting the church:

> Christian churches face a new global situation full of promise and peril. Led by new developments in economics, technology, and media, by wider and more direct contact between the world and religion, and by a wider consensus about human rights, ecological dangers, and the costs of war, new institutional and social practices are emerging on all sides.[327]

When the church forgets about the urgent redemptive needs of the world and becomes entrapped in its own self-absorption—it begins to construct ideological grounds for its distorted self-claims. The church is then transformed into a humanistic institution forgetting its true eschatological destiny. The institution of the church then becomes the center of church life. Attentions to Christ and his kingdom are diverted. Faith becomes institutional and traditional. Believers become settled within the walls of ecclesial institution. As Abraham criticizes, "Within Christianity, commitment to tradition is often seen as the great obstacle to progress in ecumenism."[328] This institutionally-centered church life could result in the disfranchisement of its true eschatological expectation. With self-claim redemptive surety within the walls of the church—the church is then regarded as the realization of the eschatological kingdom of God. This portrayal somehow is reflected in the sub-consciousness of denominations that hold on to their respective superficial traditions like heaven.

---

[326] Hanson, "The Identity and Purpose of the Church," 346.
[327] Max L. Stackhouse, Tim Dearborn, and Scott Paeth, eds. *The Local Church in a Global Era: Reflections for a New Century* (Grand Rapids: Eerdmans, 2000).
[328] Abraham, *The Coming Great Revival*, 2.

In the context of an institutionally-centered church, the church becomes just like one of the human institutions—and may even be worse than other societal institutions because it could be dogmatic while being a split-level polarized institution. This is the risk that confronts the church when it loses its appropriate eschatological orientation. Phillips and Okholm remind that:

> . . . the church has no power in and of itself, but only that mediated by Christ. The church will not bring in the consummated kingdom. That is Christ's own work.[329]

In regards to the institutionalization of the church Snyder warns:

> Institutionalization is cumulative . . . institutionalization will in time become deadening. Unless periodically reversed by institutional renewal, institutionalization will spell spiritual death for any church or movement.[330]

However Diane Knippers foresees:

> I do not think the shape of the future church will be the bureaucratic, politicized, modernist denominations of the twentieth century. In fact, I believe the church will be mature and diverse, ecumenical, theologically grounded, capable of addressing major ethical issues, and global, and it will be shaped and lived by the next generation.[331]

If the church is viewed merely as an institution—institutional renewal may not even be enough to sustain its spiritual life. But if the church is regarded in its more profound nature—and its nature is renewed—vibrant ecclesial life could just be naturally sustained. I say naturally sustained because the church will then possess internal qualities that could perpetuate holistic ecclesial life.[332]

---

[329] Phillips and Okholm, *A Family of Faith*, 120.
[330] Snyder, *The Community of the King*, 64.
[331] Diane Knippers, "God Is Working among Us," in *Pilgrims in the Sawdust Trail*, ed. George, 195.
[332] For further discussions on natural church growth refer to Christian A. Schwarz, *Natural Church Development: A Guide to Eight Essential Qualities of Health Churches* (Carol Stream, IL: ChurchSmart Resources, 1996).

Moreover, the church to be ever meaningful and significant, should not lose its appropriate place in the continuum of salvation history. And its appropriate place is its being the missional and pastoral means for guiding humanity in their spiritual journey to the Kingdom. The nearer the Kingdom is coming, the fuller it should accomplish its purpose. When the church remains static and stagnant while the Kingdom is coming, it loses its existential meanings and missional relevance.

The 1517 Reformation was a reaction to the fall of the church. However, since the 1517 Reformation, the Christian church still remains fragmented and is further falling away. In the post-apostolic church, there have been thousands of denominations fragmenting the one body of Christ. The nearness of the present time to the *eschaton*—necessitates serious considerations for denominations to transcend their respective fragmentary eccentricities and allow the Holy Spirit to transform them into prototypal ecclesial entities—fulfilling the Gospel Commission in anticipation of the soon *Parousia*. When denominations lose their sense of urgency, they remain in their respective comfort zones stiffened by traditions. Then they lost their gospel-orientation, and ironically, even redefine the evangel in terms of its denominational suppositions. Bauder warns, "When you lose the ability to define the evangel ... you lose the ability to define Christianity."[333] When the church's sense of urgency is awakened, it becomes receptive to the historical restorative operations of the Holy Spirit. The church learns to imbibe the prototypal ecclesial characteristics so that it could more efficiently fulfill its mission.

It may be conjectural to foresee the termination of the missional and pastoral election of the present church because of failure in fulfilling its very purpose due to being stunted by denominational self-centeredness. But the termination of the missional and pastoral election of the Old Testament ecclesial

---

[333] Kevin T. Bauder, "What's That You Smell?: A Fundamental Response to *The Smell of Sawdust*," in *Pilgrims on the Sawdust Trail*, ed. George, 66.

entity due to its vocational failure does pose a considerable probability. As we could now see, parachurch and transdenominational ministries are proving themselves more productive than a mere denominational effort. But will time come when established denominations because of their narrow institutionalized preoccupations will be substituted by parachurch and transdenominational ministries? And the established churches are left in oblivion?

With the urgency of humanity's need to be prepared for the *Parousia*, churches should now be seriously considering becoming more truly the church that Christ meant them to be and the Holy Spirit intended to empower. If ever there is an immediate and urgent need for global ecclesial regeneration of the Christian church—it is now. Douglas Hall sees the need for renewal at congregational level, although his call was focused on evangelicals. He writes, "Unless there is a radical theological renewal affecting the Protestant denominations at the congregational level, the remnants of classical Protestantism in North American will not survive the twenty-first century."[334] And this call is very much applicable to the whole Christian church as well.

Why the need for global ecclesial regeneration? *First*, we now have full-grown prototypal ecclesiological structures in the paradigm of Contemporary Evangelicalism. And *second*, the present time has become even more dynamic, unpredictable, and eschatological. The world is beset by more and more crises amidst false hopes on human capabilities. From moral confusions even within Christianity, to the fears of global warming, tsunami, terrorism, asteroids, new forms of diseases—the world needs more than ever a greater sense of profound hope. And there could be no more profoundly meaningful hope than hope in Christ. And there is yet no more suitable instrument of hope than the church.

Riddel poses this serious and profound challenge:

---

[334] Douglas John Hall, "The Future of Protestantism in North America," *Theology Today* 52 (January 1996): 458-465.

The church in the West is in the early stages of a massive reformation. Out in the frontiers there are pioneers of the faith, already engaging with the emerging culture . . . . But it is not enough for a few radicals to lead the way. The great mass of the Western church must shift. . . . In the process, some Christian resources will have to be reassessed. Scripture will remain central, but the way it is processed and appropriated may need to change. Holiness, worship, spirituality, conversion, evangelism and the shape of the church will be revisited. Radical surgery is more traumatic than minor surgery. It requires careful preparations, skillful intervention and extensive aftercare. But as long as it is the Spirit guiding the process, and not a self-selected group who "know what's right" for the church, we may retain confidence in the long-term prognosis.[335]

But will denominations allow themselves to be regenerated into one whole church of Christ that could more truly be proclaiming hope in Christ? Or will they still remain in their respective denominational confinements, absorbed in their respective denominational eccentricities? The answer will clearly reflect the deepness of their respective absorption in denominational preoccupations. And will predict their respective pastoral and missional election destinies. To close with Riddel's words, "Only in the relinquishing of self-assurance, pride and confidence will there be humility to learn from the Spirit."[336]

F. The Vision!

The 1517 Reformation was embryonic, and the restorative ecclesial process has been progressing since then. In Contemporary Evangelicalism we could see the paradigm of the full-grown process of ecclesial reformation. It reveals the operation of the Holy Spirit in restoring the church back to its proto-

---

[335] Riddel, *Threshold of the Future*, 173-174.
[336] Ibid., 172.

typal characteristics. The emergence of Contemporary Evangelicalism is an urgent call for the regeneration of churches into one whole church of Christ—into one regenerated people of God fulfilling their missional and pastoral purposes en route to the kingdom of God.

Logan poses this challenge—

> The need to renew the Christian ideal, to reaffirm the essential meaning of Christianity, to revive the human spirit by a return to the pristine elements of Christian living was not limited to any one period in history and was as old as Pentecost and the early church.[337]

And now—with the emergence of an apparent paradigm of Contemporary Evangelicalism for global ecclesial regeneration amidst the urgency of the present time—the time is ripe for the New Reformation! And imagine—the Christian church actually going back to its pristine state and prolificacy!

But what really is the church? Understanding the very identity of the Christian church could further open our understanding of the profound meanings and significance of what the church really is. And such understanding is very essential in regenerating the Christian church back to its prototype!

---

[337] F. Donald Logan, *A History of the Church in the Middle Ages* (London: Routledge, 2002), 105.

Part IV
Peoplehood of God as the Essence of Prototypal Church

11
The Calling of the People of God Preceding the Christian Church

God has always been calling a people since the Fall. Snyder, in the context of the Old Testament, remarks:

> This concept of peoplehood is firmly rooted in the Old Testament and underlines the objective fact of God's acting throughout history to call and prepare a chosen people, a royal priesthood, a holy nation, a people belonging to God (1 Pet 2:9; compare Exod 19:5-6).[338]

And Küng sees that, "The concept of the people of God is at the heart of Judaism."[339] Ed Hayes, in the context of the New Testament, brings out a very foundational concept in ecclesiology:

> Central to the theology of the Christian faith is an understanding of the unique work in calling out a people for Himself. Part of the good news that the apostles preached was the direct revelation from Jesus Christ that His redemptive work of grace would bear fruit in the formation of the church.[340]

The concept of the peoplehood of God is very foundational in ecclesiological understanding. It is also essential in understanding the continuum that conse-

---

[338] Snyder, *The Community of the King*, 58. R. Meyer comment, "One of the basic motifs of the OT is that of the people of God." *TDNT*, s.v. "λαός," by R. Meyer.
[339] Küng, *The Church*, 116.
[340] Ed Hayes, *The Church: The Body of Christ in the World Today* (Nashville: Word, 1999), xviii.

quently resulted in the formation of the Christian church. The concept is very necessary in understanding what the church really is. Because it is this concept that connects the church to the continuum of God's call to humanity since the Fall to the Parousia.

Immediately after the Fall, God called Adam out of the now broken world where humanity was afraid and hiding from God because of guilt. Genesis 3:8-10 narrates:

> Toward evening they heard the Lord God walking about in the garden, so they hid themselves among the trees. The LORD GOD called Adam, 'Where are you?' He replied, 'I heard you, so I hid. I was afraid because I was naked'.

Since then God has been calling humanity to come out from a fallen world to be reconciled with him. As the *Evangelical Commentary on the Bible* puts it:

> The Lord begins with a question just as the serpent had—"Where are you?" This question does not mean that God is ignorant of Adam's whereabouts. Rather, it is God's way of drawing Adam out of hiding.[341]

But also since then—humanity is always inclined to hide from God because of fear rooted in guilt. *The New American Commentary* points out:

> The anthropomorphic description of God "calling" (*mithallek*) in the garden suggests the enjoyment of fellowship between him and our first parents . . . . Yet now the man and the woman are hiding from God in fear . . . .
>
> They are pictured in the narrative like children hiding in fearful shame from their father.[342]

To assuage the feeling of guilt Adam resorted to an idiosyncratic alibi. What they "have in common is their refusal to accept personal responsibility for their

---

[341] *Evangelical Commentary on the Bible*, s.v. "Genesis 3:1-24."
[342] *The New American Commentary: An Exegetical and Theological Expositions of Holy Scripture NIV Text*, s.v. "Genesis 3:8."

actions."³⁴³ This idiosyncratic alibi did not lead Adam to be reconciled to God but drew him farther away from God. Adam's alibi was an embryo of further human ideological formulations centered on self-justification with propensity to divert the orientation of human life away from God.

That was the beginning of the humanistic perspective of life—a perspective of life that is human-centered rather than God-centered. It is a perspective that resorts to human capabilities with outright disregard of the primacy of God's creative-regenerative roles in human life. It is a secular approach to life because it attempts to find solution to the deepest human problems primarily within human realm—and outside of God. This secular- humanistic approach to life is ironical because while humans admit their deficiencies, they still resort to their deficient capabilities for finding solutions to their deepest needs.

Humans attempt to save themselves but could not. It is in the context of secular humanistic approach to life that God has been calling people to come out. First, to come out of their hidings in the broken world. Then, be reconciled to him. And eventually, be propagators of God-oriented life amidst the secular fallen world. The called out people are to experience, model and witness the forthcoming restoration of the primal harmonious relationship between God and humanity and among fellow humans. As Grenz sees it:

> God's purpose is to establish 'one new humanity' consisting of a reconciled people (Eph 2:14-19) . . . . As the fellowship of believers we enter into relationship with God and one another. This covenant relationship is a foretaste of the future community we will share in the new creation...³⁴⁴

Furthermore, since the original state of human relationship was not only characterized by perfect human-divine relationship but also by the naturally coexistent perfect human-human relationship—then the divine call is not just

---

³⁴³ *Evangelical Commentary on the Bible*, s.v. "Genesis 3:1-24."
³⁴⁴ Grenz, *Theology for the Community of God*, 461.

for people to be reconciled to God but also to be reconciled to one another. Thus the call has both spiritual and social dimensions. In the context of the church—the church is both a spiritual and social congregation. Moreover, since the call is the call to be reconciled to God and to propagate God-oriented life—thus the call has both redemptive and missional dimensions. In the context of evangelical ecclesial life—this means the interconnection of ecclesial life of faith and life of witness.

People who responded to God's call are reconciled in the love of God—to God and their fellow humans. And since their experience of divine love does not lead to self-absorption but the outpouring and sharing of divine love to others—the called out ones become missionaries of the redemptive divine love. Because of their love to God and their fellow humans—they proclaim God's love and lead others to love God—so that when they all love God they just naturally love one another.

To synthesize, God's call has both spiritual and social, and redemptive and missional dimensions. God has been calling people to come out of this fallen world and experience spiritual and social regeneration, to be saved and be missionaries of the redemptive kerygmatic call. And in all these—the overarching focus is the restoration of the centrality of God in human life.

As Noll said of the search for Christian mind in relation to the search for an evangelical mind:

> The search for a Christian mind is rather an effort to take seriously the sovereignty of God over the world he created, the lordship of Christ over the world he died to redeem, and the power of the Holy Spirit over the world he sustains each and every moment. From this perspective the search for an evangelical mind takes an ultimate significance, be cause the search for an evangelical mind is not, in the end, a search for mind,

but a search for God.[345]

A. The Calling of God's People Preceding Israel

The history of God's call shows not only the continuity of divine call progressing towards the Parousia but also the patience of God amidst human unresponsiveness or misdirected response. However, in spite of human unresponsiveness or misdirected response to the divine call, there were still those who wholeheartedly listened to God's call and pass on to succeeding generations the true heritage of faith.

Although God's call to Adam was the beginning of God's call for humanity to come out of the fallen world—in an ecclesiological sense we could regard the divine call to Noah and his family as an embryonic paradigm of God's ecclesial call. The life situation, the theology of God's call, the spiritual characteristics of the called out ones, and the intended end are paradigmatic in the history of the church. We could regard the call to Noah, being a familial call, as the precedent of succeeding God's corporate ecclesial calls.

Genesis 6: 1-22 relates God's call to Noah's family:

> When the human population began to grow rapidly on the earth . . . . Now the LORD observed the extent of the people's wickedness . . . . But Noah found favor with the LORD . . . . Noah was a righteous man, the only blameless man living on earth at the time. He consistently followed God's will and enjoyed a close relationship with him . . . . So God said to Noah . . . "I have decided to destroy all living creatures . . . . Make a boat . . . I solemnly swear to keep you safe in the boat with your wife and your sons and their wives . . . ." So Noah did everything exactly as God commanded him.

The following are the elements of the call of Noah:

---

[345] Mark A. Noll, "The Evangelical Mind," in *The Evangelical Landscape: Essays on the American Evangelical Tradition*, ed. Garth M. Rosell (Grand Rapids: BakerBooks, 1996), 38.

Life situation: The proliferation of wickedness in the world.

Theology of God's call: Calling a family who preserved their peoplehood of God, as the medium for regenerating the world with new humanity.

The called out ones: The only family with close relationship with God amidst a spiritually darkened world. They were the only people of God at that time.

The intended end: To regenerate the fallen world through radical global ecological transformation and peopling the world with a new people of God—thus the global renewal of humanity.

The mission: To be the progenitor of new humanity.

God called Noah and his family to come out of a judged world into an ark that would be their temporary refuge before the new world. Although we could viably assume Noah's missional endeavors while building the ark—but what was obvious in the call of Noah was the redemptive intent. There was an apparent divine intent to save and to renew the spiritual state of humanity through the regeneration of the people of God. Although theodicy is not the intent of this work, but suffice it to say that by virtue of God's sovereign creatorship and the eventual well-being of humanity, it was an inherent divine prerogative to radically curtail destructive human propensity and regenerate the world with new humanity. *The New American Commentary* emphasizes:

> God is grieving because this sinful "man" is not the pristine mankind whom he has made to bear his image.... But his is not regret over destroying humanity; paradoxically, so foul has become mankind that it is necessary step to salvage him.[346]

Amidst that degenerated world, God had a people—a family that did everything exactly as he had commanded them (Gen 6:22)—thus obedient to his call. And he called that family unto salvation. Here we could see the concept of God call-

---

[346] *The New American Commentary*, s.v. "Genesis 6:6."

ing a people unto salvation from expected universal judgment—in a sense a metaphor of the church anticipating the end of times.

Right after the flood, there was a new beginning of humanity. But then afterwards, again there was the resurgence of humanistic, secularist, and spiritually degenerative propensities in humanity's life. Humanity was again beginning to live in a life independent of the Creator and dependent and confident on their own human capabilities—thus the Babel phenomenon.

Genesis 11:1-8 portrays the phenomenon:

> At one time the whole world spoke a single language and used the same words. As the people migrated eastward, they found a plain in the land of Babylonia and settled here. They began to talk about construction projects. "Come," they said, "let's make great piles of burnt bricks and collect natural asphalt to use as a mortar. Let's build a great city with a tower that reaches to the skies—a monument to our greatness! This will bring us together and keep us from scattering all over the world . . . ." [But] the LORD scattered them all over the earth; and that ended the building of the city. That is why the city was called Babel, because it was there that the LORD confused the people by giving them many languages, thus scattering them across the earth.

Here we see the tragic consequences of secular, humanistic, and self-centered approach to reconstructing human wholeness—confusion, dispersion, and fragmentation. With these came further degenerative side effects of exclusion, conflicts, wars, and brutalities. And these degenerative side effects characterize not only the history of ancient Babel—but also even of the history of the church when churches became secular, humanistic and self-centered in their approach to reconstructing ecclesial "wholeness". *Zondervan NIV Bible Commentary* points out the self-centered approach of humans in Babel:

> The focus of the author since the beginning chapters of the book of Genesis has been both on God's plan to bless humankind by providing

them with that which is "good".... The characteristic mark of this failure has been the attempt by humans to gasp the "good" on their own.[347]

The New American Commentary contrasted the characteristics of Babelites and Abraham:

> The builders confess their intentions as twofold: (a) to make for themselves a "name" and (2) thereby to avoid being "scattered." They want to "empower" themselves, as we moderns say. "Make" and "name" are also proleptic of God's promise to "make" of Abraham a great nation and to magnify his "name" (12:23). The striking difference between the two examples is how the "name" is achieved. Reflexive "ourselves" and "for themselves" highlight the self-centered and independent efforts of the Babelites, but for Abraham the Lord bestows the blessing of reputation as a gracious gift.[348]

It was in that setting of humanity's fragmentary diversities which included religious and spiritual diversity that do away with the worship of one Creator-God—that God called another family. He called them out of a polytheistic locality. Genesis 12:1-4 tells the call of Abram:

> Then the LORD told Abram, "Leave your country, your relatives, and your father's house, and go the land that I will show you. I will cause you to become the father of a great nation .... All the families of the earth will be blessed through you." So Abram departed as the LORD had instructed him, and Lot went with him.

The following are the elements of the call of Abram:

Life situation: The proliferation of religious and spiritual confusion.

Theology of God's call: Calling a family who still had a spiritual inclination to become a people of God, and who could be responsive enough to regenerate the people of God amidst a polytheistic world.

---

[347] *Zondervan Bible Commentary*, s.v. "Genesis 11:1-29."
[348] *The New American Commentary*, s.v. "Genesis 11:4."

The called: An extended family that, though influenced by situated cultures, still remained relatively connected with the Creator-God, was still responsive to his call, and was willing to obey God and be his people.

The intended end: To regenerate a theistically confused world with a new generation[349] of God's people.

The mission: To be the progenitor-clan of people of God.

The world from which Abraham was called out was a confused world of multiple spiritualities and gods. It was a world that was spiritually and theistically lost. As Stanley Rosenbaum notes:

> Abraham's wife Sarah's—name is also moon-related in Akkadian (*sarratu*=Ningal, wife of Sin). Such evidence seems to suggest that Abram/Abraham's ancestors were moon worshippers, something that should come as no surprise so deep into the era that began with "farming revolution".[350]

The divine call to Abraham was a call to come out of that lost world, to be a people of God, to live in a safe zone, and to regenerate God's people who would be a blessing to all humanity.

The calling of Abraham's family to be God's people is symbolic of the calling of nominal Christians to wholehearted commitment to God's will, to live in a true life of faith, and regenerate the world with such life of faith in contrast to the degenerated worldly life. As Armerding notes, "The people of God throughout history have by their very nature provided an antithesis to the secular world."[351] Like Noah, Abraham responded with a leap of faith, obedience, and trust to the divine call even without concrete grounds for bright prospects of future life. His response was a model of faith, and his call was a missional call. He was called to live a new life of faith. And his mission was to be the progeni-

---

[349] "The religio-historical point of the passage; certainly is the call of Abram to found a new nation." *The Bible Knowledge Commentary*, s.v. "Genesis 11:27-32."
[350] Stanley Ned Rosenbaum, *Understanding Israel: A Reexamination of the Origins of Monotheism* (Georgia: Mercer University Press, 2002), 126-127.
[351] Armerding, "The Evangelical in the Secular World," 130.

tor of the people of God. Here we see the concept of missional regeneration of God's people amidst a spiritually and theistically confused world. In a sense, we could regard this being an intentional progenitor as an early stage of ecclesial mission; although more biological than socially conversional.

The story of Lot is another story of God's call to save a people from imminent judgment. As in Noah's time, we could not merely see judgment as punitive for punishment sake. But we could see the curtailment of serious destructive propensity to allow a regeneration of another people of God. Thus the intention is not punitive itself but redemptive. The difference between the call of Lot from the preceding calls is that, the missional aspect was entrusted to angels rather than to Lot. Noah had the mission to be the global progenitor of new humanity. Abraham had the mission to be the progenitor of a clan of people of God. While in the call of Lot—it was the angels who had the mission to save Lot and his family.

Genesis 19: 12-17 accounts the call of Lot:

"Do you have any other relatives here in the city?" the angels asked. "Get them out of this place—sons-in-law, sons, daughters, or anyone else. For we will destroy the city completely. The stench of the place has reached the LORD, and he has sent us to destroy it." So lot rushed out to tell his daughters' fiancés, "Quick, get out of the city!" The LORD is going to destroy it . . . . At dawn the next morning the angels became insistent. "Hurry!" they said to Lot. "Take your wife and your two daughters who are here. Get out of here right now, or you will be caught in the destruction of the city. When Lot still hesitated, the angels seized his hand and the hands of his wife and two daughters and rushed them to safety outside the city, for the LORD was merciful. "Run for your lives!" the angels warned.

The following are the element of the call of Lot:

Life situation: The proliferation of wickedness in a city.

Theology of God's call: Calling a family, through direct intervention, out of the wicked city imminently judged.

The called: Also an extended family but only the immediate four members responded with hesitation.

The intended end: Salvation from imminent destruction.

The mission: The mission of the angels was to save a righteous family.

The call of Lot brings another aspect of God's call—active missional intervention. When Lot hesitated, the angels seized his hand and the hands of his wife and two daughters. This is an incipient stage of active redemptive mission when God's act of saving humanity through divine agents was no longer a passive wait and see approach but was active and interventionist. It was like an early stage of an active evangelistic missional approach.

Again the one called out from a morally darkened world was a family that still had the sense of relationship with God. Lot and his immediate family members were the people of God in the city of Sodom. However, within that family of God there was still a falling away. This is not intended to be too allegorical, but somehow this reminds the church of the historical falling away of the called out people of Christ.[352] Further, here we see a concept of God calling a people out of a sinful world to save them from imminent destruction, in a sense a church meant for a redemptive destiny.

B. The Calling of Israel as the People of God

Now historically leaping from familial to a more corporate and more ecclesiologically paradigmatic divine call—the calling of Israel which was the progeny of Abraham's family. We see in the calling of Israel a direct precedence of Christian church. The identification of Israel and the Christian church is so

---

[352] John Carpenter criticizes evangelicalism in the backdrop of the falling away in different periods of Protestantism, see John B. Carpenter, "The Fourth Great Awakening or Apostasy: Is American Evangelicalism Cycling Upwards or Spiraling Downwards? *Journal of Evangelical Theological Society* 44(December 2001): 647-670.

close, that it even creates confusion resulting in ecclesiological conflicts. There is a view fusing Israel and the Christian church. Another one proposes continuity of the distinct election of Israel in parallel with the election of Christian church. And still another see the cessation of Israel's divine election that was transferred to the Christian church. David Smith's comment reflects this confusion:

> It is a serious error to believe that God has rejected Israel in favor of the church. Yet it is equally problematic to believe that God has two peoples—Israel and the church—and has different purposes for each. God has only one people . . . . Some maybe labeled 'Israel' and some 'church' . . . . [353]

However, the two could not be literally, spiritually, or missionally confused. The reasons are:

-One is an ethnic group and the other is not.

-Israel rejected Jesus while the church accepted him.

-And the church's mission is the proclamation of Christ as the Messiah and the only Savior—which is apparently not a mission recognized by Israel.

Exodus 19:3-6 characterizes God's call of Israel:

> Then Moses climbed the mountain to appear before God. The LORD called out to him, "Give these instructions to the descendants of Jacob, the people of Israel. You know how I brought you to myself and carried you on eagle's wings. Now if you will obey me and keep my covenant, you will be my own special treasure from among all nations of the earth; for all the earth belongs to me. And you will be to me a kingdom of priests, my holy nation."[354]

The following are the elements of the call of Israel:

---

[353] David L. Smith, *All God's People: A Theology of the Church* (Wheaton, IL: Victor Books, 1996), 205-206.
[354] Exodus 19:3-6.

Life situation: Physical and spiritual slavery of a people amidst a polytheistic society.

Theology of the call: Calling a people out of slavery to make them God's people for a special purpose.

The called: A later generation of a previously called family of Abraham that had extended into an ethnic group.

The intended end: To free a people of God from slavery and make them a kingdom of priests.

The mission: To live a free life of faith (both individually and nationally) and proclaim the goodness of the one true God amidst a polytheistic nation and the world.

The call of Israel was ecclesiologically fuller than the precedent calls and could have been the highlight of the divine ecclesial call for humanity. It was ecclesiologically fuller because of the following characteristics:

First, there were detailed volitional propositions on how the people of God should live their life of faith. The Pentateuch is replete with propositions intended to strengthen Israel's commitment to and life with God. Their new, free, and committed life was anticipated to bring about national blessings. Those propositions were pedagogical means to spiritually and morally re-educate a people acculturated by oppressive life situation and cultures foreign to their original heritage of life of faith. There was a process of transforming their internal conceptual and attitudinal psyche—so that they could think and act more truly like the people of God. The process of transforming their psyche reflects the later regenerative process in Christian faith. Here we see the concept of conversional piety. As Frederick Bush points out:

> Though rooted in God's initiative and grace, the covenant held the people of God responsible for living a life worthy of their calling . . . . It is

this quality of life that the Pentateuch's various 'codes of law' articulate.[355]

Moreover their conversional piety was volitional. Although the punitive consequence of disobedience in contrast to the blissful end result of obedience was emphasized; however, both individually and corporately, they were free to choose the kind of life they would like to live. If ever judgment was emphasized it was because their corporate identity was the people of God—and they needed to preserve the integrity of their new identity. And as such, they were expected to think and live as people of God. Otherwise, an individual, or a sub-group within, that was discordant of the corporate characteristics—would cease linkage with the whole body. In here we see the development of the concept of preserving the corporate ecclesial integrity.

Further, the pedagogical propositions were not merely conceptual but life-centered and transformational. These propositions were spiritual and moral life propositions. The pedagogical nature of these propositions was appropriate in a situation where people for a long period of time were used to being commanded as slaves. However, these pedagogical propositions were not intended as stiff end in itself. For the intention was not simply to lead Israel to mere conceptual assent—but to direct them towards a new regenerative life in God. Thus the Pentateuch teachings were not so much the tools for indoctrination—as regenerative educational means of "making disciples" of a nation. They were to be taught, become disciples of God, and, as implied by their priesthood, also to disciple other nations. In here we see the parallels of the basic religious framework of the succeeding Christian church.

In regards to the concept of covenant between God and Israel, although there are various interpretations[356] yet, it is apparent that it is the stipulation of

---

[355] Frederick W. Bush, "Images of Israel: The People of God in the Torah," in *Studies in Old Testament Theology*, eds. Robert L. Hubbard, Jr., et al (Dallas: Word, 1992), 104.
[356] For an overview of various views on covenant, see Dennis J. McCarthy, *Old Testament Covenant: A Survey of Current Opinion* (Richmond, VA: John Knox, 1972).

God's call for humanity to be his people again—as it was at creation. The *Dictionary of Biblical Imagery* sees the covenant as an image of God's dealings with his people, "The image of covenant or agreement is the primary way in which the Bible portrays the relationship between God and his people and (to a lesser extent) to the human race in general."[357] In the perspective of the divine call for the peoplehood of God, it was nothing more complex than the succinct anthropomorphic dealing of God with humans. The covenant was a call for people who still have the remnant of faith heritage, though marred, to come out of a degenerated life situation and participate in the process of regeneration. And by becoming a regenerated people of God, they in turn could be the means of guiding the rest of humanity to regenerative life.

Moreover, Israel was called not by virtue of their ethnicity but by virtue of their proximity to faith lineage. Other peoples had lost their consciousness and worship of the One true God; while Israel still believed and worshipped him. Israel's call was based on the circumstance of their faith rather than their inherent ethnic or predestinate nature. Henry Flanders, Jr. and colleagues, however, while pointing out God's election as not based on Israel's inherent greatness, emphasize divine prerogative in the call of Israel:

> Israel had no inherent greatness that caused Yahweh to choose it; its greatness may only in the fact that Yahweh had chosen it. Both existence and worth were owed to the redemptive activity of a sovereign God, who made Israel God's own people.[358]

Rosenbaum notes that:

> Paradoxically Israel's chooseness was not exactly of its own doing. Pseudo-Israelite groupings will have included a lot of 'outcasts' and 'ne'er-do-wells,' malefactors who probably joined themselves together

---

[357] *Dictionary of Biblical Imagery*, s.v. "Covenant."
[358] Henry Jackson Flanders, Jr., Robert Wilson Crapps, and Anthony Smith, *People of the Covenant: An Introduction to the Hebrew Bible*, 4th ed. (New York: Oxford University Press, 1996), 217.

through blood-brotherhood rituals.[359]

Klein also emphasizes that, ". . . Israel could not attribute her election to everything within the nation herself."[360] Although among other ethnics groups at the time of Israel's call, it was Israel that still preserved God-consciousness in a more pronounced way. We should note too that the second progenitor of humanity was just one family of Noah. And biblically, there were no dual or multiple progenitors in the post-deluvian world. Thus, basically there is only one human race. Ethnicity is incidental and superficial. And there could be no such thing as a sort of deified inherent factor in an ethnic group, for ethnicity is not the essence of human nature—the image of God is!

Of course, it would be more theologically coherent with the nature of the divine call to assume that Abraham's call (from which Israel claim ancestral and faith root) was not predestined[361] nor ethnic but was based on his responsive disposition to divine call—a disposition to faith. For Abraham was originally a Chaldean or Babylonian (Gen 11:31) and Chaldeans were polytheistic.

Thus faith-response is the basis of God's covenant with humans. *The Bible Knowledge Commentary* emphasizes, "God demanded a response by faith" if Israel "were to share in those promised blessings."[362] Coppedge comments, "Israel must respond to God's offer, choosing whether to continue with Him or to draw back." [363] He emphasizes further, "At the bottom line, as it is usually in Scriptures, God's people are called to live by faith."[364] As Klein points out:

Temporal blessings and prosperity depended upon the terms of the

---

[359] Rosenbaum, *Understanding Biblical Israel*, 137
[360] Klein, *The New Chosen People*, 29.
[361] Although God in his sovereignty and foreknowledge may seem to choose beforehand his own people. Thus Bloesch clarifies, "All are under the sign of divine predestination, all are called to liberation and salvation, but this predestination takes effect in different ways depending on whether there is a response in faith." Bloesch, *Essentials of Evangelical Theology*, I: 168.
[362] *The Bible Knowledge Commentary*, s.v. "Genesis 12:4-9."
[363] Coppedge, *The Biblical Principles of Discipleship*, 24.
[364] Ibid.

covenant. Covenant did not guarantee salvation.[365] When a people wholeheartedly respond in faith to God, they are blest, they become the people of God, and the divine purpose is fulfilled through them. They become regenerated people and agents of regeneration. The Gerald Van Groningen defines the conditions for Israel's election, "…God chose Israel to be his covenantal servants who were to live by faith and demonstrate it to the nations."[366]

Second, there was a formalization of the life of faith. Preeminent in the call of Israel was the institution of liturgy. Such liturgical institution, of course, is a necessity in a corporate ecclesial call. The institution of sanctuary services was a societal macro-projection of a more private personal or familial sacrificial liturgy. Here we see the importance of sacrificial-liturgy in the life of Israel.

However, the center of their liturgical life was neither their piety-acts nor the venue of the liturgy itself—but the sacrificial offering. The sacrificial offering was not only even the center of their liturgical life but also the central object of their everyday piety as the people of God. We could see this centrality from the sacrificial offering of Abel (Gen. 4:4), to Noah after the flood (Gen. 8:20-21), to Abraham when Isaac was a youngster (Gen. 22:13), to the Passover (Exod. 12:3). Then, in the everyday life of faith of Israel when the sanctuary was established. The sacrificial offering was the core of Israel's national psyche. Even among the later generation of Jews, the temple cultus was still central in their lives. Howard Kee notes:

> A significant number of Jews from the time of the Babylonian exile forward perceived the central model for God's people and for the maintenance of the relationship between them and God to be the Temple and its cultus. Only when the Temple cultus was being fully and properly carried out could the real Israel participate in the life God intended for

---

[365] Klein, *The New Chosen People*, 32.
[366] *Evangelical Dictionary of Biblical Theology*, s.v. "Israel," by Gerald Van Groningen.

his people.³⁶⁷

Of course, in Christian perspective, we consider the object of the sacrificial liturgy and piety as anticipating the coming of Christ. The sacrifices and liturgical piety were soteriological illustrations of the redemptive sacrifice of Jesus. The sacrificial offerings were anticipating the coming of Jesus Christ— Israel and pre-Israel liturgy and piety were prolepsis of Christ-centered life. As Bloesch points out, "The New Testament is unequivocal that the sacrifices and burnt offerings of the Old Testament priesthood are both superseded and fulfilled in the once and for all sacrifice of Jesus Christ on the cross."³⁶⁸ The formalization of sanctuary services was meant as a prolepsis of Christian faith. This view coheres with John's outright recognition of Jesus as the Lamb of God. John 1:29-31 declares:

> "Look! There is the Lamb of God who takes away the sin of the world! He is the one I was talking about when I said, 'Soon a man is coming who is far greater that I am, for he existed long before I did.' I have been baptizing with water in order to point him out to Israel."

Apparent in John's declaration is the presentation of Jesus as the anticipated Lamb of God and his act of redirecting Israel to the Lamb. *Hebrews* significantly expound the concept of Jesus as the fulfillment of the sacrificial system. It emphasizes that, "The old system . . . was only a shadow of the things to come, not the reality of the good things Christ has done for us" (Heb 10:1). The proclamation of Jesus as the ultimate sacrifice, of course, is an overarching kerygma in the New Testament, from the Gospels to the letters to the prophetic Revelation.

Thus the liturgy and piety of Israel were, as a whole, intended as preparatory Christological kerygmatic means. Since the core of their existence and life as a distinct people was not their ethnicity but their prophetic faith on the

---

³⁶⁷ Howard Clark Kee, *Who Are the People of God: Early Christian Models of Community* (New Haven, CT: Yale University Press, 1995), 19-20.
³⁶⁸ Bloesch, *Essentials of Evangelical Theology*, II: 106.

sacrificial offerings—we could viably conclude that they were being prepared for Christian faith! They were given the freewill opportunity to be the forthcoming Christian body! But because of the opportunity as being volitional, their being the proleptic Christian body was also dependent on their freewill response. Since it was dependent on their national will—it was also probable that they could lose their election and their proleptic Christian election at that—should they not faithfully respond to God and remain faithful to his calling.

Aside from liturgy, there was also the formalization of law which was, in essence—a support system for the spiritually-based overall life of the nation. Ferguson has this to say about the covenant, "God's covenant are not so much a legal relationship as love relationship, a fact shown by the marriage analogy employed by the prophets (Jer. 2:2; Ezek. 16:8-14; Hos. 2:1-3:1)."[369] It is interesting to note that instead of what we could call in present term, theological or doctrinal formulations, what Israel in Moses' time had were formulation of laws.

Although later they became legalistic and ethnocentric, and even soteriologically legalistic and soteriologically-ethnocentric—equating the means of salvation to legalistic accomplishment and ethnic election. But, at the outset these formulations of laws were intended as life-oriented principles—principles of regenerated personal and national life. It was intended to bring about order out of their bare society and lead them to a morally, socially, and religiously meaningful national life.

These formulations of laws were moral, societal, and religious legislations intended as guidelines in their transformation as the people of God. These were formulations for transformational life, rather than merely formulations for intellectual engagement or legal impositions. These life-oriented and transformational laws were their theologies, not doctrinal itself, but life-oriented teachings. Thus we could call these laws of Moses, including the Ten Commandments as means for discipleship teachings. Coppedge identifies three means in accom-

---

[369] Ferguson, *The Church of Christ*, 18.

plishing God's objectives for Israel's calling: *"learning to live under the authority of God," "living in fellowship with others who seek to follow God,"* and *"faith."* He also identifies the heart of the covenant as "the personal presence of God among his people."[370] Thus in the call of Israel we see the concept of new regenerative corporate life in God.

Third, there was a missional intent. It is interesting to note that the establishment of Israel in the promised-land was never an end in itself. But it was simply a venue for the process of transforming them, not into a kingdom *with* priests—but a kingdom *of* priests. Although a particular tribal order of priesthood (tribe of Levi) was instituted, however Israel as a whole nation of believers was intended to be the priests of God. The *Zondervan NIV Bible Commentary* points out:

> ... they were to be at once priest-kings and royal-priests ...—*everyone* in the whole nation . . . . The whole nation was to act as mediators of God's grace to the nations of the earth (cf. Gen 12:3c).[371]

Bloesch adds:

> The priesthood of the whole people of God was reaffirmed in the messianic prediction of Isaiah: "You shall be called the priests of the Lord, men shall speak of you as the ministers of our God" (Isa 61:6; cf. Joel 2:28, 29).[372]

Of course, the concept of priesthood was present in the Old Testament even before the call of Israel as a nation. However, in the call of Israel, the familial concept of priesthood was taken in its larger societal context, and was applied to the priesthood of Israel over other nations.

Israel was called to obey God so that they could be God's "own special treasure among all the nations of the earth . . . a kingdom of priests . . . ." (Exod 19:5-6). Here we see the further development of the concept of priesthood of all

---

[370] Coppedge, *The Biblical Principles of Discipleship*, 30, 33, 35, 36. .
[371] *Zondervan NIV Bible Commentary*, s.v. "Exodus 19:3-6."
[372] Bloesch, *Essentials of Evangelical Theology*, II: 105.

believers, as integral in God's act of calling people out of the world. God has a priestly purpose for his people. As Bernard Anderson states it:

> This calling [Israel's spiritual calling] is grounded on the event of the Exodus which manifested God's action in delivering Israel from Egyptian bondage ('you have seen what I did'). But Yahweh's initiative evoked response from the people. It placed them in a situation of decision, summoned them to a task within the divine purpose.[373]

Further, the intention of making Israel as a nation of priests was not ethnocentric. They were not called simply because they would be transformed into a sort of cultural exhibit amidst a community of nations. As Guder emphasizes:

> The term [*ekklesia*] refers to the fact that God's actions in salvation history include his choosing some people to carry out his purposes—for the benefit of all. Election, understood biblically, is God's purposeful action within the total scope of his gracious desire to save his erring creation. Thus, Israel is not called, or elected, for its own benefit, to be a special culture that is to enjoy privileges not given to anyone else. Rather Israel's election is functional to God's universal saving purposes.[374]

Israel's call for priesthood was a dynamic call engendering missional responsibility. As a kingdom of priests they were called to become, not a priest for themselves but, priests for others. *Eerdmans Commentary on the Bible* emphasizes, ". . . Israel is chosen and consecrated to enjoy access to God and to discharge function on behalf of the other nations of the world."[375] There priesthood was a missional priesthood. They were called to be missionaries to proclaim what God has done to them—so that other nations too would be regener-

---

[373] Bernard W. Anderson, *Understanding the Old Testament* (Englewood Cliffs, NJ: Prentice-Hall, 1975), 82.
[374] Guder, *Be My Witnesses*, 9.
[375] *Eerdmans Commentary on the Bible*, s.v. "Exodus 20:18-21."

ated and also become the people of God. The *Evangelical Commentary on the Bible* points out the missional significance of Israel's priesthood:

> She is made holy only by virtue of her relationship with God, not because of any inherent good in her. Furthermore, Israel's unique relationship with Yahweh carries with it certain "missionary" responsibilities. This point can be traced back to the purpose of Abraham's call (Gen 12:3).[376]

As Klein emphasizes, "... election was a call to serve God in the world."[377] Peter in 1 Peter 2:8-9, pointed out the missional intent of the called people of God in parallel yet in contrast with the call of Israel. It is parallel because of the same essential message; but in contrast because he indicates Israel's failure to fulfill such priesthood. He emphasized, "They [Israel] stumble because they do not listen to God's word or obey it .... But you [Christian *ekklesia*] are not like that. ..." Then he declared to the Christian church:

> ... you are a chosen people. You are a kingdom of priests, God's holy nation, his very own possession. This is so you can show others the goodness of God, for he called you out of darkness into his wonderful light.

Here we see the re-application of the call of Israel declared by God through Moses to the Christian church—due to Israel's missional failure. Here we see that indeed, the concept of priesthood is a missional concept, that is, "to show others the goodness of God." The liturgical concept of priesthood was temporal and co-terminus with the temporal nature of sanctuary services anticipating the first coming of Christ. However, Israel "conceived of that covenant [Mosaic covenant] not as the proclamation of the gospel (4:1) but in legalistic and ritualistic terms."[378] The *Evangelical Commentary on the Bible* further adds:

> The fulfillment of the promises of the better covenant is not to be found

---

[376] *Evangelical Commentary on the Bible*, s.v. "Exodus 19:3-25."
[377] Klein, *The New Chosen People*, 33.
[378] *Evangelical Commentary on the Bible*, s.v. "Hebrews 8:7-13."

in some comparative advantage enjoyed by believers in the new epoch, but rather in the consummation. These better promises are only the ancient verities of Old Testament faith, which is elsewhere in Hebrews are called "the gospel," "the inheritance," . . .[379]

With the realization of the redemptive sacrifice of Christ the liturgical sacrifice-based aspect of priesthood "is now out of date and ready to be put aside" (Heb. 8:13).

What remains as describing the priesthood of the called out ones—are the concepts of holiness and mission. The called out ones are called to be holy so that they could fulfill their mission. And their mission is kerygmatic. And their kerygmatic mission is not just the proclamation of the redemptive sacrifice of Christ but also the modeling of the new life in Christ. As priests they are to witness both in their verbal proclamation and in their everyday life—the goodness of God through Jesus. Thus Peter emphasized getting rid of malicious behavior and deceit and growing into the fullness of salvation (1 Pet. 2:1-2)—so that they could be, "showing others the goodness of God," that is, living in a life that proclaims the effects and benefits of salvation. Israel was called to be holy so that they could witness themselves for God to other nations both in words and in their daily lives. As T.F. Torrance sees it, "Israel became in a unique way the bearer of the oracles of God . . . ."[380]

The calling of Israel was not meant as an exclusive soteriological election but as a missional call. Both Jews and Gentiles have the equal privilege to avail of divine salvation. J. Baehr commenting on the theme of the letter to the Romans, points out Paul's concern, "The concern is to show that the ground of salvation has always been grace received by faith (chapters 1-7) demonstrates that Jew and Gentiles are on the same footing with regard to salvation."[381]

---

[379] Ibid.
[380] T.F. Torrance, *Reality and Evangelical Theology* (Downers Grove, IL: InterVarsity, 1982), 87.
[381] *The New International Dictionary of New Testament Theology*, s.v. "Priest," by J. Baehr

Guder comments on the concept of election:

> Election is a calling to service. God calls, and enables the response to his call, not solely for the benefit of the one called, but for a greater purpose, for which the called-out ones are now enlisted and enabled.[382]

Israel was called not to make salvation exclusive to them, but to proclaim salvation to other nations. As Klein emphasizes, ". . . the election-knowing involves a function or task and does not necessarily imply their salvation." [383] He further adds, "God's elective knowledge of Israel does not guarantee the salvation of all Israelites."[384] However, as Flanders and colleagues emphasize, "Israel . . . forgot that Yahweh had chosen it for service and not for privilege."[385] And they could only fulfill their redemptive mission, if at the outset, they themselves experienced salvation. They needed to experience national regeneration so that they could become a national missional means for global regeneration.

In all these, we see the indispensable interrelationship of ecclesial regeneration and ecclesial mission. And Contemporary Evangelicalism clearly emphasizes the need of reviving these indispensable and interrelated ecclesial components.

C. The Condition of the Call

To summarize, God has always been calling a people to himself—not only to save them but also—to send them as missionaries to the world. God's call is both soteriological and missional. Soteriological not in the sense of making salvation an exclusive right but, in the sense of calling them out to experience salvation, so that by experiencing salvation they could also witness to others of their redemptive experience.

---

[382] Guder, *Be My Witnesses*, 9.
[383] Klein, *The New Chosen People*, 32.
[384] Ibid.
[385] Flanders, Jr., et. al., *People of the Covenant*, 214.

Further, since response to God's call is volitional—the called out ones may fulfill, reject, respond, or abandon their divine call. This point is very important in recognizing the perpetuity of the divine call of a particular ecclesial entity. The perpetuity of an ecclesial call is not predestined or inherent in an ethnic or religious group—but co-terminus with its spiritual and missional faithfulness. As Larry Hart puts it:

> First, the Church is the *people of God*. As the Gaither gospel song asserts, 'God has always had a people!' In actuality, the Church is the continuation of all that God began to do through Abraham, calling out a people unto himself for the salvation of the world . . . . Tragically, God's people were not faithful . . . so that ultimately God began to speak of another and better covenant in the future (Jer 31:31-34; Ezek 37:26, 27; Heb 8:8-12).[386]

There is an essential continuity yet discontinuity of form in God's call for his people. As long as the called out ones remain faithful to God and fulfill his divine purpose—it remains as the people of God. Thus the ecclesial call is conditional.

In the call of Israel, however, we could see a developmental stage of Christ-centered life through a sacrifice-centered life, transformational piety through discipleship laws, and mission to other nations through their national priesthood. These features of the national call of Israel will become full-bloom in the call of Christian church.

But what is the significance and implications of the concept of the historical call of God in the Old Testament to the formulation of succinct present day ecclesiology that could also be paradigmatic of the whole Christian ecclesiology? These significance and implications will be presented in the next chapter.

---

[386] Larry D. Hart, *Truth Aflame: A Balanced Theology for Evangelicals and Charismatics* (Nashville: Thomas Nelson, 1999), 481.

12
The Christian Church as the New People of God

Now what are the significance and implications of the historical call of God in the Old Testament to the Christian church?

First, it shows that God has been historically and progressively calling his own people. First, God called a nuclear family. Then he called an extended family. And eventually he called an ethnic group composed of extended families with common ancestral root and faith heritage.[387] God has always been calling for particular people throughout history. Schweizer sees the importance of the concept of the peoplehood of God, "In the concept of the people of God . . . the root is in the OT people and the whole historical development up to the modern Church or the Parousia is essential."[388] And as history progresses, the called out ones take on fuller dimensions.

Second, the calling of the called out ones is conditional. When the called out ones remain faithful to their divine calling by living a life of faith and fulfilling their mission—they remain the people of God. When they fail to remain faithful—God calls another people. Thus the church as the called out people in the present time has to fulfill its piety and missional calling otherwise—like Israel it would also loss its election. As Calvin succinctly comments on 1Peter 2:9:

---

[387] The exodus people, though, could have included some non-Israelis.
[388] *TDNT*, s.v. "sw/ma," by Schweizer.

> The meaning then [of Peter's declaration] is, as though he had said, "Moses called formerly your fathers a holy nation, a priestly kingdom, and God's peculiar people: All these high titles do now far more justly belong to you [Christian believers, thus church]; therefore you ought to beware lest your unbelief should rob you of them.[389]

And *third*, the Old Testament Israel is commonly regarded as the direct predecessor of the Christian church. Thus there is a theological and ecclesiological connection between Israel as the Old Testament people of God and the church. Strathmann even sees a further link between the OT Israel, the church, and the eschatological community of the saved—thus a historical continuity of the peoplehood of God. He notes:

> ... when there is reference to the ...[people], Israel may be meant in the first instance but the ultimate application is the Christian community. Finally, in Rev 18:4 another OT verse (Jer 51:45) in which ... [your people] refers to Israel is transferred to the Christian community, and in Rev 21:3 the perfected Christian community of salvation is the ... [people of God] as foretold in Zech 2:14 and Ezek 37:27 .... [390]

However, with the failure of Israel in remaining faithful to God in the sense of accepting Jesus as the Messiah and proclaiming him as the only Savior—it ceased to be the called out people of God. Their mission was to prepare for the first coming of the Messiah, and then proclaim him when he comes—but they failed. Then God called the church. Hebrews makes it clear that, "The old system in the law of Moses was only a shadow of the things to come, not the reality of the good things that Christ has done for us" (10:1). Van Groningen points out, "Jesus Christ, who had been typified by the Old Testament mediators [Moses, David, priest] will be the mediator of the [new] covenant."[391] The *Evangelical Commentary on the Bible* comments:

---

[389] *Calvin Commentaries*, s.v. "1Peter 2:9."
[390] *TDNT*, s.v. "lao/j,"by Strathmann,
[391] *Evangelical Dictionary of Biblical Theology*, s.v. "Covenant," by Gerald Van Groningen.

The Levitical sacrifices are portrayed as inadequate in 10:1-4. They only foreshadowed the true salvation which Christ has guaranteed and will someday bring to completion.³⁹²

Thus peoplehood of God is not ethnic but spiritual, in particular— Christian. Strathmann comments on the Hebrews' use of *laos*:

> Hb. Moves wholly in the sphere of the OT cultus. When it uses . . . [*laos*], the primary reference is to Israel. But all things in the OT are only a likeness of the Christian present, whether the tabernacle, the priesthood or the cultus. Hence the Christian community continually takes the place of Israel as the . . . [people].³⁹³

Now let us discuss the calling of the church in connection with Israel's piety and missional failures.

A. The Emergence and Identity of the Christian Church

It is in the context of the conditional historical calling of God that this work proposes—that the emergence of Christian church is incidental. Stanley Toussaint brings out an interesting point:

> Because of Israel's negative response, God is now working with the Church, distinct from Israel (Rom 9-11; Eph 2:11-12; 3:1-12). The Church therefore is a mystery, never prophesied in the Old Testament (Eph 3:4-6).³⁹⁴

Toussaint here demythologizes the notion of church's mysterious preexistence in the sense of the church's incidental emergence due to Israel's spiritual and missional failures. The existence of the church is indeed incidental because there could have been no necessity of calling the church, if Israel remained faith-

---

³⁹² *Evangelical Commentary on the Bible*, s.v. "Hebrews 10:1." Further it points out, "That Christ's death had such a retroactive effect and was the basis of the gospel of forgiveness in the Old Testament." Ibid.
³⁹³ Van Groningen, "Covenant."
³⁹⁴ Stanley Toussaint, "The Church and Israel," *The Conservative Theological Society Journal* 2 (December 1998). Cited March 14, 2004, http://conservativeonline.org/journals/02-07-journal/1998v2n7-ldo1.htm.

ful to their calling. But Israel did not. Instead they rejected Christ as the object of their piety and the essence of their sacrificial system. They rejected the Lamb of God prophetically illustrated in their sanctuary, then temple, sacrificial services—that ironically were central in their national existence and life. They ended up rejecting Jesus Christ because they did not remain open and faithful to the progressive revelations.

Further, in Israel, the process of spiritual regeneration was substituted by the process of religio-ethnic ideological formulations. Their relationship to God was socially and institutionally legislated rather than regarded as a personal, spiritual and transformational experience. Conversional piety was substituted by legalistic preoccupations, and as such the object of their piety was the correctness of their religious ideology rather than faith in the prophesied Lamb of God that takes away the sins of the world.

Thus when Christ came, their national psyche was already clouded by religious ideology, so that they ended up rejecting Christ whom they presupposed did not fit in their conceptual mold. It is much like the loosing of the centrality of Christ in churches that are preoccupied with a sort of denominational and institutional ideology. Israel became exclusivist—they claimed the kingdom of God as their exclusive rights. They also became political—they even politicized their messianic expectations to mean political national deliverance from the Roman Empire rather than personal spiritual deliverance from sin. Instead of fulfilling their spiritual redemptive mission—Israel was preoccupied with political emancipation and was even obsessed of religiously and politically dominating the world. They lost the deep sense of their true calling. And they eventually lost the meaning of the Sacrifice that was central in their national life. They ended up rejecting Jesus.

Thus Jesus proclaimed that the "stone rejected by the builders has now become the cornerstone" (Matt. 21:42). Peter echoed, "He was rejected by the people..." (1 Pet. 2:4). Their rejection of Christ resulted in the loss of their special calling as the people of God. But not only did they lose their conversional piety, they also lost their mission. With their rejection of the centrality of Christ in their national life, they lost their being the chosen people of God. Thus Christ, proclaiming the Jewish rejection of him concluded—"what I mean is that the Kingdom of God will be taken away from you and given to a nation that will produce the proper fruit" (Matt. 21:43). Peter, in 1 Peter 2:5, 9-10, addressing the Christian believers reapplied the peoplehood of God to them:

> And now God is building you, as living stones, into his spiritual temple. What's more, you are God's holy priests . . . You are a kingdom of priests, God's holy nation . . . . This is so you can show others the goodness of God, for he called you out of the darkness into his wonderful light . . . . "Once you were not a people; now you are the people of God."

Peter's declaration is a clear re-application of God's national call to Israel (Exod. 19:5-6) to Christian believers. Israel's rejection of Christ resulted in the calling of a new spiritual nation—the global congregation of Christian believers. The *Evangelical Commentary on the Bible* comments on related account in Matthew:

> It is Israel's rejection of God's son that chiefly accounts for God's judgment (vv. 40-44) . . . . The new tenants (vv. 41, 43) and the building of which Jesus is the capstone (v. 42) represent the church (16:18) the New Israel consisting of Jews and Gentiles.[395]

Bietenhard points out:

> Finally the honored title of Israel, that of being God's *laos*, is transferred to the Christian . . . church . . . . He has called a church from the Jews and the Gentiles (Rom. 9:24; Hos. 1:10). This church (even as a local church, cf. Acts 18:10) is the → temple and *laos* of God (2 Cor. 6:14ff.; the quota-

---

[395] *Evangelical Commentary on the Bible*, s.v. "Matthew 21:23-39.

tions from Lev. 26:12 and Ezek. 37:27 refer in the original setting to Israel, but here applied to the Christian church).[396]

The new people of God are called to be holy and to show others the goodness of God. The life expected from them, was also the life expected from the previously called people of God. They are to be the new priests of God with apparent evangelistic mission. J. G. Millar discusses the evangelistic significance of the kingdom of priests:

> The phrase 'kingdom of priests' is difficult to interpret in its context, but the apostle Peter makes clear that it refers to the way in which God has always been committed to reaching the world through his people (1 Pet. 2:9-10). A similar idea is present in Deuteronomy 4:5-8, where God's people function as an evangelistic model for the nations.[397]

He further adds:

> There are clear similarities between the people of God before and after Christ. God chooses his people, brings them into relationship both to himself and to one another, establishes a community centered on the word of God and uses this community to reach the world.[398]

Thus God's call for Christians is also a spiritual redemptive and missional call—in evangelical terms, Christians are called to be born again and to witness for Jesus.

With the calling, response, and congregating of all those who believe and accept Jesus as their personal Savior—the phenomenon of the Christian church emerged. In Lewis Chafer's words, "By divine calling, which is efficacious (Rom. 8:30), the Church as an elect company is being gathered."[399] Thus, the calling of the Christian church is not inherent in its institutional self, but is conditional on its integrity and faithfulness as the new people of God. The

---

[396] *Dictionary of the New Testament Theology*, s.v. "lao/j," by H. Bietenhard.
[397] *New Dictionary of Biblical Theology*, s.v. "People of God," by J. G. Millar.
[398] Ibid.
[399] Lewis Sperry Chafer, *Systematic Theology* (Dallas: Dallas Seminary Press, 1948), 4:39.

church's peoplehood of God—in archetypal sense its peoplehood of Christ—is its core identity. And its identity as the people of Christ engenders Christ-centered piety and Christ-centered mission.

The church is the congregation of believers of Christ—a new chosen people who experienced salvation in Christ, who live Christ-like life, and proclaims the gospel of Christ. The various ecclesiological models are simply metaphors of the various aspects of the corporate life of the people of Christ.[400] They are not in themselves the ecclesial essences nor the core ecclesial identity. The essence of Christian church is its being the people of Christ—the people who respond to the redemptive and missional call of Christ. These believers together as one is the regenerated people of Christ called to be the agents of transformation in the world.

The concept of the church as the people of God/Christ is the core ecclesiological concept in the New Testament. Frank Frick emphasizes that the people of God "is more importantly used as the designation of the church (Rom. 9:25-26; 2Cor. 6:14; Titus 2:14)."[401] As Strathmann points out, "the community [the NT community of believers, thus the NT church] is the people of God. Chadwick notes:

> When Paul wrote letters to groups of Christians, he used various words: 'to you who are chosen and set apart in Rome' (or in Philippi, or in Colossae) . . .' to the *ecclesiae* in Galatia'. This word meant 'the people called out,' or 'chosen'.[402]

Thus, Rudolf Schnackenburg stresses, "for early Christian thought the 'Church of God'. . . is nothing else but the people of God, so that Church and people of God in

---

[400] Regarding the different aspects of the church ministerial life, Jordan categorizes these in three, "There are three kinds of occasions or ministries conducted by the Church.... They are liturgical (worship), koinonial (fellowship), and diaconal (service)." James Jordan, "The Church: As Overview," in *The Reconstruction of the Church*, ed. James B. Jordan (Tyler, TX: Geneva Ministries, 1985), 15.
[401] *The HarperColins Bible Dictionary*, s.v. "People, peoples," by Frank S. Frick.
[402] Chadwick, *A History of Christianity*, 29-30.

this perspective are identical."⁴⁰³ Küng likewise characterizes the church as a pilgrim people:

> The Church is always and everywhere a living people, gathered from the peoples of this world and journeying through the midst of time. The Church is essentially *en route*, on a journey, a pilgrimage."⁴⁰⁴

When we regard the church as the people of Christ, we begin to regard it as real and dynamic group of purpose-driven believers—a living organism. As Küng further comments, "If the Church really sees itself as the people of God, it is obvious it can never be a static and supra-historical phenomenon, which exists undisturbed by earthly space and historical time."⁴⁰⁵ Mary Sawyer, however, has this criticism, "'community' as the heart of Christian faith, as the very essence of living a Christian life, is a concept that lies dormant in more institutional churches than not."⁴⁰⁶

In regards to evangelical ecclesiology, Phillips and Okholm succinctly emphasize:

> ... the Christian family, that is, the church. They are the people of God who continue Christ's incarnate ministry by being his representatives in the world.⁴⁰⁷

They expound further the very identity of the church:

> The ecclesia of God is a specific type of people, one that God in Jesus Christ has called into existence by his work (Acts 20:28). When one accepts Jesus' offer of salvation, one is now "in Christ" (Gal. 1:22; 1 Thes. 2:14), part of his "church" (Eph. 5:23), a member of the "body of Christ" (Eph. 4:4, 15-16). In fact, our English term "church," which is related to

---

⁴⁰³ Rudlof Schnackenburg, *The Church in the New Testament* (Freiburg, Germany: Herder, 1965), 153.
⁴⁰⁴ Küng, *The Church*, 130.
⁴⁰⁵ Ibid.
⁴⁰⁶ Mary R. Sawyer, *The Church on the Margins: Living Christian Community* (Harrisburg, PA: Trinity, 2003), 13. She points out the function of community, "At the micro-level, community commonly denotes a gathering that provides nurture and mutual support." Ibid., 11.
⁴⁰⁷ Phillips and Okholm, *A Family of Faith*, 108.

the Germanic word *kirche* and Scottish *kirk*, has etymology that originally meant "of the Lord" (from the Greek *kyrios*). We who were not a people, are now a people "of the Lord." That is our primary identity.[408]

B. The Development of the Christian Church

John pointed out to the people in Jordan River that Jesus "is the Lamb of God who takes away the sin of the world" (John 1:29). After John's declaration of Jesus as the Messiah, Jesus asked John to baptize him—then came the dramatic anointing of Jesus by the Holy Spirit and the verbal confirmation of God the Father. After that public declaration, Jesus underwent the wilderness experience through which he could prove to humanity his victory over the basic yet serious temptations in human life. Thus with baptism, anointing, confirmation, and victory—he began his public ministry. And his inaugural ministry was kerygmatic. Jesus, in Mark 1:15, proclaimed:

> "At last the time has come!" he announced. "The Kingdom of God is near! Turn from your sins and believe in the Good News!"

Jesus' inaugural kerygma is paradigmatic of the redemptive call ringing throughout the New Testament—the call to be born again. In essence, the gospel proclamation is the call for people to repent and believe in Jesus as the Lamb of God who takes away the sins of the world. The call is a regenerative and redemptive call[409] with ecclesial consequence. It is the call for the people of the world to be transformed into the people of Christ. Mark, in 1:16-18, continues to tell what happened next after Christ's proclamation:

> One day as Jesus was walking along the shores of the Sea of Galilee, he saw Simon and his brother, Andrew, fishing with a net, for they were commercial fishermen. Jesus called out to them, "Come, be my

---

[408] Ibid., 110.
[409] Packer comments, "The developed biblical idea of God's calling is of God summoning man by his word, and laying hold of them by his power, to play a part in and enjoy the benefits of his gracious redemptive purpose." *Evangelical Dictionary of Theology*, s.v. "Call, Calling," by J.I. Packer.

disciples, and I will show you how to fish for people." And they left their nets at once and went with him.

After his redemptive call, Jesus called out two people to come out from their being fishermen to become his disciples and "fish for people."[410] Here we see the beginning of personal missional call. Christ was calling people not only to salvation but also to be his disciple-missionaries. Jesus was calling people not just to follow him and listen to his teachings, but also to make disciples of others.

Now what do we have here? It is a paradigm of redemptive call followed by a missional call—the same paradigm of personal and ecclesial life that Contemporary Evangelicalism is reviving. Further the call of Christ is more personal than the Old Testament call. And those who personally responded to the call came together and became a group of disciples. And the group became the core people of Christ that would become the progenitor of the global people of Christ. R. L. Omanson comments, "These twelve formed the nucleus of God's new people, the church, which like Israel of Old has been called into being to be the means by which all of humanity is restored with its creator (Acts 1:8' Matt. 28:18-22)."[411] In essence the group of disciples was the embryonic Christian church.

Christ's act of calling out people to become his disciples was an act of forming a new people of God. The group of the twelve disciples was the Christian church in its formative stage. It was in its formative stage, because the maturity of the church has still to come at a later time after the realization of the soteriological plan and the missional inauguration through the empowerment of the Holy Spirit. As reflecting the paradigm of Christ's ministry inauguration—they too needed to be anointed by the Holy Spirit before they could begin their ministry.

---

[410] For a study on the concept of "fisher of people," see Wilhelm H. Wuellner, *The Meaning of "Fishers of Men"* (Philadelphia: Westminster, 1965).
[411] *Evangelical Dictionary of Theology*, s.v. Church, The," by R.L Omanson.

The group of disciples was still an ecclesial embryo for they still needed to realize the very reason why they were called. Before Jesus' ascension they still did not have the whole redemptive and missional picture of their calling. In fact, we could viably picture out that the disciples were only beginning to realize the whole perspective of their redemptive and missional call, when Christ commissioned them to go and make disciples of all nations. Afterwards, not only them but also the rest who responded to the call of faith—congregated together and were reflecting and praying, although they still did not know how they could propagate their newfound faith to Israel, much more worldwide. Although they had the spiritual and missional conviction, they lacked the power and the linguistic capability to fulfill their mission. However, we should note that when Christ called the disciples, he did not outrightly rejected Israel. In fact, he struggled to reform them. Like the Protestant movement trying to reform the church in Rome.

While on earth Christ's ministry had two aspects, namely, kerygmatic and redemptive. He was teaching people how to live a new life. He was calling people to come out of their spiritually beclouded life situations, and teaching them a regenerative life style. He was propagating conversional piety among the now spiritually lost people of God. He emphasized humanity's need to be born again—the cliché evangelicalism has revived in the present time. And Christ emphasized that new birth is the operation of the Holy Spirit—"the Holy Spirit gives new life from heaven" (John 3:6). Christ also emphasized his redemptive mission. He proclaimed, "Salvation has come . . . . I, the son of Man, have come to seek and save those like him [Zacchaeus][412] who are lost" (Luke 19:9-10).

In the ministry of Christ we see the emphasis on humanity's need for conversional piety, salvation only in Christ, and also the believers' need for mis-

---

[412] We may regard this as a figure of people who were supposed to have spiritual heritage but was eventually lost.

sion. But note that the call for conversion, the call for acceptance of Jesus as the Messiah, and the mission was immediately directed to Israel. There was still an attempt of Christ to let Israel realize their being lost and call them back to him. As I.H. Marshall points out:

> Jesus' message was directed toward Israel and was concerned with the renewal of Israel, i.e., of the people of God. The goal was the renewal of the people as a community and not simply the repentance of individuals, although the path to the former lay through the latter.[413]

There was still an ecclesial call for Israel. Jesus, as recorded in Matthew 23:37, grieved:

> "O Jerusalem, Jerusalem, the city that kills the prophets and stone God's messengers! How often I have wanted to gather you together as a hen protects her chicks beneath his wings, but you wouldn't let me...."

Christ was reforming them amidst their degenerated national spiritual and missional life. He was trying to recall them back to their original piety and mission. However, as noted in Matthew 23:38-39, Christ foresaw their eventual rejection of him. Consequently he judged them:

> "And now look, your home is left to you, empty and desolate. For I tell you this, you will never see me again until you say, 'Bless the one who comes in the name of the LORD!'"

Here we see the eminent anticipation of the cessation of Israel as the people of God. Although the call of the disciples at the outset may not have been intended as a separatist call, that is, as a separate people from Israel, but eventually with their corporate rejection of Jesus—a new people was called. Thus, the Christian church was forming and developing. Van Gelder points out:

> The birth of the church opened as new chapter in God's redemptive work. God's presence in the world would no longer be mediated

---

[413] *Dictionary of Jesus and the Gospels*, s.v. "Church," by I.H. Marshall.

through a single nation nor located in the physical Temple in Jerusalem. God was constructing a spiritual building consisting of people from all nations.[414]

Guder sees an ecclesial heritage of the Christian church with Israel but indicates the cessation of Israel's call:

> Just as God called and set apart the nation of Israel to be blessed and become a channel of blessing to all nations, he now calls and sets apart a people, the "new Israel," to proclaim what he has done.[415]

Therefore, in essence ecclesiology is not merely a New Testament concept; although the formal Christian ecclesiology emerges only in the New Testament.[416] We could trace the historical call of God from Adam, to Noah, to Abraham, to Lot then to Israel and eventually to the Christian church. Through the historical calls of God—we could see that the call of the chosen people is always conditional. It is dependent on their faithfulness as the people of God. Thus we could also say that the calling of the church as the new people of God, or especially as the people of Christ, is also conditional. If the present Christian church does not remain faithful in its spiritual and missional calling—most probably there could be a new form of the people of Christ. Perhaps something grander that transcends denominational barriers, in a similar way the Christian church transcended ethnic barriers of the Old Testament Israel.

C. The Church as One People of Christ

The cessation of Israel as the people of God is apparent because of its apparent rejection to become the people of Christ. We could not distinguish the peoplehood of God and the peoplehood of Christ because they are essentially the same peoplehood. The concept of the cessation of Israel as the people of

---

[414] Van Gelder, *The Essence of the Church*, 103.
[415] Guder, *Be My Witness*, 16.
[416] Thus it is in this sense that Lightner could say that, "Ecclesiology is primarily a New Testament doctrine." Lightner, *Evangelical Theology*, 217.

God with the emergence of the Christian church is an issue of debate common to those whose concept of election is either ethnocentric or shaped with apprehension of nullifying the Old Testament heritage. We should however note that the heritage of the expected life of faith and witness of the called out ones is always carried over throughout the history of God's call.

As Van Gelder points out:

The church is pictured ... as the New Testament fulfillment of Old Testament prophetic expectations regarding the people of Israel.

This new people, this spiritual Israel finds its identity as God had always intended, along faith lines, not blood lines.[417]

Donald Watson supports, "The church, by faith in Jesus the Messiah, became the true Israel, the true people of God."[418] The very identity of the peoplehood of God in the Old Testament was not ethnic but messianic. So is the very identity of the church in the New Testament is not institutional but Christological. And we should also note that the rejection of Israel as the people of God does not mean that Israelites could no longer avail themselves of the salvation Jesus offers to all humanity. Salvation is open to all. Israel's missional calling as the corporate means for proclaiming the salvation of humanity through Christ—had ceased.

Who then are the new called out ones? The new called out ones, of course, are those who respond to Christ's redemptive and missional call. They are those who believe in Jesus as the Messiah and Savior, who experience spiritual conversion through the Holy Spirit, and then who witness and proclaim Christ through their verbal proclamations and exemplary life. When they naturally come together, their congregation becomes the church.[419] Thus the church

---

[417] Van Gelder, *The Essence of the Church*, 108.
[418] Donald Watson, *I Believe in Church* (Grand Rapids: Eerdmans, 1978), 78.
[419] In regards to the apocalyptic church amidst the Roman Empire, Wes Howard-Book comments, "From John's vision...*church* is used as a name for urban discipleship communities precisely so that they see themselves as people 'called out' to live God's assembly according to

emerged as the spiritual and social consequence of faith. As J. Rodman Williams emphasizes, "there is still no *church* until the people respond in faith."[420] The church does not exist independent of faith response. As John Leith puts it:

> The New Testament knows nothing of people conceiving the church and then bringing it into existence in the manner that other human institutions have come to be. The first Christians discovered that they were the church, having been created as a community by the impact of the life, death, and resurrection of Jesus Christ and by their receipt of the Holy Spirit.[421]

The identity of the New Testament church was not ethnic, geographical, cultural, or sectarian. All groups in various localities whether household, city, or province were all groups of believers in Christ—in essence the one whole people of Christ—the new people of God. Thus the called out believers were appropriately called Christians by the society they live in. This described what the society recognized in them because of their profession, everyday lifestyle, and missional preoccupations focused on Christ. They became a distinctive group of people in Christ. *Eerdman's Bible Dictionary* defines the meaning of the church—"Usually the Greek term [*church*] represents God's people as distinguished from others...." Thus Werner Kümmel writes:

> ...the primitive community expresses its claim that those who believe in Christ represent the people of God and thus have taken the place of the old people of God. But this people of God is characteristically no longer identified as "God's community" but as "Jesus community" or "Christ's community."[422]

---

a way entirely opposed to that of empire." Wes Howard-Book, *The Church Before Christianity* (Maryknoll, N.Y.: Orbis, 2001), 34.

[420] J. Rodman Williams, *Renewal Theology: The Church, the Kingdom and Last Things* (Grand Rapids: Zondervan, 1992), 3:42.

[421] John H. Leith, "Ecclesiology," in A *New Handbook of Christian Theology*, eds. Donald W. Musser and Joseph L. Price (Nashville: Abingdon, 1992), 135.

[422] Werner George Kümmel, *The Theology of the New Testament: According to Its Major Witnesses: Jesus—Paul—John* (Nashville: Abingdon, 1973), 129.

The new people of God had one faith framework, one purpose, one missional objective, and one identity. They were all believers of Jesus Christ as the prophesied Messiah and the only Savior of humanity. Their purpose was to live the life of Christ and proclaim the gospel of Jesus Christ. Their missional objective was the global discipleship of humanity. And they were appropriately and apparently identified as Christians. Thus, a new humanity emerged. As Victor Hunter and Phillip Johnson puts it, "the gathering of men and women around him [Jesus] signifies the coming of a new humanity."[423]

The experience of new life in Christ and the focus on the mission of Christ internally unites them—they become one regenerated people. The earliest Christians were one in spite of their superficial cultural diversities. They all, as one in faith, transcended their cultural and geographical enclosures. And they transcended even their previous religious culture. As transformed by Christ, their previous religious-cultural soul was also transformed into one Christ-centered psyche. Thus there was only one church, only one people of Christ, who, because of their missional zeal empowered by the Holy Spirit propagated Christian faith in many localities.

Originally there was no such thing as Eastern and Western churches distinct from each other. There were just the same Christian church located in the east and west. As *TDNT* puts it, "the congregation in different places is simply called εκκλεσια with no question of precedence or correlation."[424] *TDNT* further explains:

> ... the sum of individual congregations does not produce the total community of Christ. Each community, however small, represents the total community, the church.[425]

---

[423] Victor L. Hunter and Phillip Johnson, *The Human Church in the Presence of Christ: The Congregation Rediscovered* (US: Mercer University Press, 1985), 31.
[424] *TDNT*, s.v. "εκκλεσια," by K.L Schmidt
[425] Ibid.

The core of their oneness was their internal ecclesial faith in Jesus and their common Christ-centered Spirit-empowered missional zeal. Thus Hans Shwartz emphasizes:

> This unity [Eph. 4:5f] in Christ that Paul expresses was experienced by the Christian community and it transcended all other differences. It is therefore difficult to see in the New Testament a justifiable basis of... denominationalism.[426]

He further adds:

> The usage of the term church does not indicate that the one church is divided into churches or that an aggregate churches result in *the* church. It is rather that in different places *the* church is manifested in local congregations.[427]

The early church was not divergent churches trying to unite themselves together. They were one. There was only one church proliferating and spiritually growing in various localities. Churches were not denominational but geographical. Hodge thinks of the church's oneness in relation to one Trinitarian God, "There is no doubt if there be one God, there is but one Church; if there be but one Christ, there is but one Church; if there be but one Holy Ghost, there is but one Church."[428]

Further, there was no such thing as visible and invisible churches,[429] for all visible churches are all of one spiritual characteristic. Some theologians also approach the concept of visible and invisible churches in an integrative way. As Williams explains:

> The one and only church undoubtedly has both invisible and visible dimensions. There is the invisible dimension of not belonging to

---

[426] Hans Shwarz, *The Christian Church: Biblical Origin, Historical Transformation, and Potential for the Future* (Minneapolis, MN: Augsburg, 1982), 74.
[427] Ibid., 74-75.
[428] A. A. Hodge, *Evangelical Theology: A Course of Popular Lectures* (Edinburgh: Banner of Truth Trust, 1976), 174.
[429] Such a concept of visible and invisible church is a prejudicial concept exploited to exclude and include denominational entities based on one's denominational eccentricities.

the world: the church is *church*—"called out." There is also the visible dimension of being totally in the world and sharing fully in it as a social entity.[430]

Ian Murray sees it in a similar sense:

> With respect to her inward life the church may therefore be said to be "invisible." In another respect, however, the church is visible—in her profession of the gospel, and in her obedience to Christ's commands and ordinances. So although there are not two churches, the church may be considered under the two aspects of invisible and visible.[431]

Schmidt however, projects a pragmatic concept of the church:

> Moreover, the εκκλεσια as the assembly of God in Christ is not invisible on the one side and visible on the other. The Christian community, which as the individual congregation represents the whole body, is just as visible and corporeal as the individual man.[432]

Robert Lightner, on the other hand, speaks in terms of the local and universal church in relation to Christ:

> The local church is, in a real sense, a miniature of the universal church. To be a member of the universal church one must be divinely related to Christ.[433]

Further, there was even no distinction of apostate and true churches, for the church was truly Christian then. Those that were not truly Christian gatherings were not called the church.

Thus the church is a singular spiritual entity embodied in varied localities. It is not that Christians have churches or the churches have Christians—but that a Christian congregation is the church and the church is Christian—that

---

[430] Williams, *Renewal Theology*, 23.
[431] Iain H. Murray, *Evangelicalism Divided: A Record of Crucial Change in the Years 1950 to 2000* (Edinburgh: Banner of Truth Trust, 2001), 274.
[432] K.L Schmidt, "εκκλεσια."
[433] Robert P. Lightner, *Evangelical Theology: A Survey and Review* (Grand Rapids: Baker, 1986), 232.

is, the people of Christ. There is only one church—the church of Jesus Christ—the people who believe in Jesus Christ as their only personal Savior, and who, empowered by the Holy Spirit, live in a transformed life and witness for Jesus. In the same way that there was one humanity at creation, there will also be one new humanity at redemption—and one proleptic new humanity en route!

However, with their Christ-centered identity, they also began using other metaphors[434] to illustrate their being and life as the new people of God. They needed metaphoric conceptual aids to expound their existence, life, and purpose in Christ. They needed illustrations to explain in practical sense, the various aspects of church life. Thus as synonym of their being the new people of God, that is, the people of Christ, they referred to themselves as:

1. The children of God (1 John 3:1, Rom. 8:14).
2. A holy people (Col. 3: 12)
3. Family of believers (Gal. 6:10)
4. Flock of God (1 Pet. 5:2)
5. God's family (Eph. 2:19)
6. Kingdom of priests (1 Pet. 2:9)

As the new people of God, that is, the substitute of the failed Israel, they referred to themselves as the Israel of God (Gal. 6:16) or holy nation (1 Pet. 2:9). Here we see the spiritual continuity of the new with the old, yet the actual missional discontinuity of the old that lead to the calling of the new. Ferguson thinks in line with this perspective:

> Many of the Old Testament descriptions for Israel are taken over by the New Testament in reference to the new people of God. This fact emphasizes the continuity in the history of salvation, but it also

---

[434] Regarding ecclesiological metaphors Mudge has this to say, "Above all the biblical 'people' metaphor carries with it a note of *historical and sociological realism*. Unlike terms such as 'body' or 'temple' or 'sacrament' or even 'servant,' it requires relatively little translation into operational terms." Mudge, *The Sense of People*, 38. However, I do not see the peoplehood of God as merely metaphoric but rather the very identity of the church.

shows a newness, in that a new people is designated. Even richer blessings are said to be theirs.[435]

Ferguson listed these descriptions as indicating the New Testament claims of the new people of God:

1. Israel of God (Ps. 98: 3; 121:4—Rom. 9:6-8, 1 Cor. 10:18, Phlm. 3:3, Matt. 3:9-10).

2. Royal Priesthood (Exod. 19:6—1 Pet. 2:5, 2:9, Rev. 1:6).

3. Holy Nation (Exod. 19:6—1 Pet. 2:9).

4. Righteous Remnant (Isa. 1:9 cf. Rom. 10:20-23, Rom. 9:27-28, 11:1-5, Acts 3:14)

5. Covenant People (Luke 1:54-5, Rom. 9:4, Gal. 3:6-29, Acts 3:25-26)[436]

The Hanson's bring out similar point, although with dispensational implication:

> The fundamental and oldest account of the church in the New Testament is that it is the people of God. Just as Israel was God's people under the old dispensation so the Christian church in God's people under new.[437]

Thus in essence there is indeed no break in the continuity of the historical calls of God with the emergence of the Christian church. The Christian church is the new form of the same essence of the people of God. As the Hanson's stress, "The continuity of the church therefore must consist basically in the continuity of the people of God."[438]

To illustrate the church's charismatic-based ministerial interrelationship within the church, the early Christians used metaphors like the body of

---

[435] Ferguson, *The Church of Christ*, 77.
[436] Ibid., 77-78.
[437] A. T. and R.P.C. Hanson, *The Identity of the Church: A Guide to Recognizing the Contemporary Church* (London: SCM, 1987), 6. Orlando Costas, although seeing the people of God in a socio-political sense and as image rather than the very identity of the church itself points out that, "the foremost image of the church in the Scripture is that of God's people." Orlando E. Costas, *The Church and Its Mission: A Shattering Critique from the Third World* (Wheaton, IL: Tyndale House, 1974), 23.
[438] Hanson, *The Identity of the Church*, 42.

Christ[439] (Eph. 4:12).[440] To illustrate the church's relationship with Christ, they used the bride of Christ (Rev. 22:17). As describing the church's kerygmatic nature, they used the metaphor of the golden lampstand (Rev. 2:1).

These and other metaphors were not intended as trajectories for constructing diverse ecclesial identities—but rather illustrations of the different aspects of ecclesial life.[441] The one ecclesiological trajectory they had was their being the people of Christ. As Mudge sees it, "the trajectory of biblical thought is toward increasing realization of what is really meant by a *people of God*."[442]

Thus originally there were no diverse ecclesiological models. Diverse ecclesiologies[443] are incidental formulations based on varied aspects of ecclesial life. Thus we have liturgical churches that highlight the liturgy of the church. We have charismatic churches that highlight spiritual gifts. We have mystical ecclesiology that is preoccupied with mystery. And other wide arrays of ecclesiological formulations that are based on particular metaphors of church life or even a particular theological emphasis (like fundamentalism, dispensationalism,

---

[439] For a scientific contextual exposition with practical implications of the body of Christ metaphor, see Howard A. Snyder and Daniel V. Runyon, *Decoding the Church: Mapping the DNA of Christ's Body* (Grand Rapids: Baker Books, 2002).

[440] R. Fung comments, "The body of Christ is usually the locus of the Christian ministry." *Dictionary of Paul and His Letters*, s.v. "Body of Christ," by R. Y. K. Fung. He further adds, "The church as the body of Christ is a living organic unity composed of multiplicity of members (.i.e., individual believers, not individual congregations), each necessary to the other and to the growth of the whole." Ibid.

[441] Dulles points out the importance of ecclesiological images, "Images are immensely important for the Church—for its preaching, its liturgy, its general *espirit de corps*." Avery Dulles, *Models of the Church*, expanded ed. (New York: Doubleday, 2002), 14. He feels it so important to the life of the church that he identifies the crises of faith as rooted in the crises of image, "The contemporary crisis of faith is, I believe, in very large part a crisis of images." Ibid., 13.

[442] Mudge, *The Sense of a People*, 31.

[443] For the evolution of the church see, Eric G. Jay, *The Church: Its Changing Image Through Twenty Centuries* (Atlanta: John Knox, 1978). Michael Nazir-Ali, however, foresees that, "The shapes of the church to come and its mission and ministry will continue to be affected by the shape of the world as it is now and as it will be in the future." Michael Nazir-Ali, *Shapes of the Church to Come* (Eastbourne, England: Kingsway Communications, 2001), 22. A truly evangelical ecclesiology, however, though may have form transformation, would always remain prototypal in its essential structures.

etc). Thus Christian ecclesiology is loaded with all sorts of fragmented or fragmentary ecclesiologies that are diverted from the central and essential identity of the church as the people of Christ. So we have numerous diverse denominations. And though the varied denominations we have in Christianity recognize their being Christian—yet they are separatist and apprehensive of being spiritually and missionally united as one people of Christ. The original framework of faith of the Christian church is substituted by denominational eccentricities. Thus churches are composed of people of denominations, rather than one people of Christ itself.

Doctrinal reformulations have become so complicated that it clouded the apparent, simple and original ecclesial teachings of faith in Jesus as the only Savior, living a Christ-like life, and witnessing for Christ—all through the empowerment of the Holy Spirit. And these essentials of church life are replaced by sectarian dogmas and institutional preoccupations. By coming back to the full recognition of being one people of Christ—Christian denominations, together as one, could experience an internal regeneration. And this could eventually result in the restoration of the state of wholeness of the Christian church as one renewed people of Christ.

Here we could see the regenerative and unifying viability of the concept of the church as the people of Christ more than any other ecclesiological models. Besides, as C. Marvin Pate noted, that out of the 114 occurrences of the term *church* in the New Testament, 109 "is used of the community of God's people."[444] Grenz emphasizes a significant point:

> The choice of *church* as the designation of the Christian community suggests that the New Testament believers viewed the church as neither an edifice nor an organization. They were a people—a people brought together by the Holy Spirit—a people bound to each other through Christ—hence, a people standing in covenant with God.

---

[444] *Baker Theological Dictionary of the Bible* s.v. "Church, the," by C. Marvin Pate.

Above all, they were God's people (2 Cor. 6:16).[445]
Grenz further adds:
> The early Christians found in this term [*church*] a helpful means for expressing their self-consciousness. They saw themselves as a people called together by the proclamation of the gospel for the purpose of belonging to God through Christ.[446]

When denominations profoundly regard themselves as the renewed people of Christ—the central ecclesial focus would just be the experience of new life in Christ and the fulfillment of the Gospel Commission! In this sense experientially, spiritually, and missionally—the fragmented churches could become one people of Christ again.

D. Characteristics of a More Truly Christian Church

Assimilating the deep consciousness of the peoplehood of Christ in the soul of the church could result in the reformation of the original characteristics of church life. And these characteristics that reflect the church as more truly the people of Christ are:

First, the centrality of Christ. By this I mean the central and apparent focus on Christ, and the overarching articulations of such Christ-centeredness. As the people of Christ, the church's focus should not be institutional or denominational matters but Christ himself.[447] The proclamation of Christ as the only Savior is the missional focus of the church and not the propagation of denominational dogma or denominational expansion. Churches, of course with its Christ-centered teachings and proclamation could expand. But the expansion is not intended as institutional expansion itself, but the quantitative and qualitative fruitfulness of preparing people for God's kingdom.

---

[445] Grenz, *Theology for the Community of God*, 465.
[446] Ibid.
[447] Ferguson expresses this Christ-centered rootedness, "If the church is the people of God, it is the people of God *in Christ*. If the church is the community of the Holy Spirit, the Holy Spirit is the gift of the resurrected Christ." Ferguson, *The Church of Christ*, 72.

One of the blunders of the post-prototypal church is the ardent recognition of denominational matters as the essences of the church. Thus we have all sorts of churches founded not on the deep and wholehearted consciousness of the peoplehood of Christ, but on a particular denominational identity. Ironically though, many of the highlighted denominational identities are based on aspects of the progressive revelations of the Holy Spirit. These revelations are intended as cumulative characteristics that needed to be restored in all denominations so that together as one they could be restored as one people of Christ! When denominations recognize themselves not in terms of their supposed denominational eccentricity in contrast to, separate from, or exclusion of others—but in terms of their common peoplehood of Christ — then Christian churches together as a whole could indeed more truly reflect their being the church of Christ. The essence of the church is Christ, and the essence of churchood is peoplehood of Christ.

Second, the need for the empowerment of the Holy Spirit. By this I mean the church's dependence on the empowerment of the Holy Spirit for its life and mission. Hanson reminds that the church "must remain open to the presence of the Spirit."[448] The appropriate recognition of the church's dependence on the Holy Spirit is very essential in the life and mission of the people of Christ—because it is the Holy Spirit that directs the church to the centrality of Christ and the gospel mission.

As Jesus said:

But when the Father sends the Counselor as my representative—and by the Counselor I mean the Holy Spirit—he will teach you everything and will remind you of everything I myself told you.[449]

Thus when the early church received the empowerment of the Holy Spirit—the church was enabled to powerfully proclaim Christ. And, of course, at

---

[448] Hanson, "The Identity and Purpose of the Church," 349.
[449] John 14:26.

the outset, new life in Christ is an operation of the Holy Spirit. Thus the Holy Spirit is always the power behind conversion in Christ, living the life of Christ, and preaching the message of Christ. Coppedge brings out a paradigmatic point, "the infilling of the Holy Spirit in the lives of the disciples becomes a model of what Jesus desires in the life of everyone in any age who seeks to be a disciple and a disciplemaker."[450] As Grenz points out:

> He [the Holy Spirit] effects the union of believers with Christ and Christ's community, the reconciled people of God. At the consummation, the Spirit's mission will reach its ultimate goal as he establishes the glorious fellowship of the redeemed people living in a redeemed world and enjoying the presence of their Redeemer God. En route to that day, the Spirit nourishes the spiritual life he creates.[451]

Moreover, Volf points out the foundational role of the Holy Spirit while necessitating active ecclesial response. He writes:

> It is *the Spirit* who constitutes the church. *People*, however, must accept the gifts of God in faith (even if this faith is itself a gift of God); *they* must come together, and *they* must remain together.[452]

The empowerment of the Holy Spirit is indispensable for the church as the people of Christ. Each denomination should recognize their need for the empowerment of the Holy Spirit in their whole ecclesial life. As the people of Christ the church does not exist and live by its own self. It is not self-existent. Its existence is derived—derived from Christ and the Holy Spirit. Its existence is dependent on its responsiveness to the call of Christ and its responsiveness to the operation of the Holy Spirit! By being responsive to the redemptive and missional calls of Christ and to the regenerative and charismatic operation of the Holy Spirit—the group of respondent called out ones become more truly the people of Christ.

---

[450] Coppedge, *The Biblical Principles of Discipleship*, 122.
[451] Grenz, *Theology for the Community of God*, 379.
[452] Volf, *After Our Likeness*, 176.

As Edmund Clowney stresses:

> The church is called to God, called to be his people. By that relation to God the being of the church is defined.[453]

What draw people together to become the church are the internal Christological and Pneumatological factors—and these factors become the foundations of church life. These foundational constituents transcend denominational institutional self. Thus, for the confessing Christians to insist on the primacy of their respective denominational identity and make this as ground for ecclesial separation and fragmentation—is a denial of the primacy of the church's peoplehood of Christ.

I do not imply in this work that the church should be a-institutional or a-organizational. Because as existing in the realities of societal life; it could not realistically live without its institutional and organizational aspects. However, the institutional and organizational matters are simply means in fulfilling the very purpose of the church—not the very purpose of the church itself. Thus as Snyder said it, "While the Church is not essentially an institution it does, however, have an institutional side in the same way the family does."[454]

Third, missional vocation. By this I mean the centrality of the church's kerygmatic mission.[455] The mission of the church is an evangelical mission, that is, the proclamation of redemptive gospel of Christ.[456] Thus Bloesch reminds Christians:

> It is incumbent on us to recover the doctrine of the church, particularly with regard to its indispensable role in the communication of salvation. The church is not a mediator between God and man, but it is a veritable

---

[453] Edmund P. Clowney, "The Biblical Theology of the Church," in *The Church in the Bible and the World*, ed. D. A. Carson (Exeter, England: Paternoster, 1987), 15.
[454] Snyder, *The Community of the King*, 63
[455] Regarding a missional perspective of church Riddel has this to say, "The essence of the church has always been mission. It is created by mission, renewed by mission, and participates in mission." Riddel, *Threshold of the Future*, 174.
[456] As Hayes concisely puts it, "The church's mission in the world implies preparing people for the future kingdom." Hayes, *The Church*, 241.

means of grace to man. It cannot dispense grace as though it was in control, but it can function as an instrument of the Holy Spirit who does convey the grace of Christ to "a sinful world."[457]

The church's mission is the proclamation of Christ, not the proclamation of its denominational self. When churches are preoccupied about proclaiming itself, it becomes preoccupied with its denominational-self—thus more like a people of a denomination rather than a people of Christ. With denominational self-centeredness, churches are lead to construct what they consider protective enclosures which are sorts of religio-socio-ideological preservatives of their respective denominational-self. The ecclesial self no longer becomes Christ but their respective religious ideology. Consequently, the mission becomes the propagation of a sort of denominational ideology.

Then baptism becomes denominationally exclusivist rather than Christ-centered. Even conversional piety would consequently be defined as theological assent, rather than a process of living a new life in Christ empowered by the Holy Spirit. New life in Christ would end up even being dogmatically defined as a continuous assent to the correctness of denominational doctrines and a life coherent with denominational policies. Teachings become theoretical rather than life-oriented. And eventually, Christian life becomes mechanical, then nominal, till it resort back to secular. This scenario of backsliding would also lead to the spiritual death of liturgy. Liturgy becomes momentarily emotional if not mechanical, rather than spiritually nurturing. Then at the end of church service, Christianity dissipates throughout the week. In this setting, church life does not naturally result in sustainable Christ-centered Spirit-empowered life of faith and witness. Attendance to church service becomes a sort of periodic superficial therapy to let off steam of the pressures of everyday life. Or to assuage a conscience bothered by a sense of irreligiousness—rather than a means for developing spiritual and missional life.

---

[457] Bloesch, *Essentials of Evangelical Theology*, II:278.

In the ecclesiology of the peoplehood of Christ, the church's focus is to witness for Christ both by life-oriented exemplification and communication. With the focus on living the exemplary life of Christ and witnessing for Christ—churches are redirected to their common natural mission. Such life-oriented and kerygmatic commonality is a very viable framework that would spiritually and missionally draw altogether the one people of Christ located in different localities. Churches will no longer be regarded as different denominational entities—but localities of one people of Christ.

Thus what we have here is an internal unifying structure for the regeneration of churches to their prototypal wholeness. Watson brings out the profound kerygmatic and spiritual implications of the "people of God" ecclesiology:

> The concept of the church as "the people of God"—as God's new society, his family, his community—breaks upon many today as the most thrilling "goodnews," they could ever hear. And what a transformation it can bring when a person knows that he belongs to God and his people forever! In an age of isolation, the joy of really belonging to God and of being a part of his people throughout the world—a belonging which depends not on earning acceptance, but on receiving freely God's love—is one of the most relevant features of the Christian message of the goodnews.[458]

Fourth, transdenominational nature. By this I mean that the essence of the church transcends denominational self. As Thwaites reminds, "The containment of the church in denominations and buildings was not a part of the early Christian perspective."[459] The people of Christ ecclesiology define exclusion and inclusion not in denominational doctrinal sense but—in a universal Christ-centered sense. That is, exclusion and inclusion depending on unresponsiveness and responsiveness, respectively, of people to the redemptive and mis-

---

[458] Watson, *I Believe in the Church*, 76.
[459] James Thwaites, *The Church Beyond The Congregation* (Cumbria, UK: Paternoster, 1999), 180.

sional calls of Christ.[460]

When people respond to Christ they spiritually become the people of Christ—living the Christ-centered life of faith and witness. Their peoplehood of Christ becomes the essence of their new spiritual identity. The rest of their respective cultural identities are transformed to harmonize with their new spiritual self. The cultural elements in their individual life that do not contradict their new spiritual self may remain; and the contradicting ones are either discarded or reformed into something that cohere with their overall new identity.

Thus as Paul, in Galatians 3:24-28, succinctly puts it:

But now that faith in Christ has come . . . . So you are all children of God through faith in Christ Jesus. And all who have been united with Christ in baptism[461] have been made like him. There is no longer Jew or Gentile, slave or free, male or female.[462] For you are all Christians—you are one in Christ Jesus.

For early Christians, their peoplehood of Christ transcended their previous religious, cultural and ethnic identities. This is paradigmatic of denominational conversion—when all those who truly respond to the call of Christ become one in Christ. As one people of Christ—they would either discard or reform their respective denominational ecclesial self incoherent with their new spiritual self as the new people of Christ. This could be a bold and risky proposition for this impinges not only on denominational mindsets, but also on the established institutional components that has become synonymous with denominational existence.

---

[460] Thus Peter Hodgson regards "the image of the people of God" as "the earliest and most inclusive." Peter C. Hodgson, *Revisioning the Church: Ecclesial Freedom in the New Paradigm* (Philadelphia: Fortress, 1988), 29. However, the peoplehood of God should be regarded as the very identity of the church rather merely an ecclesiological metaphor.
[461] We should note that even with the existence of many churches in different provinces, cities, and households, baptism here never connoted separatist sectarian baptism. Baptism was just baptism in Christ. Applying this in the present would mean baptism as common entrance into the peoplehood of Christ.
[462] This term here is not primarily used in biological sense but in socio-cultural sense, where women in a very patriarchal society, were regarded with social status lower than men.

However, the full assimilation of the peoplehood of Christ into denominational church-selves is not actually a threat to the existence of churches. But on the contrary it is even unifyingand restorative of the true nature and function of the church of Christ! Churches, then as a whole becomes a renewed and revitalized body of Christ. In the same way when a born again person has to leave his old world-centered life, what is left out is not really his or her existence but the undesirable form of life he or she lived before. The true essence of human existence and life is regenerated—and this essence is the renewed existence and life in the Creator-God. Being a new child of God—a new creation of Christ—life for the converted takes on a new dimension. It is a fuller life that reflects and anticipates the archetypal state of perfection and bliss. So are churches when they leave their respective old forms of denominationally-centered ecclesial life and then be regenerated into one whole essence as the new people of God—the one whole new creation of Christ!

E. The Reason for Transcending Denominational-Self

R.G. Clouse prophetically foresees an ecclesial oneness in the *Parousia*, "the church will appear in the age to come as the one people of God united in one congregation before the throne, as the one celestial city—the New Jerusalem."[463] The church as the prolepsis of the absolutely new humanity in the Parousia should represent such eschatological wholeness in the present form of its ecclesial life.

However, in its anticipation of the Parousia, we should also make apparent distinction between the church and the Kingdom so as not to confuse a human institution with the divinely recreated cosmos. The kingdom of God that would be populated by believers of all time is sometimes confused with the church. However, as Schnackenburg reminds, "It is not the Church but the Kingdom of God which is the ultimate goal of the divine economy of salvation

---

[463] *Evangelical Dictionary of Theology*, rev. ed., s.v. "Church," by R. G. Clouse.

and redemption in its perfect form for the whole world."⁴⁶⁴ He further explains why:

> Even the New Testament people of God as it is assembled in the Church, and continues to assemble, is not yet identical with the community of the elect which enters into the perfect kingdom of God; it is still subject to test and will be scrutinized and separated at the judgment.⁴⁶⁵

The integrity of the profession of the peoplehood of Christ is still ambivalent. In a similar way, Pannenberg cautions the church, "the church must distinguish its own existence from the future kingdom of God."⁴⁶⁶ He further adds, "If the church fails to make this distinction clearly, then it arrogates to itself the finality and glory of the kingdom . . . ."⁴⁶⁷

Michael Jinkins speaks of ambiguity in Christian life that implies ambivalence of life in church:

> To speak of the church…we begin in the dwelling place of our habitation . . . paying close attention to the living texts of the people of God in the ambiguity of the lives we live under the unambiguous claim of God's reign.⁴⁶⁸

And Küng reminds the church, "For the Scripture the Church is the people of God, which, following the Old Testament people of God, is always a people of sinners, constantly in need of forgiveness."⁴⁶⁹ Thus the church should bear witness to the world "the possibility of a new kind of community"⁴⁷⁰ that is abso-

---

⁴⁶⁴ Schnackenburg, *The Church in the New Testament*, 188.
⁴⁶⁵ Schnackenburg, *The Church in the New Testament*, 156.
⁴⁶⁶ Wolfhart Pannenberg, *Systematic Theology*, trans. Geoffrey W. Bromiley (Grand Rapids: Eerdmans, 1998)3:32.
⁴⁶⁷ Ibid.
⁴⁶⁸ Michael Jinkins, *The Church: Its Changing Image Through Twenty Centuries* (Atlanta, GA: John Know, 1978), 89.
⁴⁶⁹ Küng, *The Church*, 131.
⁴⁷⁰ Richard John Neuhaus, "Why Evangelicals and Catholics Belong Together," in *Pilgrims in the Sawdust Trail*, ed. George, 104. Healy further adds that the church, "is oriented towards the ultimate goal of all humanity, indeed, of all creation." Nicholas M. Healy, *Church, World and the Christian Life: Practical and Prophetic Ecclesiology* (Cambridge: Cambridge University Press, 2000), 17.

lutely realized not in the church itself but only in the kingdom of God. The points emphasized here are very important in recognizing that the church is not the kingdom of God—thus not the destiny of Christian believers nor already perfect body of Christ. Thus a denomination is not the destiny of its congregation or the already absolute and perfect body of Christ. Therefore, church members should transcend their denominational eccentricity—and be more truly oriented to Christ and his coming kingdom. The imperfections of human nature and relationship constituting the church indicate that the church is still in the process of regeneration. And absolute perfection would only be fully realized by Christ in the *Parousia*. The church is not the absolute perfect kingdom of God.

The church is the agency providing preparation for the people en route to the kingdom; it is not the kingdom itself. Vernard Eller sees the church as a caravan rather than a commissary; he distinguishes between the two:

> ... a commissary... *is* and has its existence simply in being what it is. A caravan, conversely, has its existence only in a continual becoming.[471]

In this perspective, the church without arrogating itself as the kingdom—becomes open to the operation of the Holy Spirit. It humbles itself in the hands of the Holy Spirit and allows the Holy Spirit to restore and recreate it to what it was truly meant to be. It recognizes itself, not as a deified human creation—but an instrument for the kingdom whose usefulness depend upon the divine operation. Thus it has no reason for self-claim—but rather should humbly recognize its being a creation of the Holy Spirit. Therefore, it should ever be opened to become what it was originally designed for by Christ and the Holy Spirit.

F. The Warning Call

The aforementioned characteristics of the church as the people of

---

[471] Vernard Eller, *The Outward Bound: Caravaning as the Style of the Church* (Grand Rapids: Eerdmans, 1980), 13. He further adds, "A commissary is essentially *establishment* oriented, and a caravan eschatologically oriented." Ibid.

Christ, namely, the centrality of Christ, the need for the empowerment of the Holy Spirit, missional vocation, and trans-denominational nature—are also the very characteristics of the prototypal church that Contemporary Evangelical movement is reviving. People of Christ ecclesiology and Contemporary Evangelical ecclesiology do harmonize.

W. Ward Gasques describes the New Testament ecclesiology in a very evangelical sense, "The church in the New Testament is the assembly of believers who have been drawn together through Jesus Christ for the purpose of worshipping, serving, and obeying God in the world in the power of the Holy Spirit."[472] Hunt adds:

> If we are biblical when we think church, we think corporately—we think people. The focus is on people, on *God's people*, on a living organism, not on a building, an organization or a place. As the Christian life represents the individual aspect of Christian experience, the church represents its corporate dimension.[473]

Moreover, we could also conclude that the concept of the people of God, or in particular the people of Christ, is a not only a viable paradigm for Contemporary Evangelical ecclesiology, but also of the whole Christian ecclesiology. In a deeper and wider sense, people of Christ ecclesiology regenerates the true identity of the Christian church.

Grenz sees the relevance of the people of God ecclesiology in a postmodern context, "the postmodern, pluralist context calls for an apologetic evangelical theology that reaffirms the place of the church as a people and, in a certain sense, as a soteriologically relevant reality."[474] Mudge speaks of the people of God in a teleological sense:

---

[472] W. Ward Gasque, "The Church in the New Testament," in *In God's Community: The Church and Its Ministry*, eds. David J. Ellis and W. Ward Gasque (London: Pickering & Inglis, 1978), 2.
[473] Hunt, "New Dimensions in Church," in *New Dimensions in Evangelical Theology*, ed. Dockery, 340.
[474] Grenz, *Renewing the Center*, 308. Grenz concisely discusses the prospects of evangelicalism in postmodern culture, see "Stanley J. Grenz, "Star Trek and the Next Generation: Postmodern

> The church is that part of human whole which conveys *to* that whole *its* destiny as the space of God's reign. The church is a community in which the whole of humanity may so signified *its* calling to become a people of God.[475]

Van Der Ven sees the significance of the peoplehood of God in a wider and richer contextual sense yet internally synthesizing:

> The code *people of God* meets the requirement of all sorts of peoples and population groups to express their own social-cultural and ritual identity in a Christian sense. Through this they can develop their own spirituality: their own religious aspirations, forms of expression, language and text, dynamics, and style. It is not only a question of religious wordings or coloring; the social-cultural forms even penetrate the structure of the identity and the convictions themselves. They make the church into "something that is ours" to the extent that one could say, proceeding from a personal intrinsic impulse: "the church is all of us together," "the church is what we are," this is what essentially appeals to groups and collectives in the code *people of God*.[476]

The church is no other than the people of Christ! And the people of Christ are one! To be more truly the people of Christ the church should be one—one in living the Christ-centered Spirit-empowered life of faith and witness! When it fails to reform and continues to deform—it could lose its calling! And most probably, as seen in the history of God's ecclesial call, a new entity that would be more truly and wholly the people of Christ would emerge as the new people of Christ. Christians now need to wake up and get over with their respective institutional-denominational eccentricities—and be more truly Christ-centered, Spirit-empowered, missional and transdenominational!

---

and the Future of Evangelical Theology," *Crux* 30 (March 1994): 24-32. Jenkins expounds the situation confronting the church in a postmodern context; see Jenkins, *The Church Faces Death*.
[475] Mudge, *The Sense of a People*, 52.
[476] Johannes Van Der Ven, *Ecclesiology in Context* (Grand Rapids: Eerdmans, 1993), 196.

Summary and Conclusion

There is more to Contemporary Evangelicalism than mere parachurch missional characterization. This study shows that in fact—Contemporary Evangelicalism is reviving the paradigm of the original theological and ecclesiological frameworks of the Christian church.

The prototypal ecclesial life was more truly Christ-centered, Spirit-empowered, missionally zealous and transdenominational. But these prototypal characteristics were seriously marred when the church succumbed to secular influences. However, since the Reformation the Holy Spirit has been progressively restoring these prototypal ecclesial characteristics. And this restorative process has been embedded in ecclesial movements from Reformation onward to Contemporary Evangelicalism. Thus, the Reformation and succeeding movements are not intended as denominational and separate movements, but part of one and long process of regenerating the whole Christian church.

In Contemporary Evangelicalism we see the climax and the full-bloom paradigm of this prototypal ecclesial regeneration. It reveals the following characteristics of the original theological and ecclesiological frameworks:

A. Theological Framework
    1. Christ-centered focus
    2. Life-oriented theology
    3. Bible-based faith

B. Ecclesiological Framework

1. Christ-centeredness
2. Spirit-led life
3. Missional zeal
4. Transdenominational operation

And on the personal level, Contemporary Evangelicalism emphasizes the necessity of new birth through repentance and acceptance of Jesus as personal Savior through the empowerment of the Holy Spirit. This emphasis redefines Christianity back to its original life-oriented and holistic transformational perspective.

Further, as reflecting the original identity of Christian church—Contemporary Evangelicalism *re*-presents the church—as the new people of God, or in particular, the people of Christ. This very identity of the Christian church transcends denominational enclosure. Thus, Christian believers as the people of Christ need to transcend their exclusivist and separatist denominational eccentricities—and be more truly the people of Christ rather than diverse peoples of denominations. Contemporary Evangelicalism presents a model of a more truly Christ-centered transdenominational church.

However, the Christian church in general has missed the integrative framework of ecclesial regeneration. Thus each ecclesial movement is regarded as separate denominational entity. This study presents an integrative perspective of ecclesial movements and emphasizes the need of integrating all the essential ecclesial revelations embodied in the history of ecclesial movements. When this assimilation happens—then there will be a grand New Reformation! Then begins—the internal and holistic regeneration of the present day churches back to one whole prototypal Christian church!

BIBLIOGRAPHY

Part I: Evangelicalism
A. Books
Abraham, William J. *The Coming Great Revival: Recovering the Full Evangelical Tradition.* San Francisco: Harper & Row, 1984.
Barr, James. *Escaping from Fundamentalism.* London: SCM, 1984.
Bebbington, D.W. *Evangelicalism in Modern Britain: A History from the 1730s to the 1980s.* London: Unwin Hyman, 1989.
Billy Graham Center. *An Evangelical Agenda: 1984 and Beyond.* Pasadena, CA: William Carey Library, 1979.
Bloesch, Donald G. *The Evangelical Renaissance.* Grand Rapids: Eerdmans, 1973.
_____. *The Future of Evangelical Christianity: A Call for Unity Amidst Diversity.* Colorado Springs, CO: Helmers & Howard, 1988.
_____. *Essentials of Evangelical Theology.* 2 vols. Peabody, MA: Prince, 2001.
Bock, Darrell L. *Purpose-Directed Theology: Getting Our Priorities Right in Evangelical Controversies.* Downers Grove, IL: InterVarsity, 2002.
Boyd, Gregory A., and Paul R. Eddy. *Across the Spectrum: Understanding Issues in Evangelical Theology.* Grand Rapids: Baker Academic, 2002.
Cameron, Nigel M. de S., ed. *The Challenge of Evangelical Theology: Essays in Approach and Method.* Edinburgh: Rutherford House, 1987.
Carpenter, Joel A. *Revive Us Again: The Reawakening of American Fundamentalism.* New York: Oxford University Press, 1977.
Cray, Graham, et al. *The Post-Evangelical Debate.* London: SPCK, 1997.
Davis, John Jefferson. *Foundations of Evangelical Theology.* Grand Rapids: Baker Book House, 1984.
Dayton, Donald W., and Robert K. Johnson. *The Variety of American Evangelica-lism.* Downers Grove, IL: InterVarsity, 1991.
Dockery, David S., ed. *New Dimensions in Evangelical Thought: Essays in Honor of Millard J. Erickson.* Downers Grove, IL: InterVarsity, 1998.
Dorrien,. Gary. *The Remaking of Evangelical Theology.* Louisville, KY: Westminster John Knox, 1998.

Ellingsen, Mark. *The Evangelical Movement: Growth, Impact, Controversy, Dialog.* Minneapolis: Augsburg, 1984.

Evangelical Synod of North America. *The Evangelical Catechism.* Cleveland, OH: United Church Press, 1985.

Fraser, David A., ed. *Evangelicalism: Surviving its Success.* Princeton: Princeton University Press, 1987.

Freston, Paul. *Evangelical and Politics in Asia, Africa and Latin America.* Cambridge: Cambridge University Press, 2001.

George, Timothy, ed. *Pilgrims on the Sawdust Trail: Evangelical Ecumenism and the Quest for Christian Identity.* Grand Rapids: Baker Academic, 2004.

Grenz, Stanley J. *Renewing the Center: Evangelical Theology in a Post-Theological Era.* Grand Rapids: Baker Academic, 2000.

Grothius, Douglas. *Truth Decay: Defending Christianity Against the Challenges of Postmodern.* Downers Grove, IL: InterVarsity, 2000.

Harris, Harriet A. *Fundamentalism and Evangelicals.* Oxford: Clarendon Press, 1998.

Hart, D. G. *Reckoning with the Past: Historical Essays on American Evangelicalism from the Institute for the Study of American Evangelicals.* Grand Rapids: BakerBooks, 1995.

———. *That Old-Time Religion in Modern America: Evangelical Protestantism in the Twentieth Century.* Chicago: Ivan R. Dee, 2002.

Henry, Carl F.H. *Evangelicals in Search of Identity.* Waco, TX: Word Books, 1976.

Hodge, A.A. *Evangelical Theology: A Course of Popular Lectures.* Edinburgh: The Banner of Truth Trust, 1976.

Horton, Michael Scott. *Made in America: The Shaping of Modern American Evangelicalism.* Grand Rapids: Baker Book House, 1991.

Hunter, James Davidson. *Evangelicalism: The Coming Generation.* Chicago: The University of Chicago Press, 1987.

Humphrey, Fisher, ed. *Nineteenth Century Evangelical Theology.* Nashville, TN: Broadman, 1983.

Hutchinson, Mark, and Ogbu Kalu, eds. *A Global Faith: Essays on Evangelicalism & Globalization.* Sydney: Centre for the Study of Australian Christianity, 1998.

Johnston, Jon. *Will Evangelicalism Survive It's Own Popularity?* Grand Rapids: Zondervan, 1980.

Kantzer, Kenneth S., ed. *Evangelical Roots: A Tribute to Wilbur Smith.* Nashville, TN: Thomas Nelson, 1978.

Lightner, Robert P. *Evangelical Theology: A Survey and Review.* Grand Rapids: Baker Book House, 1986.

Lovegrove, Deryck W. *The Rise of the Laity in Evangelical Protestantism.* London: Routledge, 2002.

Marsden, George, ed. *Evangelicalism and Modern America.* Grand Rapids: Eerdmans, 1984.

_____. *Reforming Fundamentalism: Fuller Seminary and the New Evangelicals.* Grand Rapids: Eerdmans, 1987.

McGrath, Alister. *Evangelicalism & the Future of Christianity.* Downers, Grove, IL: InterVarsity Press, 1995.
_____. *A Passion for Truth: the Intellectual Coherence of Evangelicalism.* Downers Grove: IL: InterVarsity Press, 1996.
Murray, Iain H. *Evangelicalism Divided: A Record of Crucial Change in the Years 1950 to 2000.* Rep. ed. Edinburgh: The Banner of Truth Trust, 2001.
Nash, Ronald A. *Evangelicals in America: Who They Are, What They Believe.* Nashville, TN: Abingdon, 1987.
_____. *Evangelical Renewal in the Mainline Churches.* Worchester, IL: Crossway Books, 1987.
Nelson, Rudolph. *The Making and Unmaking of an Evangelical Mind: The Case of Edward Carnell.* Cambridge: Cambridge University Press, 1987.
Noll, Mark A. *The Scandal of Evangelical Mind.* Grand Rapids: Eerdmans, 1994.
_____, and David F. Wells. *Christian Faith and Practice in the World: Theology From an Evangelical Point of View.* Grand Rapids: Eerdmans, 1988.
_____, and Ronald Thiemann, eds. *Where Shall My Wond'ring Soul Begin?: The Landscape of Evangelical Piety.* Grand Rapids: Eerdmans, 2000.
_____. *The Rise of Evangelicalism: The Age of Edwards, Whitefield and the Wesleys.* Downers Grove, IL: InterVarsity Press, 2003.
Packer, J.I. *Fundamentalism and the Word of God: Some Evangelical Principles.* Rep. ed. Grand Rapids: Eerdmans, 1972.
Phillips, Timothy, Jr., and Dennis L. Okholm. *A Family of Faith: An Introduction to Evangelical Christianity.* Grand Rapids: Baker Academic, 2001.
Porter, Stanley E. and Anthony R. Cross. *Semper Reformandum: Studies in Honour of Clark H. Pinnock.* Cumbria, UK: Paternoster Press, 2003.
Quebedeaux, Richard. *The Young Evangelicals: Revolution in Orthodoxy.* New York: Harper & Row, 1974.
Ramm, Bernard. *The Evangelical Heritage: A Study in Historical Theology.* Grand Rapids: BakerBooks, 2000.
Rausch, Thomas P., ed. *Catholics and Evangelicals: Do They Share a Common Future?* Downers Grove, IL: InterVarsity, 2000.
Rawlyk, George A., and Mark Noll, eds. *Amazing Grace: Evangelicalism in Australia, Britain, Canada, and the United States.* Grand Rapids, MI: BakerBooks, 1993.
Rosell, Garth M. *The Evangelical Landscape: Essays on the American Evangelical Tradition.* Grand Rapids: BakerBooks, 1996.
Rubey, Steve, and Monte Unger. *50 Events of the 20th Century that Shaped Evangelicals in America.* Nashville, TN: Broadman & Holman, 2002.
Smith, Christian. *American Evangelicalism: Embattled and Thriving.* Chicago: The University of Chicago Press, 1998.
_____. *Christian America? What Evangelicals Really Want.* Barclay, CA:

University of California Press, 2000.

Sproul, R.C. *Getting the Gospel Right: The Tie That Binds Evangelicals Together.* Grand Rapids: BakerBooks, 1999.

Stackhouse, John G., Jr., ed. *Evangelical Futures: A Conversation on Theological Method.* Grand Rapids: BakerBooks, 2000.

_____. *Evangelical Landscapes: Facing Critical Issues of the Day.* Grand Rapids, MI: Baker Academic, 2002.

Storey, Graham, ed. *The Evangelical and Oxford Movement.* Cambridge: Cambridge University Press, 1983.

Stott, John. *Evangelical Truth: A Personal Plea for Unity, Integrity, and Faithfulness.* Downers Groove, IL: InterVarsity Press, 1999.

Tidball, Derek J. *Who Are the Evangelicals: Tracing the Roots of the Modern Movements.* London: Marshall Pickering, 1994.

Tinker, Melvin. *Evangelical Concerns: Rediscovering the Christian Mind on Issues Facing the Church Today.* Ross-shire, UK: Christian Focus, 2001.

Torrance, T.F. *Reality & Evangelical Theology.* Downers Grove, IL: InterVarsity, 1982.

Trueman, Carl R., Tony J. Gray and Craig L. Blomberg, eds. *Solid Ground: 25 Evangelical Theology.* Leicester, England: Apollos, 2000.

Walker, David S. *Challenging Evangelicalism: Prophetic Witness and Theological*

Webber, Robert E. *Common Roots: A Call to Evangelical Maturity.* Grand Rapids: Zondervan, 1978.

_____. *Ancient-Future Faith: Rethinking Evangelicalism for a Post Modern World.* Grand Rapids: Baker Books, 2003.

Wells, David F., and John D. Woodbridge, eds. *The Evangelicals: What They Believe, Who They Are, Where They Are Changing.* Nashville, TN: Abingdon, 1975.

Wells, Williams W. *Welcome to the Family: An Introduction to Evangelical Christianity.* Downers Grove, IL: InterVarsity, 1979.

Williams, D. H. *Retrieving the Tradition and Renewing Evangelicalism: A Primer for Suspicious Protestants.* Grand Rapids, MI: 1999.

Williamson, Clark M. *Way of Blessing Way of Life: A Christian Theology.* St. Louis, MS: Chalace Press, 1999.

Woodbridge, John D., Mark Noll, and Nathan O. Hateh. *The Gospel in America: Themes in the Story of America's Evangelicals.* Grand Rapids: Zondcrvan, 1979.

B. Periodicals

Armerding, Hudson T. "The Evangelical in the Secular World." *Bibliotheca Sacra* 127 (April 1970): 129-139.

Arnold, Clinton E. "Early Church Catechesis and New Christians' Classes in Contemporary Evangelicalism." *Journal of Evangelical Theological Society* 47 (March 2004): 39-54.

Bauman, Michael. "Why the Noninerrantist Are Not Listening: Six Tactical Errors Evangelicals Commit." *Journal of Evangelical Theological Society.* 29 (September 1986): 317-324.

Bebbington, D.W. "Evangelical Christianity and the Enlightenment." *Crux* 25 (December 1999): 29-36.

Beck, James R. "Evangelicals, Homosexuality, and Social Concern." *Journal of Evangelical Theological Society* 40 (March 1997): 83-97.

Carpenter, John B. "The Fourth Great Awakening Or Apostasy: Is American Evangelicalism Cycling Upwards Or Spiraling Downwards?" *Journal of Evangelical Theological Society* 44 (December 2001): 647-670.

Diehi, David W. "Evangelicalism and General Revelation: An Unfinished Agenda." *Journal of Evangelical Theological Society* 30 (December 1987): 441-455.

Gaebelein, Frank E. "Evangelicals and Social Concern." *Journal of Evangelical Theological Society* 25 (March 1982): 17-22.

Grenz, Stanely J. "Star Trek and the Next Generation: Postmodern and the Future of Evangelical Theology." *Crux* 30 (March 1994): 24-32.

Hall, Douglas John. "The Future of Protestantism in North America." *Theology Today* 52 (January 1996): 458-465.

Hitchen, John M. "What it Means to be an Evangelical Today—An Antipodean Perspective—Part One—Mapping Our Movement." *Evangelical Quarterly* 76 (January 2004): 47-64.

Killen, R. Allen. "The Inadequacy of the New Evangelicalism and the Need for a New and Better Method." *Journal of Evangelical Theological Society* 19 (Spring1976): 113-120.

Lane, Belden C. "The Spirituality of the Evangelical Revival." *Theology Today* 43 (July 1986): 169-177.

Lazenby, Henry F. "The Mythical Use of the Bible by Evangelicals." *Journal of Evangelical Theological Society* 34 (December 1991): 485-494.

Lovelace, Richard F. "Evangelical Spirituality: A Church Historian's Perspective." *Journal of Evangelical Theological Society* 31 (March 1988): 25-35.

McCune, Rolland D. "The Formation of the New Evangelicalism (Part One): Historical and Theological Antecedents." *Detroit Baptist Seminary Journal* 3 (Fall 1998):3-34.

_____. "The Formation of the New Evangelicalism (Part Two): Historical Beginnings." *Detroit Baptist Seminary Journal* 4 (Fall 1999): 109-150.

McGrath, Alister E. "The Challenge of Pluralism for the Contemporary Christian Church." *Journal of Evangelical Theological Society* 35 (September 1992): 361-373.

_____. "The Christian Church's Response to Pluralism." *Journal of Evangelical Theological Society* 35 (December 1992): 487-501.

_____. "Evangelical Apologetics." *Bibliotheca Sacra* 155 (January 1998): 3-10.

Moltmann, Jurgen. Christianity in the Third Millennium." *Theology Today* 51 (April 1994): 75-89.

Mouw, Richard J. "Evangelicals In Search of Maturity." *Theology Today* 35 (April 1978): 42-51.

Muether, John R. "Contemporary Evangelicalism and the Triumph of the New School." *Westminster Theological Journal* 50 (Fall 1988): 339-347.

Noll, Mark, Cornelius Platinga, and David Wells. "Evangelical Theology Today." *Theology Today* 51 (January 1995): 495-507.

Neff, David. "Inside *CT*." *Christianity Today* 43 (June 14, 1999): 5.

Payne, William P. "The Social Movement Dynamics of Modern American Evangelicalism." *Ashland Theological Journal* 35 (2003) 37-54.

Peters, George W. "An Evangelical Response to Theological Issues in Mission." *Bibliotheca Sacra* 135 (July 1978): 253-262.

Phillips, W. Gary. "Evangelical Pluralism: A Singular Problem." *Bibliotheca Sacra* 151 (April 1994): 140-154.

Pinnock, Clark H. "Theology and Myth: An Evangelical Response to Demythologizing." *Bibliotheca Sacra* 128 (July 1971): 215-226.

Scott, J. Julius, Jr. "Some Problems in Hermeneutics for Contemporary Evangelicals." *Journal of Evangelical Theological Society* 22(March 1979): 67-77.

Smith, Gary Scott. "The Men and Religion Forward Movement of 1911-12: New Perspectives on Evangelical Social Concern and the Relationship Between Christianity and Progressivism." *Westminster Theological Journal* 49 (Spring 1987): 91-118.

Tracy, David. "Theology and the Many Faces of Postmodernity." *Theology Today* (April 1994): 104-114.

Ward, Ted W. "Metaphors of Spiritual Reality." *Bibliotheca Sacra* 140 (January 1983): 3-10.

Part II: Ecclesiology
A. Books

Alston, Wallace M., Jr. *Guides to the Reformed Tradition: The Church*. Atlanta: John Knox, 1984.

Barna, George. *The Second Coming of the Church*. Nashville, TN: Word, 1998.

Berkouwer, G.C. *The Church*. Grand Rapids: Eerdmans, 1976.

Bloesch, Donald G. *The Reform of the Church*. Grand Rapids: Eerdmans, 1970

_____. *The Church: Sacraments, Worship, Ministry, Mission.* Downers Grove, IL: InterVarsity, 2002.

Boice, James Montgomery. *What Makes a Church Evangelical?* Wheaton, IL: Crossway Books, 1999.

Braaten, Carl E. *Mother Church: Ecclesiology and Ecumenism*. Minneapolis: Fortress, 1998.

Carmody, Denise L., and John Carmody. *Bonded in Christ's Love: An Introduction to Ecclesiology*. New York: Paulist Press, 1986.

Carson, D.A., ed. *The Church in the Bible and the World*. Exeter, England: Paternoster, 1987.

Clapp, Rodney. *A Peculiar People: The Church As Culture in a Post-Christian Society*. Downers Grove, IL: InterVarsity, 1996.

Clowney, Edmund P. *The Church: Contours of Christian Theology*. Downers Grove, IL.: InterVarsity, 1995.

Colson, Charles. *The Church*. Dallas, TX: Word, 1992.

Conzelmann, Hans. *History of Primitive Christianity*. Nashville, TN: Abingdon, 1973.

Costas, Orlando E. *The Church and Its Mission: A Shattering Critique from the Third World*. Wheaton, IL: Tyndale, 1974.

Dieter, Melvin E., and Daniel M/ Berg, eds. *The Church: An Inquiry into Ecclesiology from a Biblical Theological Perspective*. Anderson, IN: Warner, 1972.

Dulles, Avery. *Models of the Church*. New York: Doubleday, 2002.

Eller, Vernard. *The Outward Bond: Caravaning as the Style of the Church*. Grand Rapids: Eerdmans, 1980.

Ellis, David J., and W. Ward Gasque, eds. *In God's Community: The Church and Its Ministry*. London: Buckering & Inglis, 1978.

Evans, G.R. *The Church and the Churches*. Cambridge: Cambridge University Press, 1994.

Ferguson, Everett. *The Church of Christ: A Biblical Ecclesiology for Today*. Grand Rapids: Eerdmans, 1996.

_____. *Early Christians Speak: Faith and Life in the First Three Centuries*, 3rd. ed. Abilene, TX: ACU, 1999.

Flew, R. Newton. *Jesus and His Church: A Study of the Idea of the Ecclesia in the New Testament*. London: Epworth, 1960.

Frost, Michael, and Alan Hirsch. *The Shaping of Things to Come: Innovation and Mission for the 21st Century Church*. Peabody, MA: Hendrikson, 2003.

Giles, Kevin. *What on Earth Is the Church?: An Exploration in New Testament Theology*. Downers Grove, IL: InterVarsity, 1995.

Grenz, Stanley J. *Theology for the Community of God*. Grand Rapids: Eerdmans, 1994.

Guder, Darrell L. *Be My Witnesses: The Church's Mission. Message, and Messengers*. Grand Rapids: Eerdmans, 1985.

Hanson, A.T., and R.P.C. Hanson. *The Identity of the Church: A Guide to Recognizing the Contemporary Church*. London: SCM, 1987.

Harrison, Everett F. *The Apostolic Church*. Grand Rapids: Eerdmans, 1985.

Hayes, Ed. *The Church: The Body of Christ in the World Today*. Nashville, TN: Word Publishing, 1999.

Healy, Nicholas M. *Church, World and the Christian Life: Practical-Prophetic Ecclesiology*. Cambridge: Cambridge University Press, 2000.

Hodgson, Peter C. *Revisioning the Church: Ecclesial Freedom in the New Paradigm*. Philadelphia: Fortress, 1988.

Horton, Michael Scott., ed. *Power Religion: The Selling Out of the Evangelical Church?* Chicago: Moody, 1992.

Houtepen, Anton. *People of God: A Plea for the Church*. London: SCM, 1984.

Howard-Book, Wes. *The Church Before Christianity*. Maryknoll, NY: Orbis, 2001.

Hunter, Victor L., and Phillip Johnson. *The Human Church in the Presence of Christ: The Congregation Rediscovered.* US: Mercer University Press, 1985.

Jay, Eric G. *The Church: It's Changing Image Through Twenty Centuries.* Atlanta, GA: John Knox, 1978.

Jinkins, Michael. *The Church Faces Death: Ecclesiology in a Post Modern Context.* New York: Oxford University Press, 1999.

Jordan, James B., ed. *The Reconstruction of the Church.* Tyler, TX: Geneva Ministries, 1985.

Karkkainen, Veli-Matti. *An Introduction to Ecclesiology: Ecumenical, Historical & Global Perspectives.* Downers Grove, Il.: InterVarsity, 2002.

Kee, Howard Clark. *Who Are the People of God: Early Christian Models of Community.* New Haven: CT, Yale University Press, 1995.

Klein, William W. *The New Chosen People: A Corporate View of Election.* Grand Rapids: Zondervan, 1990.

Koenig, John. *The Feast of the World's Redemption: Eucharistic Origins and Christian Faith.* Harrisburg, PN: Trinity Press, 2000.

Küng, Hans. *The Church.* New York: Sheed and Ward, 1967.

Lathrop, Gordon W. *Holy People: A Liturgical Ecclesiology.* Minneapolis: Fortress, 1999.

Lebacqz, Karen, *Word, Worship, World, and Wonder: Reflections on Christian Living.* Nashville, TN: Abingdon, 1997

Logan, F. Donald. *A History of the Church in the Middle Ages.* London: Routledge, 2002.

Lovegrove, Deryck, W., ed. *The Rise of the Laity in Evangelical Protestantism.* London: Routledge, 2002.

Martin, Ralph P. *The Family and the Fellowship: New Testament Images of the Church.* Grand Rapids: Eerdmans, 1979.

Minear, Paul S. *Images of the Church in the New Testament.* Philadelphia: Westminster, 1960.

McKinion, Steven A., ed. *Life and Practice in the Early Church.* New York: New York University Press, 2001.

Moltmann, Jurgen. *The Church in the Power of the Spirit: A Contribution to Messianic Ecclesiology.* Minneapolis: Fortress Press, 1993.

Mudge, Lewis S. *The Sense of a People: Toward a Church for the Human Future.* Philadelphia: Trinity Press, 1992.

_____. *The Church as a Moral Community: Ecclesiology and Ethics in Ecumenical Debate.* New York: Continuum, 1998.

_____. *Rethinking the Beloved Community.* Geneva: WCC Publications, 2001.

Nazzir-Ali, Michael. *Shapes of the Church to Come*. Eastborne, England: Kingsway Communications, 2001.

Newlands, George M. *The Church of God*. Hants, UK: Marshall Morgan & Scott, 1984.

Pannenberg, Wolfhart, Avery Dulles, and Carl E. Braten. *Spirit, Faith, and Church*. Philadelphia: Westminster, 1970.

Reno, R. R. *In the Ruins of the Church: Sustaining Faith in an Age of Diminished Christianity*. Grand Rapids: Brasos, 2002.

Riddel, Michael. *Threshold of the Future: Reforming the Church in the Post-Christian West*. ondon: SPCK, 1998.

Sawyer, Mary R. *The Church on the Margins: Living Christian Community*. Harrisburg, PA: Trinity, 2003.

Schnackenburg, Rudolf. *The Church in the New Testament*. Freiburg, Germany: Herder, 1965.

Schwarz, Hans. *The Christian Church: Biblical Origin, Historical Transformation, and Potential for the Future*. Minneapolis: Augsburg, 1982.

Smith, David L. *All God's People: a Theology of the Church*. Wheaton, IL: Victor Books, 1996.

Snyder, Howard A. *The Community of the King*. Downers Grove, IL: InterVarsity, 1977.

_____., and Daniel V. Runyon. *Decoding the Church: Mapping the DNA of Christ's Body*. Grand Rapids: BakerBooks, 2002.

Stackhouse, John G., Jr., ed. *Evangelical Ecclesiology: Reality or Illusion?* Grand Rapids: Baker, 2003.

Stackhouse, Max L, Tim Dearborn, and Scott Paeth, eds. *The Used Church in a Global Era: Reflections for a New Century*. Grand Rapids: Eerdmans, 2000.

Thwaites, James. *The Church Beyond the Congregation*. Cumbria, UK: Paternoster, 1999

Van Der Ven, Johannes A. *Ecclesiology in Context*. Grand Rapids: Eerdmans, 1993.

Van Gelder, Craig. *The Essence of the Church: A Community Created by the Spirit*. Grand Rapids: Baker Books, 2000.

Vogel, Joseph M., and John H. Fish III, eds. *Understanding the Church: The Biblical Ideal for the Twenty-first Century*. Neptune, NJ: Loizeaux, 1999.

Volf, Miroslav. *After Our Likeness: The Church as the Image of the Trinity*. Grand Rapids: Eerdmans, 1998.

Watson, Donald. *I Believe in the Church*. Grand Rapids: Eerdmans, 1978.

Webber, Robert E. *Evangelicals on the Canterbury Trail: Why Evangelicals Are Attracted to the Liturgical Church*. Wilton, CT: Morehouse-Barlow, 1985.

Wells, David F. *The Bleeding of the Evangelical Church*. Edinburgh: The Banner of Truth Trust, 1995.

Westerhoff, John H. III. *Living the Faith Community: The Church that Makes a Difference.* San Francisco: Harper & Row, 1985.

Williams. J. Rodman. *Renewal Theology: The Church, the Kingdom, and Last Things.* Vol. 3. Grand Rapids: Zondervan, 1992.

Wingren, Gustaf. *Gospel and Church.* Trans. Ross Mackenzie. Edinburgh: Oliver & Boyd, 1964.

B. Periodicals

Brueggemann, Walter. "Rethinking Church Models Through Scriptures." *Theology Today* 48 (July 1991): 128-138.

Cameron, Evan K. "The Soul Both Saved and Simple, The Church Both Faithful and Flawed: Reflection on Reformation Church History." *Union Seminary Quarterly* Review 57:1-3 (2003): 1-16.

Dabney, D. Lyle. "The Church as a Community of (Un)Common Grace: Toward a Postmodern Ecclesiology." *The Christian Theological Research Fellowship Papers* 4 (July 1991). Cited March 28, 2004. http://home.apu.edu/sCTRF/papers/1997_papers/dabney.html

DiNoia, J. Augustine. "The Church in the Gospel: Catholics and Evangelicals in a Conversation." *Pro Ecclesia* 13 (Spring 2004): 172-188.

Farstad, Arthur L. "We Believe in: Church." *Journal of Grace Evangelical Society* 5 (Spring 1992): 3-10.

Fish, John H. III. "The Life of the Local Church." *Emmaus Journal* 6 (Summer 1997): 3-42.

Gangel, Kenneth O. "Marks of the Church." *Bibliotheca Sacra* 158 (October 2001): 467-477.

Grenz, Stanley, "The Community of God: A Vision of the Church in the Postmodern Age." *Crux* 28 (June 1992): 19-26.

Grubb, Luther L. "The Church Reaching Tomorrow's World." *Grace Journal* 12 (Fall 1971): 13-33.

Hall, Douglas John. "The Church Beyond the Christian Religion." Cited March 14, 2004. http://www.religion-online.org/cgi-in/relsearchd.dll/showarticle?item_id=529.

Hanson, Paul D. "The Identity and Purpose of the Church." *Theology Today* 42 (October 1985): 342-352.

Hargrove, Barbara. "Churches as Mediating Structures." *Theology Today* 39 (January 1983): 385-394.

Hodgson, Peter C. "Ecclesia of Freedom." *Theology Today* 44 (July 1987): 222-234.

Kent, Homer A. "The New Covenant and the Church." *Grace Theological Journal* 6 (Fall 1985): 289-298.

Kostenberger, Andreas J. "The Mystery of Christ and the Church: Head and Body, 'One Flesh'." *Trinity Journal* 12 (Spring 1991): 79-94.

Larkin, William J., Jr. "The Recovery of Luke-Acts as 'Grand Narrative' for the

Church's Evangelistic and Edification Tasks in a Postmodern Age." *Journal of Evangelical Theological Society* 43 (Spetember 2000): 405-415.

Lewis, Gordon R. "The Church and the New Spirituality." *Journal of Evangelical Theology Society* 36 (December 1993): 433-444.

Jacobson, Nolan P., and William E. Winn. "A New Theology for a New Missiology." *Theology Today* 25 (April 1968): 43-80.

Mackay, John A. "Let the Church Live On the Frontier." *Theology Today* 40 (April 1983): 39-43.

Marshall, Bruce D. "The Disunity of the Church and the Credibility of the Gospel." *Theology Today* 50 (April 1993): 78-89.

McIntosh, Mark A. "Ecclesiology and Spirituality: The Church as Noetic Subject." Society for the Study of Theology, 2001 Annual Conference Paper.

Mills, Gene. "The Pneumatological *Ekklesia*." *Quodlibet Journal* 5 (July 2003). Cited March 28, 2004. www.Quodlibet.net.

Morrison, John D. "Trinity and Church: an Examination of Theological Methodology." *Journal of Evangelical Theological Society* 40 (September 1997): 445-454.

Packer, J.I. "A Stunted Ecclesiology? The Theory and Practice of Evangelical Churchliness." Fellowship of St. James, 2002. Cited April 21, 2004. http://www.touchstonemag.com/docs/issues/15.10docs/15-10pg37.html.

_____. "Church: God Plants His People In a New Community." *Concise Theology:*
A Guide to Historic Beliefs. Cited April 21, 2004.
http://www.monergism.com/thethrshold/articles/onsite/packer/church.html.

Plummer, Robert L. "Imitation of Paul and the Church's Missionary Role in 1 Corinthians." *Journal of Evangelical Theological Society*. 44 (June 2001): 219-235.

Rhodes, J. Stephen. "The Church as the Community of Open Friendship." *The Asbury Theological Journal* 55 (Spring 2000): 41-49.

Robra, Martin. "Moral Community: Reflections on Ecclesiology and Ethics, Notes from Common Journey." *Union Seminary Quarterly Review* 58:1-2 (2004): 83-96.

Roof, Wade Clark. "The Church in the Centrifuge." *The Christian Century* (November 8, 1989): 1012-1014.

Rose, Stephen C. "Shape and Style of the Church Tomorrow." *Theology Today* 25 (April 1968): 64-80.

Stott, John R.W. "Christian Ministry in the 21st Century: Part 1: The World's Challenge to the Church." *Bibliotheca Sacra* 145 (April 1988): 123-132.

_____. "Christian Ministry in the 21st Century: Part 2: The Church's Mission in the World." *Bibliotheca Sacra* 145 (July 1988): 243-253.

Toussaint, Stanley. "The Church and Israel." *The Conservative Theological Society Journal* 2 (December 1998). Cited March 28, 2004.

http://conservativeonline.org/journals/02_07_journal/1998c2n7_id01.htm.
Vlach, Michael. "Ecclesiology in Church History." Cited January 25, 2004. http://theologicalstudies.org/ecclesiology.html.
Westhelle, Vitor. "The Church's Crucible: *Koinonia* and Cultural Transcendence." *Currents in Theology and Mission* 3 (June 2004): 211-218.
World Council of Churches. "The Nature and Purpose of the Church: A stage on the way to a common statement." *Faith and Order Paper No. 181* (November 1998). Cited March 28, 2004. http://wccx.wcc-coe.org/wcc/what/faith/nature1.html.
_____. "Becoming a Christian: The Ecumenical Implications of Our Common Baptism." *Faith and Order Consultation Paper* (France, 1997). Cited March   28, 2004.
http://www.wcc-coe.org/wcc/what/faith/faverg.html.
_____. "The Unity of the Church: Gift and Calling. *The Canberra Statement* (Canberra, 1991). Cited March 28, 2004.
http://wccx.wcc-coe.org/wcc/what/faith/canb.html.

Part III: General Systematic Theology and Other Related Books
Anderson, Bernard W. *Understanding the Old Testament*. Eaglewood Cliffs, NJ: Prentice-Hall, 1975.
Barrett, Charles D. *Understanding the Christian Faith.* Englewood Cliffs, NJ: Prentice-Hall, 1980.
Berkhof, Hendrikus. *Christian Faith: an Introduction to the Study of Faith*. Trans. Sherd Woudstra. Rev. ed. Grand Rpaids, MI: Eerdmans, 1986.
Bushwell, James Oliver, Jr. *A Systematic Theology of the Christian Religion*. Vol. 2. Grand Rapids, MI: Zondervan, 1963.
Chafer, Lewis Sperry. *Systematic Theology*. Vol. 4. Dallas: Dallas Seminary Press, 1948.
Chaunu, Pierre, ed. *The Reformation*. New York: St. Martin's, 1986.
Clark, Francis. *Eucharistic Sacrifice and the Reformation*, 2nd ed. Oxford: Basil Blackwell, 1967.
Coppedge, Allan. *The Biblical Principles of Discipleship*. Grand Rapids: Francis Ausbury, 1989.
Dixson, Scott G. *The Reformation in Germany.* Qxford: Blackwell, 2002.
Erickson, Millard J. *Christian Theology.* Grand Rapids: Baker, 1985.
Fulbrook, Mary. *Piety and Politics: Religion and the Rise of Absolutism in England, Wurttemberg and Prussia*. Cambridge: Cambrdige University Press, 1983.
Garrett, James Lee, Jr. *Systematic Theology: Biblical, Historical, and Evangelical*. Vol. 2. Grand Rapids, MI: Eerdmans, 1995.
Gonzalez, Justo L. *The Story of Christianity*. San Francisco: HarperSanFrancisco, 1985.
Green, Vivian. *A New History of Christianity*. New York, NY: Continuum, 1996.

Grimm, Harold J. *The Reformation Era: 1500-1650,* 2nd ed. New York: Macmillan, 1973.
Grudem, Wayne. *Systematic Theology: An Introduction to Biblical Doctrine.* Leicester, England: InterVarsity, 1994.
Hart, Larry D. Truth *Aflame: A Balanced Theology for Evangelicals and Charismatics.* Nashville, TN: Thomas Nelson, 1999.
Hubbard, Robert, Jr. et al, eds. *Studies in Old Testament Theology.* Dallas: Word, 1992.
Kelly, J.N.D. *Early Christian Doctrines.* Rev. ed. Peabody, MA: Prince Press, 2003.
Kümmel, Werner George. *The Theology of the New Testament: According to Its Major Witnesses: Jesus-Paul-John.* Nashville: Abingdon, 1973.
McCarthy, Dennis J. *Old Testament Covenant: A Survey of Covenant Opinion.* Richmond, VA: John Knox Press, 1972.
Musser, Donald W. and Joseph L. Price, eds. *A New Handbook of Christian Theology.* Nashville: Abingdon, 1992.
Oxtoby, Willard G., ed. *World Religions: Western Traditions*, 2nd ed. Ontario: Oxford University Press, 2002.
Pannenberg, Wolfhart. *Systematic Theology.* Vol. 3. Trans. Geoffrey W. Bromiley. Grand Rapids: Eerdmans, 1998.
Pinson, Koppel S. *Pietism as a Factor in the Rise of German Nationalism.* New York: Columbia University Press, 1934.
Porter, Stanley E. and Anthony R. Cross. *Semper Reformandum: Studies in Honor of Clark H. Pinnock.* Cumbria, UK: Paternoster, 2003.
Rosenbaum, Stanley Ned. *Understanding Biblical Israel: A Reexamination of the Origins of Monotheism.* Georgia: Mercer University Press, 2002.
Spickard, Paul R and Kevin M. Craig. *A Global History of Christians: How everyday Believers Experienced Their World.* Grand Rapids: Baker Academic, 1994.
Thielicke, Helmut. *Prolegomena: The Relation of Theology to Modern Thought Forms.* Vol 2. *The Evangelical Faith.* Trans. and ed. Geoffrey W. Bromiley. Edinburgh: T&T Clark, 1982.
Thiessen, Henry C. *Lectures in Systematic Theology.* Rep. ed. Grand Rapids, Eerdmans, 1989.
Tracy, Joseph. *The Great Awakening: A History of the Revival of Religion in the Time of Edwards and Whitefield.* Edinburgh: The Banner of Truth Trust, 1976.
Williamson, Clark M. *Way of Blessing, Way of Life: a Christian Theology.* St. Louis, MS: Charles Press, 1999.

www.ingramcontent.com/pod-product-compliance
Lightning Source LLC
Chambersburg PA
CBHW061636040426
42446CB00010B/1440